INTIMACY BETWEEN MEN

"Combining sexuality and intimacy in one relationship is a powerful experience, and these processes can enhance each other. If you think you've had great sex before, wait until you try it with a partner who has been angry with you and then forgiven you, held you when you cried . . . the trust and depth of such a connection can bring new heights of sexual ecstasy . . . ."—from the book

For single men seeking to create permanent partnerships and for couples who want to strengthen existing relationships, this provocative, groundbreaking work is a wonderfully supportive and enlightening guide to celebrating life and building lasting love.

JOHN H. DRIGGS received his M.S.W. from the University of Minnesota. He has been a Clinical Associate at Lesbian and Gay Community Services and is currently in private practice in Minneapolis, where he makes his home. STEPHEN E. FINN received his Ph.D. from the University of Minnesota. He has also served as a Clinical Associate at Lesbian and Gay Services in Minneapolis and is currently on the faculty of the Clinical Psychology Training Program at the University of Texas in Austin, where he also maintains a private practice.

INTIMACY
BETWEEN MEN

HOW TO FIND AND KEEP GAY LOVE RELATIONSHIPS

JOHN H. DRIGGS, M.S.W.,
AND STEPHEN E. FINN, Ph.D.

A PLUME BOOK

PLUME
Published by the Penguin Group
Penguin Books USA Inc., 375 Hudson Street, New York, New York 10014, U.S.A.
Penguin Books Ltd, 27 Wrights Lane, London W8 5TZ, England
Penguin Books Australia Ltd, Ringwood, Victoria, Australia
Penguin Books Canada Ltd, 10 Alcorn Avenue, Toronto, Ontario, Canada M4V 3B2
Penguin Books (N.Z.) Ltd, 182-190 Wairau Road, Auckland 10, New Zealand

Penguin Books Ltd, Registered Offices: Harmondsworth, Middlesex, England

Published by Plume, an imprint of New American Library, a division of Penguin
Books USA Inc. Previously appeared in a Dutton edition.

First Plume Printing, November, 1991
10 9 8 7 6 5 4

Copyright © John H. Driggs, M.S.W. and Stephen E. Finn, Ph.D., 1990
All rights reserved.

Acknowledgment
Excerpt from FORGIVE AND FORGET by Lewis B. Smedes. Copyright © 1984 by
Lewis B. Smedes. Reprinted by permission of Harper & Row, Publishers, Inc.

Ⓟ REGISTERED TRADEMARK—MARCA REGISTRADA

LIBRARY OF CONGRESS CATALOGING-IN-PUBLICATION DATA
Driggs, John H.
    Intimacy between men : how to find and keep gay love relationships
/ John H. Driggs & Stephen E. Finn.
    p.   cm.
    Originally published: New York : Dutton, 1990.
    ISBN 0-452-26696-3
    1. Gay male couples—United States.   2. Interpersonal relations.
3. Intimacy (Psychology)   1. Finn, Stephen Edward.   II. Title.
HQ76.2.U5D75   1991
306.76'62—dc20   91-31449
                                                          CIP

Printed in the United States of America
Original hardcover design by Steven N. Stathakis

To Bonnie, in celebration of our love and commitment. Your heart, voice, and touch have given me new life.

To Jim, with love and thanks for all we've learned together.

To protect confidentiality, people described in this book are composites of many clients we have seen. Names and essential identifying characteristics are fictitious, and any resemblance to a single person is coincidental.

CONTENTS

ACKNOWLEDGMENTS

This book rests on the support and wisdom of many people. We are enormously grateful to all of them.

We wish to thank the former staff of Lesbian and Gay Community Services in Minneapolis for their trust in us as we learned about gay male intimacy. Special thanks are due Grace Kuhns, for her keen clinical insights and her appreciation for the absurd.

We give thanks to our teachers, Ken Hampton, Ada Hegion, Millie Huttenmaier, Carl Kirsch, and Marilyn Peterson. The lessons we learned from them are woven throughout these pages.

We are grateful for the material and emotional support of many friends. Glenn Lindsey, Frank Hirschbach, and David Sanford graciously provided hospitality during Steve's numerous visits to Minneapolis. Dave Wood taught us about the nuances of the English language and encouraged us to publish our thoughts. Carla Dunn, Mark Ehrke, Dan Goldblatt, Lauren Newton, and Millie Smith provided encouragement and faith when it was sorely needed.

We are indebted to our literary agent, Jonathan Lazear, for his encouragement, vision, and resourcefulness in getting this book in print. We would like to thank Gary Luke and the editors of Dutton for their realistic guidance in organizing our text while promoting warmth and connection with our readers.

Dr. Arnold Buss at the University of Texas generously gave of his time to read and extensively comment on the first draft of the manuscript. He greatly contributed to the clarity of our writing.

We are grateful to our partners, Jim and Bonnie, for their love and patience during the years this book was in progress. They've never let us get too big for our britches and continually reminded us that having their love is more important than talking about love. Jim also read many drafts of the manuscript and kept numerous embarrassing errors from appearing in print.

Finally, we extend special thanks to the many men who cannot be thanked by name—clients whose stories are reflected in these pages and who taught us much of what we know about intimacy. It was a privilege and a joy to relate to these men in psychotherapy and relive our relationships with them through this book.

INTRODUCTION

Intimacy is a basic human need. It also makes your life richer and more rewarding. Close relationships will support you in times of trouble and cushion you from life's stresses. They will also help you discover more options in life. If you have intimate friendships you will be more secure with yourself and more aware of your inner needs; you will have a deeper connection to the world and to your own spirituality. In our experience, personal sharing is an exhilarating step toward becoming more fully alive.

But intimacy may sometimes seem impossible, exhausting, intimidating, or not worth your effort. Maybe you've been hurt once too often and long for the life of a hermit. Or perhaps you truly want a close relationship but don't know how to find one. Intimacy is wonderful, but how do you make it past the first month? This book makes sense of the ups and downs of close relationships and guides you toward your goal of intimacy.

You are a special audience: gay men. While gay male relationships are similar to those of heterosexuals or lesbians, you have certain strengths and weaknesses in developing closeness that are the result of growing up gay and male in our society. Through reading this book, you and those you love can understand your relationships better and develop deeper, more fulfilling ties.

Although all kinds of people struggle to gain intimacy, the frequency of AIDS (Acquired Immune Deficiency Syndrome) among gay men has given urgency to this book. The despair and isolation you and your friends may feel because of AIDS can be as psychologically devastating as the disease is physically debilitating. However, this anguish also challenges you to get closer to friends, family, or a lover to share your grief and renew your spirit. Building intimate relationships celebrates life; in the face of AIDS, such celebrations are needed even more.

HOW WE CAME TO WRITE THIS BOOK

The ideas in this book originally took form when we were co-therapists in short-term support groups for gay men in Minneapolis. These groups, which began in 1982, typically had five to eight men who met for ten to twelve weeks to discuss intimacy. We selected men without severe emotional or psychiatric problems. They were well-adjusted gay men who wished to examine their relationships to improve their ability to be close to others.

Most had struggled with relationships for years. How could a twelve-week experience have any impact? Frankly, at first we were skeptical. But after running several groups, we became confident that twelve sessions did produce lasting changes in group members' ability to be intimate. Men continued growing emotionally after they left our groups, and the experience reverberated in their lives for months to come. We were inspired and intrigued and began to wonder, "How can we share this experience with other gay men?"

The next step toward writing this book took place in March 1984 during a University of Minnesota conference called "Developing a Positive Lesbian or Gay Identity." Drawing on our experience with gay men's groups, we presented a workshop on intimacy in gay male relationships. We scheduled two presentations, each limited to twenty-five men, hoping to give attenders an experience of intimacy. Both times, more than seventy men crowded into the small room we were assigned, insisting that our workshop was their top choice. This experience reinforced what we had learned in our groups: gay men hunger for intimacy.

A second event sparked the idea of writing a book. We attended a workshop by David McWhirter and Andrew Mattison just prior to the publication of their study *The Male Couple*. At the end of the presentation, one man stood and said, "You've told us a lot about couples who've been together longer than five years. But can you tell us how to make it past the first month?" A murmur ran through the room, and we knew this man spoke for many others as well. This book is our answer to his question.

Yet another reason for writing the book was purely selfish. In the summer of 1984, Steve moved to Texas where he accepted a job. Both of us grieved the change in our friendship and looked for a way to continue to learn from one another. Writing a book seemed a good way to maintain a vital connection. In retrospect, there would have been easier ways to keep contact; we got more than we bargained for. In writing a book about intimacy, we frequently had to reexamine our relationship and find new strengths in our friendship.

You may be surprised that a heterosexual man (John) and a gay man (Steve) would be partners in writing a book on gay intimacy. However, our affection for each other is a cornerstone of our writing, and our cooperation has matured us as individuals and strongly influenced this project. John has repeatedly reminded us that gay men share important similarities with heterosexual men in their approach to relationships. Steve has been a voice for the unique experience of gay men. Thus, you are offered two perspectives on one of the most important issues in your personal life.

THREE CAVEATS

Although based on our experiences with others, this book comes from us. As such, it is not a purely objective or scientific account of intimacy. The exhilaration, distress, frustration, and hope that we have felt in our relationships with gay men, heterosexual men, women, and our families will be evident as you read through these pages. These emotions are the source of our greatest wisdom and the best guide to having good relationships.

This is not the final word on gay male relationships, nor do we see ourselves as the final experts on the subject of intimacy. Intimacy is a process that unfolds throughout life, and each of us continues to learn from relationships. By sharing our personal efforts and insights with you, we have erected some landmarks that may aid in your journey. Of course, no one can do the work for you. The joy and frustrations of your quest are held in trust for you alone.

A paradox for us in writing this book has been that, although we have something vital to say about intimacy, its essence extends beyond words. Thus, we do not encourage you to use this book as a bible, a measuring device, a love potion, or a magic wand. Like many people, we are constantly on the lookout for these tools, so contact us immediately if you find any. In the meantime, you may find that the magic is within yourself.

PART ONE
■
INTIMACY

1

INTIMACY AND PSEUDO-INTIMACY

It was Thursday night, and the Gay Men's Support Group was partway through its sixth meeting. "How are we ever going to set this group on fire?" we asked ourselves. Thoughts like "Intimacy is too threatening for men" and "This is just too hard" ran through our heads. If we felt like this, imagine how the men in the group felt. An eerie politeness had set into the weekly sessions. No one disagreed, interrupted, or caused trouble. Every meeting was the same. Instead of comforting us, the predictability of the group worried us. Would the group stay together when conflict inevitably came? Could we ever trust the sincerity of what was being said in the group?

The individual men had character all right. Sam was blunt, claiming, "Gay men are good for only one thing." Mark was prudishly provocative. He religiously wore tight jeans to each group meeting while insisting that sex was the last thing on his mind. Chico was a macho biker who hated queens, and Ted insisted that nobody leave the group with hurt feelings. Then there was George, who came across as a dumb blonde. His favorite line was, "Hey, don't tell me. It must be Thursday because it's group night." Each man's style had its own shortcomings, but was as dependable as clockwork.

Ted had started off the sixth meeting with his usual,

"Let's go around and find out how the week went for every-body." He talked on and on about his Aunt Florence's visit and how rude she'd been to him and how lonely he felt over the weekend because nobody called him. He rallied with a discussion about decorating his apartment with rose-colored wallpaper. After he talked, a long silence fell over the group like a shroud. We sank more deeply in our chairs.

Out of the blue, Chico piped up, "Hey, man, I'm bored to death with this group." We couldn't believe our ears! Mark immediately replied with, "How can you say a thing like that?" Then everybody got on the bandwagon. Sam said, "That's your problem. All you ever talk about is sissies and queers." Playing the peacemaker, Ted suggested that we quit arguing and let Chico have his own opinion. Silence and panic ensued, and Chico hung his head in shame.

Of all the people to show insight, George proposed, "That's not his problem. Chico is speaking for everybody. We're all gay. We know what it's like. Why pretend?" One by one, the group members looked at each other and knew he was right. Over the next hour, some amazing disclosures took place. Sam said he was bored with going from lover to lover. Mark recalled the mixed messages he got from his family about being gay and showed some tears. Ted said he felt burdened to keep the group together. Chico perked up, claim-ing, "I've never felt more respected by men in my life."

The group had temporarily reached a new level of close-ness and commitment. When we asked the men how this had happened, they were stumped. They knew what didn't work in relationships, but not what did. Chico looked to us and again spoke for the group, "What is intimacy, anyway?"

WHAT IS INTIMACY?

Intimacy is a process in relationships enabling individuals to meet personal needs while accepting differences in each other.

"INTIMACY IS A PROCESS . . ."

Intimate relationships constantly change as people know each other over time. Just as you can always learn more about yourself, there is always something new you can share with a partner. And even in the best relationships there may be peaks and valleys of closeness. Because intimacy is a process, it is something you never completely attain, nor is it ever truly absent in your relationships. Ironically, you make the least progress toward intimacy when you think you have no more to learn.

Intimacy is subtly reflected in how we talk to each other, how we communicate nonverbally with each other, and how we regard each other. Perhaps this subtlety is most clear when a friend says, "It's not *what* you are saying, but *how* you are saying it that matters to me." Because the level of intimacy constantly changes in a relationship, you may find it hard to decide whether your relationship is growing in intimacy. But then again, hearing and seeing a waterfall at dusk and feeling its spray on your face is a lot more satisfying than talking about it.

"INTIMACY IS A PROCESS IN RELATIONSHIPS . . ."

In general, intimacy is something you experience with other people. If you desire the excitement and challenge that closeness brings, you must reach out. Intimacy rarely comes to find you alone in your room. Because intimacy involves relationships, at least two *willing* participants are needed. Perhaps you have had the sad experience of trying to force closeness on another person, with no success. Intimacy requires mutual consent and effort.

"INTIMACY IS A PROCESS . . . ENABLING INDIVIDUALS . . ."

The better you know yourself—your likes and dislikes, strong points and weak points, and all the things that make you uniquely *you*—the more you will be able to be truly close to others. Intimacy is a powerful experience. You need to feel sure that your identity won't get lost or be destroyed before risking closeness with another person. In a mature intimate relationship, two people rarely lose the sense of being separate individuals, and each partner feels that his individuality is affirmed.

". . . TO MEET PERSONAL NEEDS . . ."

You can be fulfilled through being close to others. Many of your basic needs are *interpersonal*; they require other people for satisfaction. These include the need to be held, the need to be sexual, and the need to play. Some people are content with a life of solitude, but most of us require close relationships to feel satisfied. Of course, even in the best of relationships, there are needs your partner cannot meet or times that he cannot be available to you. Intimacy will not completely shield you from those lonely moments, but it will minimize them. As Sheldon Kopp wrote in *No Hidden Meanings*, "Love is not enough, but it sure helps" (p. 29).

". . . WHILE ACCEPTING DIFFERENCES IN EACH OTHER."

When you are close to someone, while maintaining your individual identity, you will inevitably have different tastes, opinions, and philosophies of life. For intimacy to occur, each of you must recognize these differences and more or less accept them. This is partly why close relationships are personally validating. That someone can know you in all your peculiarities and still accept you is tremendously rewarding. In its most positive form, this acceptance is not begrudging ("Oh, well, I guess I'm going to have to learn to live with this part of you."), but is a celebration of the differences that have arisen ("By your being different from me, I have the opportunity to learn new things and grow.")

Let's also say what intimacy is not. First, it is not restricted to sexual relationships. It can occur whether or not two people are aware of and overtly express sexual feelings toward each other. No one denies the special satisfaction that comes in an attachment that is both intimate and sexual. However, you are nurtured by a variety of people, including family, heterosexual male friends, and women. These relationships can also be intimate.

Neither is the length of a relationship a measure of its intimacy. There are long-term relationships that are not particularly close, and some relationships become quite intimate after relatively little time. On the other hand, a brief personal encounter probably would not be intimate, no matter how intense or satisfying it was. Intimacy requires time, but time is not enough.

How do I evaluate the intimacy in my relationships? Now that you know what intimacy is, you may say, "That sounds great! Let me at it!" We admire your enthusiasm. But before you set off on a new journey, you need to know exactly where you are and what you may meet along the way.

Use the following questions about your relationships as a road map. Read through these questions or reflect on them more systematically, perhaps taking notes in a journal. Consider each of your important relationships separately and then look for similarities among them. Our questions may disturb you and leave you with unresolved feelings. If you can muster enough courage, share your exploration and results with a trusted friend.

How do you and your partner nurture each other and make each other feel safe? Feelings of trust and safety are essential to intimacy. The openness and vulnerability of a close relationship are impossible unless each of you knows that your partner will not hurt you or treat you disrespectfully. It may be difficult to determine whether you are being nurtured by your partner. You may talk yourself into feeling loved even when you are not, because you feel undeserving of affection. Or your current relationship may be better than past ones: even crumbs are a feast when you're used to being starved.

Compare notes with friends whose relationships you admire. If you feel that you must always be on your good behavior around the other person, or that you must always be strong in relating to your partner, trust and safety may be lacking. Ask yourself these questions: Do we turn to each other for comfort and support when upset? Do we deal with each other honestly, without fear of rejection or disapproval? Do I feel that our relationship is strong and that we are committed to each other? Is there an overall balance of give and take?

How do you express conflict and tension? Some friction is inevitable in close relationships. If you and your friends deal with each other honestly, while attempting to meet your individual needs, there will always be times when you do not see eye to eye. By openly dealing with the tension that results from these conflicts, you will learn and grow. For example, in writing this book, we sometimes disagreed sharply. The process of working out these differences was often stormy and trying. Yet, because of our struggles, our friendship is deeper and more meaningful. Also, we've written a book that neither of us could have produced alone, or that would have less impact had we been polite and not spoken our true feelings. Strong relationships are produced in this fashion. Both partners have unique and valuable contributions to offer and must have the courage to challenge each other. Paradoxically, you sometimes get closer to another person through heartfelt arguing. Ask yourself: Do I let others know when I disagree, or do I routinely keep quiet to avoid conflict? Do I encourage friends to let me know their true feelings? When I'm angry do I try to control or intimidate my partner?

How do you resolve conflict and tension? Although openness about differences is essential to intimacy, both partners must develop methods for settling disagreements. Unresolved conflicts breed anger and tension. In such an atmosphere, differences between you are threats, not opportunities for further understanding. The stress of living in a hostile environment makes it harder to solve the original conflicts. You eventually become hopeless and give up.

Not all disagreements need to be solved. Instead of compromising, you and your partner can also agree to disagree. This is most successful when a difference isn't crucial. If you find yourself holding a grudge, you definitely need to renegotiate.

To evaluate conflicts in your relationships, answer the following questions: What helps me and my partner settle conflicts? Are we equally committed to resolving tension between us? Do we forgive past misunderstandings and accept differences for which we find no compromise? Can we use anger to explore personal issues or is there such tension that I feel like I'm walking on eggshells?

To what degree do you and your partner show mutual respect? Mutual respect means you're concerned with your best interests *and* the best interests of the other person. Of course, your interests may conflict. Such situations set the stage for difficult choices. Mutual respect simply means that you act with an awareness of the possible effects your actions will have on the other person.

Mutual respect also means that each partner has something valuable to contribute to the other. Respect cannot be a lopsided affair in which one person always gives and the other only takes. Each individual possesses a special dignity and worth that expands the other's life in a valuable way. Mutual respect is not limited by differences in age or ability between two partners. If this seems impossible to you, use this trade secret of teachers and therapists. In a successful teacher-student relationship, the teacher learns from the pupil just as the pupil learns from the teacher. Similarly, in a successful therapy relationship, it is not only the client who changes and heals, but also the therapist. As therapists, if we are not challenged personally and do not grow from our work with a client, we probably are closing off part of ourselves and not fully respecting the client. Realizing this usually helps remedy whatever internal block exists.

Do you openly express warmth, affection, and tenderness? The joys of close relationships include hugging, touching, and being complimented. You may crave close relationships to satisfy your need for these types of contact. Unfortunately, some people are very uncomfortable giving or receiving admiration and love. This part of intimacy is often especially difficult for gay men who have learned, as a survival mechanism, not to show affection to other men. Are there moments when you're embarrassed expressing or receiving affection? Does this happen when you're alone with your partner? Do you and your partner discuss how you like to be touched? Do you receive affection freely or feel unworthy and wonder what hidden strings are attached?

Are you and your partner comfortable with asking and offering? A wise therapist once said, "Intimacy means asking for things you might not get, and offering things the other person might not accept." Asking and offering are essential if both partners are to meet their needs. These acts also show that each partner has a separate identity, in effect saying: "I ask for what I want because we are different and you can't read my mind; I offer what I can because you don't know exactly what I'm willing to give." Asking and offering have uncertain outcomes, which shows that risk and trust are essential to intimacy. By asking for what you need and offering things to your partner, you communicate respect for yourself and your partner. Do you know the difference between something you'll give if asked, but don't want to offer? If you ask and are turned down, do you blame yourself for asking? Do you fault yourself if you don't receive what you ask for?

Do you welcome change and growth in yourself and your partner? Truly close relationships promote emotional growth and teach you new things about yourself. If you're intimate, you'll constantly face changes in yourself, your partners, and your relationships. Such changes are often irksome. You're never free from new challenges, nor can you rest, knowing that you've made it, and take it easy. You may feel that you're playing a game in which someone's constantly changing the rules without warning. To the extent that you see change as a positive and integral part of intimate relationships, you'll be exhilarated by the challenge and the chance to grow in ways never imagined. Ask yourself: Do I encourage change and growth in my partner, or do I dread the challenges it will bring? Have I postponed or abandoned my own growth to stay in this relationship? How is this relationship growing and changing?

Now that you've completed your assessment you may say to yourself: "How can anybody live up to these standards?" or "I thought I was depressed *before* I started this book." Well, take a deep breath and pat yourself on the back. No relationship could live up to these standards. The mere fact that you've examined a close relationship speaks well of you. You may feel annoyed or put off by our questions, scared or ashamed, or perhaps despairing. No one has escaped these feelings. How else would we be able to write about them? Remember, you're more than the sum of all your relationships. Completing this section means that you have strengths that will sustain you far beyond this assessment. What are your strengths?

MASQUERADES OF INTIMACY

I'm Barry. Alex and I met at a friend's house two years ago just when I desperately needed to get away from my lover. It seems unreal to talk about it now. I was being battered. Alex saved my life by

*offering me a place to stay. He refused to let me
leave, so after three days I moved in for good. Now
we spend evenings together and often have lunch at
work with each other. We both collect antiques and
like the same sorts of books and movies. We go out
with a lesbian couple every so often, but Alex and I
are just homebodies, I guess. We have to watch out
for Alex's blood pressure, so we don't eat out with
friends. And when I'm unhappy with his spending
habits I remind myself what life was like before Alex.
After all, what can two fatties expect from anyone
else? Who would have us?*

As psychotherapists we often see a pattern in relationships,
sometimes called "dependency," "co-dependency," "enmesh-
ment," or "relationship addiction." We call this pattern *pseudo-
intimacy* because although it resembles intimacy, it is not
true intimacy.

Barry and Alex are in a pseudo-intimate relationship.
They appear happy and spend much time together, and their
attachment fulfills many needs. But both have sacrificed much
of their individual identities to be together. Differences in
their relationship are suppressed, not expressed and resolved.
They have few friends apart from each other, suggesting that
each expects his partner to meet all his needs. Also, hidden
tension in their relationship may contribute to their weight
and health problems. Barry views himself as unworthy of
others, and Alex apparently felt responsible for keeping Barry
alive. The relationship has the desperate, static feel of two
people who cannot risk any change for fear the whole thing
will fall apart. These are the hallmarks of the pseudo-intimate
relationship: loss of individuality, suppression of conflict, and
resistance to change and growth. Of course, neither intimacy
nor pseudo-intimacy exists in a pure form; most relationships
have elements of both.

Yet there are positive aspects of pseudo-intimacy. Ignoring individual needs, suppressing conflict, and keeping things
the same are important skills in relationships, particularly
when a life crisis confronts you or your partner. At such
times, pseudo-intimacy may temporarily sustain your relationship. Also, pseudo-intimacy is a normal stage of relationships
for many gay male couples. A survey found that in their first

year, many gay male couples show characteristics of pseudo-intimacy. Typically, after about a year, a couple progresses from pseudo-intimacy to a more stable foundation for relating. [1]

As a step toward intimacy, pseudo-intimacy may be preferable to solitude, and it can serve as a rehearsal or learning ground for close relationships. Pseudo-intimate relationships can inspire you and provide needed motivation when you're discouraged. Finally, pseudo-intimacy may tempt you to tackle the challenges of intimacy and keep you engaged while you struggle through periods of intimacy-building.

Problems arise when couples confuse pseudo-intimacy with true intimacy. Such couples stay stuck in pseudo-intimacy, and their relationship may not mature. The partners may not know enough to hope for anything more in their relationship, or, as in the case of Alex and Barry, may feel that they don't deserve anything better. As Sheldon Kopp wrote in *What Took You So Long?*, "It's all right to pretend sometimes. The only danger lies in pretending that you are not pretending" (p. 21).

As psychotherapists we have often seen the unfortunate results of confusing intimacy and pseudo-intimacy. In a pseudo-intimate relationship personal growth stops, taking a toll on the partners. Some people develop physical symptoms, like Alex and Barry—obesity, high blood pressure. Others are stricken in a spiritual sense. As you till your garden of relationships, remember: intimacy is recognized by the effort it entails and by the considerable fruits of the labor.

WHAT ARE THE REWARDS OF INTIMACY?

At this point you may be thinking, "This sounds like a lot of work! What's in it for me?" If you're wondering if intimacy is worthwhile, just review some of the benefits of closeness. This list is especially useful when you're discouraged or bitter about relationships.

Joy. Being loved and accepted by someone you admire may feel like walking on air, hearing bells ring, or floating on clouds. Our word for this phenomenon is *joy*, but whatever you call it, it is wonderful. You may feel joy in solitary situations: strolling in a beautiful garden, during deep meditation or prayer, or after completing a creative piece of work.

But for most people, intimate relationships are the best source of lasting, intense joy. Closeness is so invigorating that it can even help some forms of mild depression. A Sufi master was once asked the key to happiness. He replied, "Surround yourself with those whom you love and who love you."

Self-awareness. Close relationships teach you about yourself in two ways. Intimate partners give you feedback, which helps you identify not only problems, but also the positive, unique parts of your personality. What others say is not always true, but such feedback tells you how others see you and challenges your perceptions of yourself. Second, your interactions with others enable you to reach conclusions about who you are. You might be able to increase your self-awareness without being in a close relationship, but it would be as hard as learning how your face looks without a mirror.

Healing. Unfortunately, connections to others are opportunities not only for joy but also for hurt. But as you were hurt, so you may be healed. Intimacy is perhaps the most powerful way to overcome pain from past relationships.

How can close friendships heal old wounds? One way is by helping you correct mistaken ideas about yourself. For example, after a particularly hurtful relationship, you may believe, "There is something wrong with me. No one will ever love me." It takes only one later friendship based on mutual love and respect to change your mind. And loving partners can help you overcome old patterns that caused problems in past relationships. As an example, consider Mark.

Mark grew up in a formal British family that never dealt with anger directly and this has been a problem in all his relationships. In the past few years, he has lived with a fiery Latin lover, Carlos, and one of their major problems has been their different styles of dealing with conflict. Carlos was accustomed to passionate arguments about disagreements. Mark was more likely to sulk in his room. Recently, Mark proudly announced that he and Carlos had their first real fight. Apparently, in the midst of his shouting, Mark realized what a sign of progress it was for him to raise his voice. It dawned on him that his anger had been helped by living with Carlos. He then was so happy and appreciative that the original issue was quickly resolved.

Enhanced Self-Esteem. Intimate relationships help you feel good about yourself. This is a gift you retain even when you're alone: as you come to know more about yourself, and to heal your past hurts, your self-esteem is raised. But intimate relationships influence your self-esteem in other ways, too.

One of the most rewarding things about a close relationship is realizing that you have something valuable to offer others. A client who was shy and retiring recently said, "A friend thanked me profusely for giving him a sketch I had done of wildflowers. I didn't think it was such a big deal. But when I saw how much it meant to him, I realized my sketch had value."

Showing your love for others is an important way of confirming your worth and of building respect for yourself. In this way you discover inner strengths you had no idea you possessed. Intimate relationships, with their emphasis on asking and offering, are the ideal context in which to learn about your inner worth.

More Options. People who are involved in intimate relationships are cushioned from life's stresses and have more options when hardship visits their lives. Such options range from the very practical to the less tangible. For example, if you must suddenly attend a family funeral, intimate friends may water your plants, feed your pets, and give you a ride to the airport. Without such support, your choices are much more limited. Also, if you have taken the risk of telling a good friend that you are HIV+, he may provide a shoulder to cry on or a warm hand to hold when you are worried that your health is worsening. Friends and lovers cannot shield you from pain, but they can make it more manageable by giving you ways to confront adversity.

Pseudo-intimate relationships are so costly because instead of increasing your options they restrict them. People in pseudo-intimate relationships rarely build support networks independent of their partner. They put all their eggs in one basket which leads them to carry that basket very carefully. If you have several relationships in your life with different degrees of intimacy, it's easier to take risks in new areas of personal development.

Personal Growth. In brief, intimacy is a road to personal growth. Although there are several ways of developing your human potential, you will probably require close relationships at some point in the process. Erik Erikson, the famous psychoanalyst, strongly believed that intimacy was an essential task of adulthood. According to Erikson, those people who do not experience closeness in adulthood undergo repeated attempts and repeated failures in their relationships and do not enjoy productive and satisfying lives until they achieve intimacy.[2]

How do relationships help us grow and mature? Well, imagine that we are all like rough diamonds that need to be shaped and polished for the incredible hidden beauty to emerge. Like the diamond, each of us needs shared intimacy to shape and polish the many facets of our personality. In relationships, as we get close to one another, the precious gem at the core of us emerges for all to see.

Of course, there are other steps to personal growth that are as important as intimacy. You have to take time away from others, to regroup and reflect on what you have learned in relationships. You need to balance being alone and being with others.

Spiritual Fulfillment. The word *spirituality* has several connotations. For some, it brings visions of fundamentalist ministers preaching messages of damnation; for others, seances and Ouija boards in dimly lit rooms. By spirituality, we mean a sense that there is something intangible that is larger than us and that connects us to others and gives meaning to our lives. You may call this something God, your higher power, the Goddess, Allah, or the Inner Light, or you may call it nothing at all. You may seek connection with your spirituality through an organized religion or on your own. Whatever the name and form your spiritual search takes, we believe that it is essential to a balanced, rich life.

"How can other people help me find God?" you ask. "I thought I had to do it all myself." One answer lies in what we've said before: By helping you heal yourself and realize your full potential, others aid in your spiritual growth. But there is more to it than this. In our lives, some of our most powerful spiritual experiences have come through other people. There was the time a lover gave up jealousy to hold one of us as we cried over an old relationship. Or the courage it took for a proud friend to offer a sincere apology. Or the compassion an estranged father found as a friend died of AIDS. Such moments are eternal, and they glow with the mark of the divine.

Finally, others can help you develop spiritually by discussing spiritual matters and insights with you. You may find it more difficult to discuss personal spiritual experiences than to discuss sex. If you openly share your spiritual journey in a safe relationship, however, you can compare notes, receive guidance and support, and strengthen your faith. Discussing spirituality in your relationship is a sign of trust and a way of furthering closeness.

WHEN IS INTIMACY NOT A GOOD IDEA?

You might get the impression from our glowing description of intimacy that we see it as something to be sought under all circumstances and in all relationships. Not so. There are undoubtedly situations in your life that require you to be in frequent contact with people you do not or cannot like, for example, in your family or in your office. Avoiding these people might require drastic changes, such as quitting your job or leaving home. Also, some of these people may be completely incapable of intimacy. For example, you may have an abusive parent who humiliates you when you show your feelings. Or your boss may resist all change and retaliate if you express any anger. Establishing intimate relationships with these people is not only *not* wise but may be more self-destructive than productive in the end.

When is it fruitless to pursue intimacy? If you've repeatedly found little in common with another person or repeatedly failed to resolve your differences with that person, then it's probably best to maintain a distant relationship. Accepting limitations in relationships is healthier than hoping for what cannot be. If intimacy is not possible with a particular person, don't blame yourself or despair. Remember, there are other people who you can turn to for intimacy.[3]

All relationships in your life cannot be intimate. None of us has the time and energy to be close to all the people we meet during the day. Imagine trying to have a deep, intimate relationship with each member of your family, your work crew, and bowling club, as well as your barber, mechanic, and plumber! You very soon long for solitude. Not only is it impossible to make every relationship an intimate one, there is no reason to try. Part of the richness of life is having a variety of people to relate to. One evening you may want simple, mindless fun with a new acquaintance, while the next you may feel the need of a heart-to-heart talk with an old friend. As long as you have some relationships that meet your intimacy needs, you don't need to force each personal contact into a close one.

Finally, intimacy is not for everyone. The effort required for interpersonal closeness may seem inordinate. You may simply decide, "I don't want to!" Also, when you're sick or facing a crisis, you may not have the energy to expend on intimate relationships. At these times, you may fall back on old standbys and find solace and support.

Intimacy is a rewarding, thrilling, and frightening experience. It may change your life or your view of yourself, and it may lead you to exotic places you otherwise would never have explored. Intimacy is certainly not for the fainthearted.

NOTES TO CHAPTER 1

[1]This initial stage of gay male relationships is described by D. P. McWhirter, and A. M. Mattison, in *The Male Couple: How Relationships Develop* (Englewood Cliffs, N.J.: Prentice-Hall, 1984).
[2]E. H. Erikson, *Identity and the Life Cycle.* (New York: W. W. Norton, 1980).
[3]For a fuller discussion of this question see H. Halpern, *How to Break Your Addiction to a Person* (New York: McGraw-Hill, 1982).

ROADBLOCKS TO INTIMACY

You might think that achieving intimacy should be easy, that closeness should occur simply because you want it or because you have paid your dues of loneliness and now deserve the rewards of companionship. But often there are roadblocks on the path to close relationships. Some of these are more common or more intense in the relationships of gay men, but all can be overcome. Dealing with your own roadblocks to intimacy is like carving a fine sculpture; the labor is part of the artistry and satisfaction, and you will need lots of effort and commitment.

Once upon a time, two neighbors quarreled and each decided to build a fence between their homes. One was built of old stones and earth and the other of shrubbery. Determined to outdo each other, the men produced fences that were works of art. Naturally, each man disdained the other's fence and disparaged it whenever possible. This conflict endured for years; their mutual contempt and rivalry became legendary. One day a group of neighbors decided enough was enough. They pointed out to the two men that their fences had grown together, and that they now had something in common. Shocked, the

*two men took a fresh look at the other's fence, each
realizing the beauty and care of the others construc-
tion and how well the two walls fit together. They
stopped to trade shy compliments about the fences.
This led to long conversations, first about masonry
and gardening, then about other topics. Finally, one
neighbor invited the other over to tour his property.
Eventually, the men became close friends. Apparently their jealousy had really been admiration. In
the end, the fences remained, but the two neighbors
no longer saw them as barriers and visited back and
forth quite freely.*

As therapists, we discovered something wonderful: The men
in our support groups initially became close by learning to
appreciate the ways they were pushing each other apart! As
they recognized the various maneuvers we all use to avoid
intimacy, they typically became intrigued and excited about
calling each other on such behaviors: "Hey, why does it feel
like a cruise bar in here tonight?" "Sam, when you're so
stoic, I almost see Clint Eastwood standing there." "Oh, my
God! I'm doing it again, aren't I? Why is it so hard for me to
ask for what I want?" Inevitably, the joy, humor, and depend-
ability of men blocking intimacy became a source of brotherhood instead of a way of perpetuating aloneness. Our discovery
remains an intriguing paradox for us and proves that roadblocks to intimacy do not conceal love and affection. What
psychological fences or walls have you built between yourself
and others? Your walls have served you well and should be
cherished before moving beyond them. Our descriptions of
various types of walls may help you appreciate them.

"TELL ME WHO YOU WANT ME TO BE"

*I don't understand why John left me. I tried as hard
as I could to give him whatever he wanted. I learned
to cook his favorite dishes. He didn't like it that I
smoked, so I quit cigarettes right away. I got my hair
cut the way he liked it even though it wasn't my
favorite style. I was sure this time I had found my*

prince. But after five months he told me he couldn't take it anymore—that he was bored. How could anyone be bored with me? All my friends say I'm a real card. I sure can keep 'em laughing. I'm a great one to have at parties. I'd be pretty lonely now except for my job at the restaurant. People say I'm a fabulous waiter; I know what they want even before they ask for it.

Often the methods we use to invite intimacy impede its development. This is glaringly true if you ask others to define who you are. You can adopt the clothes, appetites, and dislikes of friends or lovers and sometimes even juggle several conflicting personal styles in an attempt to satisfy everyone. In this way you appear available for a relationship and ready to make any sacrifice in order to be close to someone, but your generosity is not what it appears to be, because you offer so little of your inner self to a partner. You cannot honestly use a lover for a seeing-eye dog; after all, you can see, too. By taking risks and speaking your mind, you can discover your inner wealth and offer it to others.

Asking others to define your individuality stifles intimacy in relationships. To be intimate, you need to be aware of and to assert your feelings, beliefs, and thoughts, even when there is no one around to support these assertions. Men who have little awareness of their inner lives can never really be close to others. They are always protected in their relationships by their chameleon's skin. Typically, partners of men like this report being bored or feeling constricted in the relationship, although at first they may be flattered by their partners' accommodations. They may feel scorn or disdain for the chameleon, whose behavior is evidence of his own lack of self-respect.

"IF YOU REALLY KNEW ME, YOU'D GO AWAY"

You would never have recognized me a year ago. I would cry whenever I looked at myself in the mirror. I couldn't even open my mouth at the Friday folk dances. I felt like blending into the wallpaper. Some-

how I got up enough courage to flirt with this gorgeous man, Marcus. After six months he finally approached me and even started to act like he cared about me. I could barely believe it. Do you know what I did then? I treated him like dirt. I guess I couldn't respect him for wanting me. When I was little, my dad and older sister used to call me "the little fag." In high school gym class, the teacher would taunt me in front of the other boys and ask me to wiggle. I hated myself in those days. Now I'm changing. I don't know why. Maybe because of AIDS. I got so enraged at what the fundamentalists were saying, about AIDS being God's punishment on gays, I decided I wasn't going to be ashamed any longer. It's been a long hard struggle, but I'm getting there. I started enjoying the folk dances and found out that my body can do lots of graceful and creative things. I even get my fair share of attention now. I still feel shy, but I talk to people and look them in the eye. I don't have to hate myself for somebody else.

A fairly common block to intimacy is shame, a topic on which we could write another entire book. Indeed many gay men may feel they have already written the book on shame. Shame is a secret feeling that "I am a bad person," that "It would be better if I had not been born," or that "There is something basically horrible about me, if only people knew." Shame prevents intimacy because you feel you have to continually protect yourself from being known by others. You may believe, if the truth came out, the game would be over and all your friends would abandon you. Because it involves secrecy and isolation, shame is very resistant to change.

Sadly, many gay men in our support groups have histories of personal shame. Lacking self-respect, they cannot offer or accept closeness or have relationships based on mutual respect. After all, if you feel worthless, how can you respect your friends and lovers for choosing you? Shame is fueled by the erroneous belief that lovability is something earned and not a birthright of your existence. Without an intrinsic feeling of self-worth, you are obliged to keep proving yourself to others. As you might expect, the feedback from others is never perfectly reassuring, thereby reinforcing your feelings of shame.

A man who feels intrinsically ashamed of himself requires constant approval and cannot believe that others really love him. Such a man is trapped by his self-hate and cannot enjoy the loving benefits of intimacy. Attempting to nurture a person whose self-concept is impoverished by shame may feel like emptying the ocean with a teaspoon: generous efforts but no results. Men who feel ashamed tend to be guarded and secretive in relationships, fearing to reveal the awful secrets of their inner lives. Some eventually find partners who beat them or treat them badly, thereby confirming to themselves their basic unworthiness.

Shame is not inborn but a mirror of the inadequacies of our families and society. People shame others in an attempt to stifle behavior that they feel helpless to control in other ways. Unfortunately, the shame you receive from others is internalized while growing up. The more experiences of disapproval, humiliation, conditional love, and enforced secrecy you have experienced, the more likely it is that you will have a substantial residue of shame. Also, the more shame you have, the harder it will be to face a partner in total honesty and vulnerability, and eventually be healed of your shame.

"I DON'T KNOW HOW"

Jeff and I have been seeing a counselor for a month now. We were having some problems and wanted to work them out. Those meetings are so confusing to me. I always feel upset afterwards. The counselor keeps asking me to describe how I feel or to say what I want from Jeff. This might seem like a line, but I just don't know how to do those things. I've never talked to somebody about my insides before. Sometimes I feel like there's nothing there. I'm doing the best I can right now, but Jeff keeps telling me he needs more from me. Last time, I started crying right there in the middle of the room—you'd think I'd have better control. I don't know what's happening to me . . .

Like playing a musical instrument, being in a relationship requires skill, commitment, and practice. But few of us are taught relationship skills. We learn to play by ear, only to find out later that there are arpeggios of feeling and grace notes of relatedness that are simply beyond our ability. Don't worry. With patience and preparation and this book's guidance you can expand your relationship skills enough to play the music of intimacy.

What are the skills so essential to close relationships? Start with the ability to recognize and talk about feelings, to listen to others and empathize with their situations, to ask for things you need, negotiate differences, and turn down requests from others. With this rigorous curriculum, is it any wonder that most people do not succeed at their first intimate adult attachment?

"I CAN'T SAY NO . . . I CAN NEVER SAY YES"

Mark is like a breath of fresh air, so open and easy to be with. I've had bad experiences with lovers trying to run my life. Mark isn't like that at all. The one thing that really bothers me is how often Mark changes his mind at the last minute. Hell, last week we were all set to go out for a nice dinner and he canceled because his parents dropped in unexpectedly. The other night we were supposed to spend a romantic evening at home, but that bombed because two of Mark's friends dropped over. I was really mad because I had something important to talk to him about. But he just had to invite his friends in. Well, no one's perfect and I'll just have to put up with it. Oh, the other thing is lately our sex just doesn't have any zing in it.

■　■　■

People will bulldoze you to get what they want, you know. I've learned this the hard way; it's happened to me more than once. I used to get lonely and decide to give it one more try. Now I don't really need anybody. No, nobody's going to get the best of old Tom again. All those animals running around out there have only one thing on their minds. And I'll thank you to know it's not gardening! Nowadays, after my cooking class at the center I just go home to my apartment. If I feel tempted to have a little fling, I just remind myself about AIDS. I think being alone is just part of being a gay man today. My cats and my plants keep me company. What do I need anybody else for? Sometimes I worry about the gray hairs I see in the mirror. But with all I have to offer, what are a few imperfections? Yes, I'm not going to let anybody into this house again until I'm sure they realize I'm the chance of a lifetime.

One category of relationship skills deserves special mention because it presents difficulties for so many people. This is the ability to set boundaries in relationships: to know when to say yes, when to say no, and when to say you've simply had enough. All of the men described previously have problems setting personal limits in relationships, although in very different ways. Mark sees his life as an open house where guests are free to come and go. Mark's lover is not sure what is fair to expect in a relationship or whether his wishes are exorbitant. Tom's personal style may seem vastly different; he keeps other men at arm's length and is essentially imprisoned by his own rules. But you get the sense that in the past Tom may have operated very much as Mark does now. Often individuals flip-flop back and forth between these two extremes—never being able to say no, and never being able to say yes—without ever reaching a happy medium. Running your life like an open house or a prison, or switching back and forth between these two extremes impedes intimacy in relationships.

Those with the open-house style in relationships confuse love with total accommodation to the wishes of others. Certainly relationships require flexibility, but a consistent pattern of accommodation and denial of feelings leads to hidden resentments. As with Mark and his lover, these resentments may surface first in a couple's sexual relationship. You get the sense that these two men are tiptoeing around intimacy issues. Such politeness can kill passion in a relationship and result in destructive sexual liaisons outside the relationship. Mark and his partner could probably restore the passion in their relationship by learning to set limits with each other and facing the conflict that might result.

Sometimes one partner is skilled at setting personal limits and the other is not. In these relationships, one person typically tries to set limits for himself *and* his partner. The controlling partner tries to prop up, cajole, or threaten the other into being firm. With time, he depends on the inadequacy of his lover to feel secure. One partner is like a doctor and the other his patient. Intimacy cannot flourish here.

If you set rigid limits, like Tom, you may despair about life passing you by. More commonly, men with this style take a sour grapes stance and fool themselves into believing that there is no one worth relating to. They may develop an overly conservative life-style as both a compensation and a reminder that life is threatening. The safe retreat quickly becomes a prison. These men frantically shut everyone out because they fear they lack the judgment to screen their friendships. They have decided they won't get hurt yet another time, so these men insist on proof of utter trustworthiness before they will open the tiniest chink in their defensive cynicism. But no one can offer airtight proof, especially not to a hardened skeptic.

Part of the wonder and excitement of intimate relationships lies in the risk you take in investing your affections. Setting personal boundaries means learning to evaluate the wisdom of various investments. You would not put your life savings in the hands of a total stranger, nor would you hoard them beneath your mattress. As with your money, invest your heart wisely and you will reap many returns. Later in the book, we'll show you how.

"RELATIONSHIPS ARE MADE IN HEAVEN"

I still remember that first night with Sean. We ate dinner at my place, with candles and wine, and danced alone in the dark to Barbra Streisand's "People Who Need People Are the Luckiest People in the World." We made love in front of the fireplace and afterwards he gave me a white rose from his garden and a poem he had written. I was happier than I had ever been in my life. He seemed so tender and so

*strong. What a shock it was to find out later about
his mean streak. It took me months to realize that he
and I were not meant for each other. I still miss him,
but I guess he just wasn't the right one.*

We are all capable of being romantic and theatrical. It can be
thrilling to fantasize about being loved by a special person.
And in enduring relationships, shared romantic play and
adventure can rekindle earlier excitement and be a way of
saying, "If we had it to do all over again, we would choose
each other." As a creative use of your imagination, romance
can considerably enhance intimacy in relationships.

Romance, however, should not be confused with intimacy. Perhaps, like Sean, you believe the romantic myth
promoted by society: There is one person out there who is
meant for you. If you find that person, all of your needs will
be taken care of and you'll live happily ever after. This
relationship will be effortless because it is made in heaven.
Advertising, movies, television programs, novels—all teach us
this romantic myth.

The romantic myth damages many relationships by creating unrealistic expectations of partners. It leaves people
unprepared for the challenges that accompany intimate relationships. When the reality of the hard work of intimacy
becomes clear, many people feel disappointed and cheated.
Furthermore, the romantic myth teaches you that someone else
possesses qualities you can never attain and that this person
will be responsible for your happiness. Such beliefs may meet
fantasy needs but actually undermine self-respect and intimacy.

The romantic myth may be expressed in relationships in
seemingly opposite ways. Some men abandon a succession of
partners, each time convinced at the slightest difficulty that
this is not the right one; they must keep looking. Other men
persist in destructive and stifling attachments, afraid to part
with the fantasy lover created in their minds.

Many people in the world have the potential to love and
be loved by you. Out of this multitude you may choose one
or even several people to challenge you and participate in
your growth. These people will not protect you from the
difficult personal tasks that confront you from time to time,
but they will provide opportunities for joy and balance in
your life. Celebrating this life adventure is truly romantic.

"I WON'T MAKE THAT MISTAKE AGAIN"

Several years ago we were in a coffee shop sharing stories and sympathy about blunders we had made in past relationships. One of us noticed the following message on an empty sugar packet discarded on the table: "Experience is a wonderful thing. It enables you to recognize a mistake when you make it again." Of course we broke out laughing and felt touched in a special way. We realized that, despite all we had learned as therapists, we had fallen into the trap of self-pity.

Some men do not allow themselves to experience intimacy because, like the two of us at the coffee shop, they are still living in the past. So many of us never fully forgive ourselves for having had problems in a relationship. So many of us never fully forgive others for having hurt or disappointed us. Even the vague possibility of present or future closeness brings up our unfinished business from the past and sends us scurrying back into hiding, to lick old wounds.

Men who are stuck in the past often avoid relationships entirely. In their determination not to make that mistake again they cut themselves off from the possibility of making new mistakes. It's as if they live by the motto "Nothing ventured, nothing lost." Sometimes these men bore their friends with an endless litany of the wrongs they have suffered at the hands of others. The underlying message seems to be: "Don't try to convince me to trust anyone again. And lest I be tempted, I will remind myself once more of the reasons I dare not do this." These men are beyond the comfort of a loving relationship until they choose to live in the present. Unless they leave the past behind, any experiences that contradict their negative view of others will go unnoticed.

Major unresolved issues from the past can also be seen in the man who has a steady series of relationships, each demonstrating the same difficulties and lack of insight. Such men are also often fiercely determined not to make the same mistake again. Uncannily, however, they chose partners who turn out to be exactly what they most fear. For example, a former client had been involved with a series of married men. Each time, he believed his lover would eventually leave his wife and children to be with him. Each time, he was disappointed, and vowed never to date a married man again. Even more tragic was a second client, Duane, who consistently chose partners who physically abused him. This man was not a masochist—he had no conscious desire to be hurt—just a dangerous sixth sense for finding lovers who beat him.

Past mistakes can be helpful if you take note of them, become curious about them, and try to alter them. When this happens, what appears to be an obstacle can be a stepping-stone to greater intimacy. If you look closer, there may be many possible reasons for destructive patterns in your relationships. You may pick unavailable men because you feel they are no threat to you. Or unavailable men may seem easier to control. Or you may feel undeserving of lovers with a healthy self-concept. Underlying this feeling may be years of empty or exploitative relationships with significant males—a father, brothers, uncles, or lovers. Repeating old patterns can be an unconscious way of denying earlier abandonment and exploitation: "As long as I keep doing what I've always done and don't dwell on the past, everything will be fine." What is repeated remains forgotten; past hurts are frozen in time.

Of course, there is a serious price to pay for such denial; frequently it keeps you from developing emotionally. Men like Duane can feel desperately trapped in a pattern that seems beyond their control. Such men may appear cool; but inside they typically despair, believing they will always be trapped. Duane, feeling his future relationships with men were predetermined, eventually moved back home with his parents and denied that he was gay. With such dire consequences, you might ask what would happen if you let yourself feel old hurts.

On a more hopeful note, if you fear intimacy because of past mistakes, you can eventually improve your relationships by grieving over old losses. Grieving is difficult, but it will free you from past mistakes. Deciding to grieve is the first step.

"ALL THAT GLITTERS IS GOLD"

Kevin and I had lived together for five years and things were going really well. Of course, there were ups and downs, but we had reached the point of knowing how to encourage each other, even if we didn't exactly agree. Several of our friends commented we got along better than any couple they knew. Then the bomb hit. Within a week we each got an offer of a huge promotion, the chance of a lifetime, except they were in two cities thousands of miles apart. We didn't know whether to laugh or cry, and did a lot of both. I know I tried everything I could think of to convince myself to go with Kevin or him to come with me, and I guess he tried the same thing. Nothing worked. Finally, we decided the only thing to do was for each of us to take the new job for a trial period and see how it went. Boy, that was a hard one. I had a secret fear that Kevin would leave me or that we would simply drift away from each other. We spent six long months apart, with lots of phone calls and one weekend visit. Funny, it wasn't as bad as I expected. Even though we were separated, I had the feeling of being connected to Kevin. Then at Christmas, the miracle happened. Kevin flew in to visit me and I was bursting to tell him my decision. I had realized my new job was more glitter than gold and I wanted to leave it and be with him. Before I could open my mouth, Kevin told me he had decided the same thing. That was a Christmas to remember!

Paying attention to spirituality will help you attain a balanced, rich, and joyful life and improve your relationships. Abandoning spiritual ideals and values can prevent you from successfully making intimate connections with others.

How does spiritual impoverishment show up in relationships? Individuals who have given up their personal spiritual search often seem hung up on appearances. They choose lovers and friends by looks alone, by position in life, or by the wealth they have. These criteria say nothing about a person's capacity for intimacy, of course, and often lead to disappointments. The emphasis on external things may also show up once a relationship has formed. One couple we knew used any disagreement or discomfort in their relationship as the occasion for expensive gifts, lavish dinners, or luxury holidays. Obviously, this couple soon suffered from financial as well as spiritual deficits.

If you are out of touch with your spiritual source, you may attempt to re-create it in a lover. You may insist that your partner be all knowing, utterly reliable, and close to perfect—in short, a god. This expectation may temporarily shelter you from the anxiety and despair generated by difficult existential questions. Of course, no lover can live up to these standards, and your shelter may disappear, leaving you enraged at human shortcomings. As C. S. Lewis so aptly warned in *The Four Loves*, "Love, having become a god, becomes a demon" (p. 83).

There is sometimes a direct relationship between spiritual abandonment and pseudo-intimacy. Partners may cling to each other out of fear of loneliness and from a desire to find life's meaning in another person. You need not feel so alone, and your relationship will be more meaningful, if you are aware of your connectedness to all creation.

Cultivating your spirituality enhances your ability to appreciate fully the wonders of life, including your partners. As with Kevin and his lover, you may discover the miracle of another person choosing something difficult out of his integrity and love for you. You may be more in touch with the progress of your relationships, more patient, and more forgiving of yourself and others. Being grounded spiritually can help you see the world as alive, exciting, and full of meaning. Such a view can fill you with hope and help you be with others.

Finally, let's face it, there are times when no matter how hard you and your intimate partner try to connect, it just doesn't work. You can use all of the tools in this book, be self-aware, and still not get past a relationship conflict. Like the men in our example, you may even face a separation. At these times, it's possible the only way you and your partner can unite is through your joint and individual awareness of an inner reality. If each of you has a strong spiritual life and can share this with your partner, it can help your relationship through these hard times and, in any case, sustain you as individuals. An active spiritual life provides a foundation for coping with things that are out of your control, including aspects of intimate relationships.

If you recognize yourself in this chapter, be comforted to know that all of us encounter roadblocks on the path to intimacy. Discovering these impediments and struggling to overcome them is a way you love yourself and others. What fun would it be to have a relationship with a perfect lover who had nothing to learn? Don't worry, no such person exists.

We caution you against rushing to fix any of the problems this chapter helped you to name. Overcoming a roadblock to intimacy requires a compassionate understanding of how it helped you get where you are now. In the next chapter we discuss how obstacles to intimacy are artifacts of the rich cultural heritage of growing up gay. This legacy is entrusted to gay men and, if properly invested, yields wisdom and strength for intimate relationships.

PART TWO

■

GAY MEN

3

COMMON EXPERIENCES OF GAY MEN

Gay men are incredibly diverse: of different races, ages, religions, educations, and types of families; some have been married and have children, others have never had sex with women; some become aware of gay feelings at a very early age, and others only late in life. Any generalizations about the "gay male experience" inevitably gloss over these rich differences.

In this chapter, we pick out common themes from the stories of gay men, following them from early childhood, through coming out, to their assimilation in the gay community. Read these descriptions of other gay men. Do you identify with these men? You may appreciate the courage it takes to survive as a gay man and feel a common bond with other gay men. If you don't relate to these stories, your history may have been different from that of other gay men. Perhaps you'll understand why you feel out of sync with other gay men. Whether or not your experiences are typical, your history as a gay man vitally affects your loving other men.

BEING DIFFERENT

*The other boys pegged me as a "queer" long before I
knew what that meant. But as far back as I remember, I knew I was different. They played baseball; I
liked to dress up my sister's dolls. They hunted frogs
in the creek; I wanted to stay in the house where it
was safe. My parents always pushed me to be outside, and sometimes the other boys would let me tag
along. In the end, I always wished I hadn't. Either
they picked on me until I cried or simply ignored me.
When I got home, my father would tell me I was a
crybaby and that he was embarrassed by me. Once
he teased me himself in front of his poker buddies. I
was so humiliated I wanted to die.*

Some gay men pass through early childhood uneventfully,
unaware of the challenge that will face them when their
sexual feelings develop. But these gay men are actually the
minority. More and more evidence indicates that most gay
men—at least 50 percent and probably more—remember
intense feelings of being "different" from other boys and
being labeled "sissies" by other children and adults.[1] Remarkably, this may happen as early as two or three years of age,
long before you develop mature sexual feelings or children
know what it means to be gay.

    If you were called a sissy while growing up, you may
know about the difficulties that accompany such labeling.
Even young children refuse to play with a sissy. And very
possibly your father rejected you, being afraid that your effeminacy would tarnish his own masculinity. If she did not
ridicule you, maybe you clung to your mother, leading you
to be less independent than other boys and less social. The
end result of being called a sissy is often your feeling inadequate and ashamed, and despairing of being accepted by
other boys and men.

    You might think childhood experiences like these would
result in irreversible psychological damage for many gay men.
This does not appear to be true. But, many gay men are faced
with a Catch-22: you want to be intimate with other men, but
it was men and boys who rejected you, taunted you, and

despised you as a sissy in the past. This dilemma makes establishing trust and intimacy a complex undertaking. This point was made painfully clear by Erin, a seven-year-old boy who was very effeminate from the age of two, and who was referred to one of us for psychotherapy. One day, Erin tearfully told his mother that other boys in school had teased him and called him a faggot. He asked what this meant. She hesitated and then told him, "A faggot is a boy that loves boys and not girls." "But," Erin exclaimed vehemently, "I don't even *like* boys!" Many gay men may find themselves exactly in this position: they love men, but never even liked boys.

If you were effeminate as a child and therefore felt different from the other boys, you may have a strong desire to fit in as an adult and be tempted to suppress your individuality and not make waves. This desire can hardly be faulted, but it can be detrimental to intimacy; your relationships are likely to be more pseudo-intimate than intimate because you are too afraid to let your partner really know you. And if men and boys rejected you as a boy, the adult you become may feel starved for approval from men. "Tell me who you want me to be" in which you change yourself to suit your partner can seem like a good approach to seeking this approval but it is only a short-term answer. You cannot have a close relationship if you do not share yourself. As we discuss later in this chapter, one source of healing if you grew up feeling different may be the sense of belonging that comes from joining the gay community.

DENIAL, SECRECY, AND SHAME

I still remember the exact moment it hit me that I was gay. I was in sixth grade. There was a boy in my class, Phil, who was athletic and well-liked, and I always daydreamed that we were best friends. One day, after gym class, I couldn't keep my eyes off Phil as he showered. I had discovered how to jack off several months before, and that night in bed I fantasized touching and kissing him in the shower. After I came, I suddenly realized: "This is what it means to be gay—to be interested in sex with men." I had

always known that I was different from the other
boys. Now I understood why. It was good to have
figured this out. But I was furious that what they
had been calling me for so many years was true.
And I made a pact with myself: no one, not anyone,
would ever know my horrible secret.

Even if as a boy you knew you were different from other boys, it is quite another thing to come to terms with mature sexual feelings when they begin to appear in early adolescence. Almost every gay man or boy goes through some period of denying his sexual attraction for other males. Gay feelings are so clearly against the rules for men in this culture that a natural first impulse is to think, "It can't be true! I'm not gay!" and to hunt desperately for evidence confirming your heterosexuality. Feelings of attraction toward the same sex may hover in the background of your consciousness. These feelings may occasionally surface in your dreams, or daytime fantasies, or you may briefly feel attracted to another man. For some men, the attempt to block out gay feelings may result in severe psychological symptoms, such as depression, anxiety or sexual dysfunction.

Although some men never break through their denial, obviously many do eventually admit their sexual feelings for other men. Even after this courageous step, however, there may be lingering effects from the period of denial. This is especially likely if the denial lasted for a long time. If you suppress your gay feelings over years, you also numb yourself—you lose your ability to feel by blunting your anger, compassion, and empathy. The resulting insensitivity obviously creates problems toward achieving intimacy.

For example, Aaron, a 31-year-old man in one of our groups, spent almost fifteen years denying his sexual feelings for men and convincing himself that his inner fantasies were of no consequence. When we first met Aaron, he had been exploring his gayness for several months and had recently been taken advantage of by a lover. This man had blatantly used Aaron and then run off with several thousand dollars. Amazingly, Aaron claimed to have no angry feelings at all toward this lover. The other group members could not believe Aaron was being truthful about his feelings, but Aaron's reaction made perfect sense given his personal history. By discounting his sexual feelings for so many years, Aaron had also blocked other feelings, like fear and anger. Thus, Aaron had no internal signals to tell himself when he was being violated or abused by another person. He gave whatever was asked of him, with no awareness of whether it was something he really wanted to give. Aaron's attitude was a prime example of the open-house style of relating described in Chapter 2, and it left him vulnerable to exploitation.

Are you continually being hurt by others? Maybe you are ignoring some of your own feelings. Perhaps years of hiding your sexuality, although necessary and lifesaving at the time, has dampened your other emotional responses. If so, don't despair. Aaron eventually made progress. You can too.

You have gone beyond the denial stage when you admit to yourself, "Yes, I am sexually attracted to men." Most gay men come to this awareness around age 13 or 14. This step, although courageous, is typically followed by another conflict: How can you be open about your sexual feelings when everyone around you disapproves? Initially, you may cope with this dilemma by having a hidden inner life. In this private world, you engage in elaborate fantasies of imaginary lovers. In public you hide your sexual feelings or even openly scorn gay men. During this period of enforced secrecy, many gay men develop skills worthy of international spies. They invent imaginary girlfriends, appear to fit in to society's expectations, and may even seem happy. Parents and friends often never suspect that what they see is, in part, a charade. This phase may last a few months or endure for many years.

If you spent time in a private world, see this as a smart choice; you did what you had to do to survive. Most likely, you feared dire consequences if your sexual feelings were to suddenly become public. Let's face it: this fear was quite realistic! As an adolescent you were especially vulnerable if your sexuality was disclosed, because you were dependent on others (like your parents) for emotional and financial support. Also, teenage boys are notoriously homophobic. By keeping quiet about your sexuality, you showed your awareness that you can't trust everyone to be supportive of gay feelings.

Although having a private inner world may have been the best solution to a bad situation, it can have lasting consequences for later relationships. If you spent years imagining white knights in coats of armor, it often is hard to give up the ideal that "relationships are made in heaven." Although real lovers may now be available, you may find that imaginary lovers are still more attractive. The real ones may never seem as sexy, strong, or understanding as the ones you created in your mind during your loneliness.

How you feel about hiding your gay identity also affects your self-esteem and therefore, your relationships. The rare individual may believe, "My gay feelings are not bad or evil, but I'm going to hide them from other people because it will make my life easier and it's none of their business anyway." Probably more common is the feeling: "If others know about my gay feelings, they will no longer love me. This means these feelings are a shameful (or horrible, sinful, sick) part of me and I must never let anyone know about them." Such beliefs need not be conscious to powerfully affect your life, and they may persist even after you come out and are around people who accept your being gay.

In Chapter 2, we described the belief, "If you really knew me, you'd go away," in which you are afraid to reveal your true nature because your self-esteem is so low. For some gay men, this block to intimacy stems from the period when they hide their sexuality. Once you get into hiding your innermost feelings and desires from others, it can be a difficult habit to break. Also, after years of viewing the world as threatening and seeing yourself as flawed, you may find it hard to accept another perspective.

A prolonged period of hiding gay feelings can leave you confused about issues of secrecy and privacy, especially when it comes to sexual matters. You may ask yourself: Who has the right to know about my sexual behavior? When is it safe to be open about my sexuality? Should I feel guilty if I don't tell my friends and lovers everything about my past? Being unable to answer these questions poses an obstacle to having intimate relationships. Your relationships will be more successful if you have a clear idea of what information is legitimately kept from friends and partners.

Much of what we are discussing has to do with shame. Gay men are particularly prone to shame because a vital part of themselves is so clearly condemned by our culture. And although other groups are looked down upon by society (e.g., blacks, handicapped people, women), gay men are different in being able to hide that part of themselves that is frowned upon. When a *secret* part of you is disapproved of, intense shame is almost always the result.

Shame that stems from early childhood is the most destructive kind because it is so firmly embedded in our view of ourselves. Think back: At what age did you become aware of gay feelings? Boys who are acutely aware of gay feelings before puberty and who experience ridicule and humiliation early in life often seem to grow into men full of shame. Late bloomers, who first recognize their gay feelings in adulthood, often did not feel different during childhood or did not feel that they had anything to hide. These men are less likely to have deep-seated shame.

Family attitudes are also related to the shame you carry with you into adult relationships. Consider not only your family's stance about homosexuality, but also how your family handled other ways of being different. Sadly, some families are threatened by any small deviation from the norm. There is an implicit rule, "Everyone must be the same," and different behaviors result in severe punishment. Perhaps you were forced to play a musical instrument, just because others in your family did. Or maybe you got heat because, in a family of athletes, you liked to read. Mandatory sameness is usually an attempt to cover up problems within a family by forcing everyone to toe the line. The most serious offense in a family like this is to be different in a way that is frowned upon by the neighbors, for then the family as a whole loses prestige. As a result, being gay can feel like a terrible way of letting everyone down.

Gay men are not more likely than other people to come from restrictive families. If your family was restrictive, however, you might be especially prone to feelings of shame in adulthood. If you came from a family where differences were viewed as natural or even desirable, you may be somewhat immune to the shame directed at you by society. A good family can immunize you against shame.

If shame was important in your family background, you'll also see it in your siblings, even if they're not gay. Typically, everyone in such a family feels ashamed. Perhaps a brother or sister was less successful in school or less attractive than the rest of the family, and feels inadequate as a result. Sometimes a sibling who was more attractive or more successful than the others feels shame. In families that feel threatened by differences, even positive attributes can make you feel ashamed if they set you apart from others. Talk with your siblings about your family. If you recognize restrictive patterns in your own family, you can see where your feelings of shame came from. When you know why you feel shame, you can work to free yourself of it.

Another way that shame affects closeness is through its deep tie to anger. Not surprisingly, if you come from a family in which shame was a dominant theme, you may carry within you a large reservoir of rage. In intimate relationships, this anger is likely to surface from time to time, and many a partner may be scared away. Shame also affects your ability to express anger directly to others. After all, if you think you're not worth the time of day, why would you say anything when other people treat you badly? Men whose anger is inhibited by shame sometimes are abused in relationships. They may see this as confirmation of their worst fears, that they are unlovable and relationships are sources of hurt.

Many of the gay men in our groups believed that shame was no longer a concern after coming out. You may feel this way too. In our view, shame is something most gay men deal with throughout their lives. First, past shame lingers and affects relationships for years. Also, understandably, you may have situations in your life where you hide your sexuality. Even if you live in a gay neighborhood and have supportive friends, you may still feel the need to keep your sexuality secret from your boss, your travel agent, or your grandmother. Such situations can generate shame and thereby affect your intimate relationships. By recognizing shame, you take the first step toward overcoming it.

GROWING UP MALE

Even though I knew I was gay, I was determined that nobody else would know, and I did my best to play the biggest macho dude around. When I was in the service I drank more, screwed more, fought more, and raised more hell than anyone else in my company. If any man so much as hinted that he was tougher than me, I'd force him to prove it with his fists. And all this time I was hurting so bad inside I could barely stand it. I just wanted to have some guy hold me and let me cry on his chest. Of course, I couldn't let on to this; it wasn't manly.

GM, 24, wants hot male action. Me: good-looking and straight acting; you: macho, hairy, well-hung. Not into mushy romantic evenings. No fats, fems, or weirdos.

It may seem self-evident, but it's easily overlooked: gay men are brought up in the context of all of society's rules and expectations for males. While these norms probably affect all men in their attempts to be closer to others, they are especially important for gay men, because gay men want to be in love relationships with other men. You may believe that in rejecting one part of your male socialization—by acknowledging your gay feelings—you rejected all other parts of the male role as well. Although there is some truth to this, you probably have been influenced by society's standards of masculinity. In some respects, maleness may be more important than gayness in understanding gay male relationships.

One of the first lessons of social behavior you probably learned is to be stoic or subdued about certain emotions. "Big boys don't cry," and the boy who shows fear, distress, or tenderness after a certain age is likely to be ridiculed by adults and peers. All too soon, you learn your lesson, and as adults many men are unable to experience feelings of vulnerability or pain. Expressions of affection or caring are seen as queer and needs for touching and affection as signs of weakness.

A related message that you probably received is that intimacy is dangerous. From early on, most men are taught not to get too close or they will be smothered or swallowed alive by partners. The ideal man is fiercely independent and somewhat distant, and at the end of the movie he rides off alone into the sunset. "Make my day" leaves little room for close relationships. Some psychologists believe that boys learn a fear of intimacy mainly from their fathers and other adult men.[2] In part, this dynamic may help a boy separate from his mother and develop his identity as a man. If intimacy with your mother is replaced by intimacy with your father, later relationships do not suffer. But, most fathers also fear closeness and are not very involved in child rearing. They provide no counterbalance to the message that intimacy is threatening. Gay men who were effeminate boys, and whose fathers rejected them for being different, are especially prone to this message that intimacy is not safe.

Internalizing these ideas—"Big boys don't cry" and "Intimacy is dangerous"—can cause difficulties for men in any type of adult relationship. In heterosexual couples, the woman most often becomes the intimacy expert for the pair in order to resolve the difficulty. She is attentive to subtle cues concerning her partner's feelings, thereby relieving him of the responsibility of expressing his emotions. Also, she learns to carefully gauge the degree of closeness she asks of her partner so that he doesn't feel threatened or smothered. In a gay male couple, these same role options may not exist if both men have successfully learned the lessons of male socialization of "big boys don't cry" and "intimacy is dangerous." Observing two such men interact is like watching two characters in a Clint Eastwood movie: terse, unemotional dialogue, stony faces, feigned boredom. The understatement is almost comical.

If you attended the Clint Eastwood school of relationships, you may say "I don't know how" when it comes time for intimacy. You may also react with the "I can't say yes" pattern, refusing to allow anyone close, reflecting your terror of what closeness would bring. You may find yourself choosing partners who have better intimacy skills than you do, in an attempt to make up for your deficiencies. But this solution rarely works in the long run. Intimacy requires two willing participants and each person must do his share toward achieving intimacy on his own.

Although men in our society are discouraged from connecting with others emotionally, they are encouraged to be as sexual as they want. Sexual exploration is severely frowned upon for women, but for men it is desirable. Men in our society often associate their self-worth with the amount of sexual experience they have. Sexual exploits are seen as a proof of one's maleness. And even if such behavior is not totally approved of, it is usually tolerated for, after all, "boys will be boys."

Some years ago, the gay men in one of our groups showed this belief when they began bragging about the number of sexual partners they had had. A contest quickly developed about who had had the most partners. The less sexually experienced men in the group felt "green" and ashamed. Since then, AIDS has certainly caused a change in the sexual behavior of gay men, but not, we suspect, in society's expectations. Some gay men now struggle with how to maintain their self-esteem as men, while severely restricting their sexual contacts.

An amusing place to find other "sex-pectations" of men is in gay male pornography, for here these beliefs are so exaggerated as to be easily visible. Real men are supposed to be well-hung, have tremendous endurance and sexual skill, and to drop their pants at every opportunity. Woe be to those of us who are sexually shy, have average endowments or little experience, and who fall asleep immediately after the first round of making love. Gay men sometimes reinforce these beliefs in each other because, after all, they are trying to impress another man.

What happens when society's expectations and sexual stereotypes affect gay male relationships? When sex becomes a competitive arena, instead of a way to joyfully experience closeness with another person, it often splits off from intimacy. Sex can be a wonderful path to closeness, but only when it is not viewed as a measure of your adequacy as a man.

The combination of sexual license and emotional restraint among men also creates a distinctive pattern of behavior in our society. Maybe you've encountered men who cannot distinguish sexual feelings from other feelings. When another person might be sad, they feel sexual. When you might expect to be scared, they feel sexual. When they could be happy, they feel sexual, and so on. These men have oversimplified their emotional lives to the point that they only have sexual feelings, those feelings permitted by society for men. By sexualizing even nonsexual issues, such men feel they constantly need sex, but find that it does not satisfy their inner cravings. Gay men are no more prone to this pattern than heterosexual men, but neither are they immune to it.

Another aspect of traditional masculinity is a fear and hatred of homosexuality, sometimes called "homophobia." Homophobia is a cultural phenomenon and it is particularly strong in the United States. You may think that because of your same-sex feelings, you are automatically free of such attitudes, but this is not true. Many gay men harbor a deep-seated hatred and disdain for their sexuality.

Homophobia is widely visible in gay male culture. As shown in the ad at the beginning of this chapter, "straight acting" and "no fems," are frequent lines in gay personals, and homophobic insults often appear in the dialogue of gay male pornography. Some of the cruelest gay jokes we've heard were told to us gleefully by gay men, and many gay men call each other "queen" and "faggot" when they are angry. Such epithets sometimes express familiarity or affection, but more often they show an underlying disdain for gay identity.

Ask yourself: How have I internalized homophobic attitudes? Showing scorn for your partner when he is soft or swishy, or constant vigilance can be indicators of your own homophobia. Deep down you may fear that you are not a real man and that you do not deserve love and respect. Or, like some gay men, you may prefer heterosexual men to gay men as sexual partners, or at least gay men who appear to be heterosexual. Such preferences can greatly reduce the number of partners available for close relationships.

Mutual respect is an essential part of intimacy, and homophobic attitudes are inherently destructive of respect in gay male relationships. Also, homophobia contributes to a sense of shame and may lead to the belief "if you really knew me, you'd go away." If you look down on homosexuals and avoid gay functions you are unlikely to become part of the gay male community. You may perpetuate biases against gay men, maintain your self-contempt, and miss out on a major source of support and healing for your relationships.

It is worth noting that some experts see homophobia as being rooted in a fear and scorn of men, as well as of homosexuality. In this sense, homophobia can interfere with all expressions of tenderness and closeness between you and other men, even when it is clear that such behavior is not sexual. Whether a hatred of maleness or a fear of homosexuality, homophobia is a challenge for gay men to love themselves.

ACHIEVEMENT AND COMPETITION

In our society, men primarily base their self-worth on their jobs and their status relative to other men. In contrast, women generally define their identities in terms of their relationships with significant others. Closeness is not expected to be a priority for men. In fact, men who value relationships may be viewed as lacking drive, purpose, or masculinity. If you blindly adopt society's beliefs about masculinity, you put yourself in a no-win situation and limit your capacity for intimacy.

Keeping achievement in its proper perspective may be particularly difficult for gay men. Gay men lack many of the conventional ways of gaining status, such as having a lovely wife and 2.2 kids in the suburbs. Without these measures of success, some gay men push themselves to achieve more than other men. Such compensation has its costs. As a man in one of our groups put it, "I've struggled my whole life to get respect from men, and now that I've finally gotten it through my work, I have no time for friends or lovers." This dilemma can be resolved by keeping work and relationships in a healthy balance and broadening your definition of what it means to be a man.

Competition is another aspect of the male emphasis on achievement, and it is one of the primary ways that men and boys relate to each other while growing up. In its proper perspective, competition can be a positive force, leading to greater growth on everyone's part and a sense of camaraderie among members of the same team. You don't need to give up your desire to excel at tennis, bridge, or painting to be intimate with others. If you excessively emphasize achievement and competition, however, it can interfere with trust and safety in relationships.

To be close, there must be times when you can just be yourself. If you've accepted the male competitive ethic, you may have difficulties letting down your guard because you're convinced that people are constantly rating you and comparing you to others. This can contribute to the "I can't say yes" scenario described in Chapter 2, in which you cannot trust another man for fear of getting hurt. If you expect to fail when others rate you, you might develop "If you really knew me, you'd go away." In this case you block intimacy because you are afraid that you don't really measure up. The competitive ethic also produces the man who constantly needs to show that he is smarter and more desirable, or a better cook, lover, or runner than his partners. Constant competition in the bedroom, kitchen, and neighborhood park makes your relationship feel unsafe, desperate, and empty. Intimacy is not possible under these conditions.

Of course, competition can occur between partners in any type of relationship, but relationships involving two men are particularly susceptible to constant competition. "It takes two to tango," and competition escalates when both partners know the dance well. If there was intense sibling rivalry in your family during your childhood, you might be especially prone to competitive relationships as an adult. If your parents compared you to your heterosexual brothers, you are among the group of men who often feel most competitive with adult lovers. Understanding these dynamics is useful if you are struggling with competition in your intimate relationships.

Competition is generated by the belief that, "There is only so much love to go around." This message leads to desperation for both winner and loser, for even if you win, it's always possible to lose the next round. Cooperative relationships give a different message: "No matter how much (food, love, money) there is to go around, we will share it." This message is much more compatible with the mutual respect and security that is essential to intimacy.

COMING OUT

There was a gay students' group my freshman year in college, but I was too scared to attend the meetings. Then, in my sophomore year, something shifted. More and more I thought, "Maybe it isn't so bad to be gay," and I started fantasizing about meeting other gay men. Then one day, I did it. I had just sung in a very successful concert and was feeling good about myself. Afterwards, I went to a gay party that was advertised in the school paper. I was shaking as I walked in but felt more comfortable when I recognized a few people. I never knew there were so many gays and lesbians on campus! I talked a long time to a cute guy, and two days later he called and asked me to a movie. My first date! I was flying high for a week and began to think about telling my best friends my secret.

Just as most gay men go through a period of hiding their sexuality, most also experience the joy of eventually coming out of hiding and sharing their inner life with significant others. You may remember your coming out as a time of joy, honesty, new freedom, and excitement. You may have had other feelings, among them fear and anger, at the same time, although they may have been less obvious to you.

The joy that comes from disclosing your sexuality to someone else and being accepted is a sign of the growth toward self-acceptance. Self-acceptance is essentially an internal decision to love and cherish a part of yourself that may be scorned by others. It's when you can say, "I have to be me, no matter what other people think." Although self-acceptance is partly a personal process, no one can develop feelings of being valued, accepted, and worthwhile in complete isolation. You must take risks to gain the acceptance of others, and the benefits of coming out are often very much in proportion to these risks. For example, the least threatening people to tell about your sexual feelings for men are usually other gay people, but their acceptance may also mean the least to you. Telling heterosexual friends and family that you are gay can be very threatening, but also may yield the most benefits. Thus, self-acceptance, while essentially personal, can be fostered by courage, responsibility, and trusted friendships.

Of course, there is no guarantee how friends, family, and co-workers will respond when you tell them you are gay. However, you may find you can predict fairly accurately who will accept you. General discussions about homosexuality or a newspaper article relating to AIDS can help you introduce the topic and decide whether you wish to trust a person further. Such planning is important to ensure that your first experiences with coming out are rewarding, that is, that the persons you tell you are gay will be accepting of your sexuality. Having a few positive experiences in coming out will decrease the pain of rejection if it occurs.

Sometimes, the coming-out process is accompanied by

frequent sexual activity and exploration with alcohol and drugs. This stage is like the rebellion and exploration common in adolescence and may simply be delayed for gay men. If initial attempts at coming out are postponed long past the average age of mid-adolescence, this period of exploration may be especially intense and prolonged. Now, because of AIDS, such behavior is a risky way for you to come to terms with your sexuality.

You may think of coming out as a process that occurred for a short time in your life, never to return. Actually, being open about sexuality is an issue that you will face repeatedly throughout your life. For example, if as an adult you change jobs or move, you may find yourself in exactly the same situation you encountered during your teenage years—with few friends who know about your sexuality. If you wish to deepen new friendships, you must gather your courage against possible rejection and once again reveal that you are gay. Even if you live in the same place your whole life, you will encounter new people from time to time and will need to decide about being open about yourself.

Think of the coming-out process as a model for intimate relationships. Although your friends and lovers know that you are gay, if you seek intimacy you will always be revealing something. It may involve disclosing that you were sexually abused as a child, that your father was in prison, or that you are HIV positive. Or you may be a Republican among Democrats, or a science fiction lover whose friends are all literature snobs. Each time you take the risk to disclose personal information to build relationships, you are coming out.

We have found this view of coming out helpful to gay men in our groups in thinking about intimacy. Gay men are experts at disclosing their sexuality, and many of the same guidelines apply to other types of revelations. For example, test the waters before sharing other information, and you probably shouldn't share everything with everyone. Just as with disclosures about sexuality, start with safe people before moving on to riskier ones. The benefits of this broader revelation are very similar to those of coming out as a gay man: an increased sense of self-acceptance and of connection to those around you.

Cherish these many small moments of self-disclosure, just as you may remember and feel proud about the times you were open about your sexuality. Building intimacy is a life-long process that requires courage and dignity. By congratulating yourself on your strength and honesty so far, you set the stage for further acts of bravery.

DIFFICULTIES WITH FAMILIES

My heart was pounding as I ate my salad. I was sure I would choke if I didn't get this over with soon. I took a deep breath and swallowed hard.

"Mom," I stammered, "I have something to say to you."

She immediately tensed, her lips pursing and her shoulders hunching a bit. Even before, I could tell that she was nervous too. Obviously, she knew something was up when I invited her to lunch three days before I left for graduate school.

"I've been waiting to tell you for a long time, but I've been too scared. Now the dishonesty is really bothering me. I don't feel comfortable coming home anymore, and I miss the talks I used to have with you and Dad. I feel like I'm losing my family and I don't want that to happen. Mom, I'm gay and Paul is my lover."

■　■　■

No, I don't see my family, but I don't miss 'em. We never had anything in common and were always at each others' throats. Even when I was little, they couldn't stand it that I wasn't like my brother. Sure, there was a time when I wanted it to be like in the fairy tales: ". . . and they all lived happily ever after." I even told my parents I was gay. That was a mistake. My mom started crying hysterically and my dad came after me with his fists. I went over to a friend's house for the night, and the next day I couldn't get in the house. They had changed all the locks. My things were out in the garage with a note: "Manny, we never want to see you again." I moved to the city and tried to call them once or twice. They

*always hung up as soon as they heard my voice. I
went through a bad time, but now I think it was for
the best. What do I need a family for anyway? If it
were up to me, we'd take children away from their
parents when they were born and raise them some-
place else.*

Whether or not you've been through the experience of
telling your family you are gay, you may understand our
point in this section: gay men face certain difficulties with
their families simply because they are gay and because they
are men. These difficulties may exist whether or not homosexuality is ever openly discussed in your family.

For some gay men, family difficulties begin in childhood. As we mentioned, if you were considered effeminate as
a boy, your father may have rejected you or ridiculed you in
an attempt to get you to act masculine. These reactions are
especially likely if your father firmly held traditional male
values. Having a brother or sister who fit in better than you
did may have caused more than normal rivalry between the
two of you, especially if your parents made shaming comparisons: "Why can't you be like your brother?" And if your
siblings' friends taunted them about you, they may have
strongly resented your being different. Finally, if you were
considered effeminate as a boy, your mother may have tried
too hard to shelter you from the hazing of society. This may
have inadvertently given you the message: "You will not be
safe unless I am around."

These types of strains exist not only in your past; they
can result in lingering hard feelings between you and your
family, thereby robbing you of one source of support and
closeness in adulthood. Also, the family patterns that develop
around boys who are effeminate can affect their close relationships as adult men. A rejecting father can leave you
feeling insecure as a man. Rivalrous relationships with brothers and sisters set you up for competitive relationships with
friends and lovers. And an overprotective mother can leave
you thinking that you can't survive life's demands without the
protection of one particular person, a belief that predisposes
you to pseudo-intimate rather than intimate adult relationships.

Luckily, some families don't respond in these ways to
boys who are different, and only a portion of gay men are

considered effeminate as boys. Nevertheless, if the family patterns described here fit for you, they can be strongly influencing your adult relationships.

You probably also faced considerable challenges while hiding your homosexuality from your family. During this time, many gay men have a sense of emotional distance from their families. They spend little time with their families, get little emotional support, and often move far away from home. This emotional distance is not surprising. Intimate relationships require trust and honesty. If you feel that you must hide an essential part of yourself from your family in order to be loved and accepted, how can you possibly maintain real closeness with them?

Sometimes, there is a spiral of hurt and distrust generated by secrecy within a family: you do not tell your parents that you are gay and start spending less time at their home the better to keep your secret. They are upset that you no longer seem to care and are cold and distant when you call. This makes you want to visit them less and discourages you from breaking your silence, and so on. Patterns like these can take on a life of their own and are sometimes broken only when one party takes the courageous step of showing how much she or he cares.

If you do tell your family you are gay, the reaction you get can have profound effects on your self-esteem. If your family reacts negatively or gives you little support (for example, ignores your disclosure), you are challenged to value yourself fully without help from your family. Gay men whose families support their sexuality probably feel self-confident, independent, and hopeful, and they often desire more contact with their families. These positive reactions are partly a result of a healing of shame because loved ones accepted a part of yourself that you always feared they would reject.

Even the healthiest of families may not react joyfully to the news that you are gay. Typically, you can expect the same feelings that arise when someone important to you dies: shock, denial, anger, guilt, shame, confusion, depression, and acceptance. These reactions are a normal part of the grief process, a process that families are exposed to repeatedly in a number of small ways. In this instance, no one has actually died, but your family is mourning beliefs, hopes, and desires that they now must let pass. Facing up to the knowledge that you are gay is painful because so many significant hopes are now lost to them.

For example, your parents may have hoped that you would marry a beautiful woman, make lots of money, have 2.2 children and a dog, and buy a house in a nearby community. They may have spent years envisioning this future. Your siblings and grandparents may have had similar expectations. Now, the news that you're gay appears to significantly alter these plans. No wonder they're upset. A challenge arises: will your family members allow themselves to experience and pass through the intense feelings associated with the grief process, or will they reject you as a way of avoiding these feelings?

Knowing more about the grief process helps you understand your family's reactions to your coming out. For example, after the initial discussion of your sexuality, your family may seem to ignore the topic: "We're going to act as if this never happened. Please don't force us to face this." This response is an example of *denial*, an initial stage in mourning in which people pretend a loss never happened. If your family is intent on denial, they may be furious if you insist on continuing to discuss your sexual lifestyle. Often families are reluctant to move out of this stage because they have an unconscious sense of the feelings that await them: anger ("How could you do this to us?"), guilt ("What did we do to cause this?"), hope ("If you go to see a psychiatrist, you can be changed"), and disappointment ("We thought you would grow out of this!"). Eventually, they may feel depression ("This is the end of the world") and acceptance ("This is the way you are, and we can't change you"). There isn't an orderly progression from one stage to another. Your family may repeat earlier stages or switch back and forth between two stages. As grief progresses, however, they probably will move closer to acceptance.

Telling your family about your sexuality means reaching out to them for closeness; it demonstrates many of the things we have said about intimacy. For example, coming out is a risk and a way of openly acknowledging differences between you and your family. There is likely to be some conflict and tension as a result of your disclosure, and the tension is likely to be resolved if there is an acceptance of differences on both sides and a recognition that people can disagree and still be close. Revealing your gay feelings to your family can teach you a lot about intimacy in general.

Thinking of coming out as an act of intimacy may help you decide whether you wish to come out to your family. Remember, it's not possible to be intimate with everyone, and some people are clearly inappropriate for intimacy. Also, intimacy requires an investment of energy and time. Only you can decide whether your family members have the qualities necessary to join you in pursuing real closeness and whether the work it would entail is worth the benefits you might obtain. Remember that intimacy is not an all or nothing thing. You can tell your mother and father, but not your grandparents. Or you can tell your mother and father that you are gay, but not invite them to spend spring vacation with you and your lover. You can choose how much intimacy you desire with your family.

If you think of disclosing your sexuality to your family as a challenge to intimacy, it may also help you predict how they will react to your disclosure. Many families are able to meet the challenge, at least partly, but some are not. The families that cope best are comfortable with differences between family members, have a strong base of warmth and affection, the skills to deal with anger and other strong feelings, and a solid shared spiritual life. In short, your family is most likely to react well to your coming out if it has already established some intimacy.

If you decide not to tell your family about your sexuality at this time, consider other, less threatening ways to get closer to them. If these efforts go well, you can always reconsider telling them later. On the other hand, if you can't spend an enjoyable evening playing cards or watching a movie with your family, the chances are less promising that coming out will be a positive experience for you. As with other forms of intimacy, take slow, gradual risks with your eyes wide open. This usually brings the best results for everyone involved. The rest is up to your family.

There is one other way that knowing about intimacy can help you reveal your gay feelings to your family. Earlier we discussed how coming out could positively affect you. In fact, your family may also benefit from a coming-out experience. This is illustrated by the following letter, received by a gay man from his sister:

Dear Richard,

I just wanted to bring you up to date on happenings at home after your visit, and to thank you again for the courage you showed in telling us all about your being gay. As you know, Mom and Dad were pretty upset initially—they had always planned for you to carry on the family brains and name—but I think they are starting to come around now. Last night, Mom talked to me about it for the first time without crying, and today, I caught Dad reading one of the books you left for them. I'm not saying that everything's hunky-dory, just telling you not to get discouraged and to give them time to get used to your news.

Really the major reason I'm writing is to let you know how I'm feeling. You know, I've always admired you terribly, Richard, and this has just increased my respect for you. You were so patient and clear in answering everyone's questions that night. It made me really proud to be your sister. I've missed you over the past four years and felt a rift growing between us. I was afraid to say anything before, but now I understand what it was about. I hope that now that everything is out in the open, we'll see more of each other again.

Perhaps the best thing to come out of this so far is that I've begun to think about the ways that I hide myself in our family. Remember Dan, and how I was afraid to tell Mom that I was on birth control pills? Don't take this wrong, but if Mom and Dad can learn to deal with their son being gay, they should be able to accept their daughter having sex with a man! Your honesty has set an example for us all.

I hope you are well and that you haven't suffered many sleepless nights since you left. I love you and look forward to see you soon.

                                                    Love,
                                                    Ann

Coming out tests the emotional well-being of a family and challenges every member of that family to deal with broader issues. As you can see in the preceding letter, when family members are able to do this, the benefits are many and varied. No matter how your family responds, respectfully telling them that you are gay is a precious gift.

How does it affect you and your family if you must continue to hide your sexuality or if your family is unable to accept the challenges of intimacy? Some men in this situation will tell you that they suffer no ill effects. Like Manny, the second man quoted at the beginning of this section, they often have a "who needs them?" attitude about their family. This is a painful way to cope with the profound grief that comes from losing one's family ties, for Manny has lost his family just as surely as if they all had died in a horrible accident. A loss like this can leave you without the practical support—emotional, financial—available to men who are in contact with their families. But such losses can have less obvious consequences that deeply affect your other relationships.

In his support group, Manny's every action showed his belief that honesty leads to loneliness. Whatever the topic, he never expressed his opinion but only agreed with other group members as a way of saying, "Tell me who you want me to be." Finally the group picked up on this and confronted Manny, asking what he really thought and felt, why wouldn't he ever give his own opinions, but felt he had to agree with someone else? Manny admitted that he was afraid that if the others didn't like him, he would be booted out the door, just as he was in his family. This is an example of the "I won't make that mistake again" approach to intimacy. With much support from this group, Manny was eventually able to find and express his likes and dislikes.

If your family rejects you because you are gay, they themselves may suffer ill effects. Their action strengthens the belief that it is not okay to have differences in the family and that any violations of this rule will be severely punished. This type of threat can make it difficult for other family members to assert their independence while keeping family ties. Some may choose lives of quiet resignation, never expressing their individual potential. Others may break away from the family entirely, an action that may allow them to reestablish contact with you later on. Neither of these options leads to healthy, intact families. The way your family reacts to your coming out shows the current strength of the family and influences the well-being of every individual in it.

BETRAYALS BY ORGANIZED RELIGION

I was so proud of being an altar boy. I learned the Latin faster than any of the other boys and loved to put on the long black cassock and starched white surplice and serve Mass. I felt happy up there on the altar and somehow closer to God. Father Andrew liked me and often asked me to help out on special occasions. I was more careful than the other boys and always arrived early for Mass. I had a bit of a crush on him, although I didn't know it at the time. For several years I even wanted to be a priest. My parents were ecstatic. Every Irish family is supposed to give one son to the Church. When I started having sexual dreams about the other boys, I didn't know what to do. I knew that it was a sin, but I couldn't help it. Those feelings felt like such a deep part of me that I didn't know how to stop them. I spoke to Father Andrew about it in confession and he told me I should stop being an altar boy for a while. I cried for a week and couldn't tell my parents why. Eventually, as it became clear to me that I was gay, I stopped going to church. I wanted nothing to do with a God who would make me gay, and then reject me for it.

Organized religions' rejection of gay people epitomizes the failing of the larger culture: An institution that promised solace and spiritual support for all has become an instrument of pain and oppression. In no other context can the betrayal of gay men and lesbians be seen more clearly. Perhaps even more unfortunate, this betrayal has led some gay men to reject all spiritual practices and aspire to a completely secular, atheistic existence. This is tragic because an active spiritual life is of great benefit in maintaining intimate relationships. We believe that being close to others often requires spiritual discipline and guidance.

The persecution of gay men and lesbians by organized religion is especially heartbreaking, because many gay men and lesbians have great sensitivity to spiritual experiences. Throughout history, gay people have occupied prominent places as healers, priests, and counselors. Perhaps, as several writers have hypothesized, there is some way that being "different" specially prepares you for a life of service and ministry.[3] In our own work, we have observed that a number of gay men report very strong spiritual interests in childhood or just before coming out. Often, after deciding to be open about their sexual orientation, they reject all religious involvement.

The affinity or talent of gay men for spiritual experiences may explain their strong rejection of religion after coming out. The vehemence you hear from some gay men about religion clearly does not indicate indifference. Rather, such feelings are reminiscent of someone who has been deeply hurt by a cherished lover. When many gay men discuss their estrangement from traditional (especially Christian) churches, they emphasize the hypocrisy of these churches. It is disturbing to be presented with a gospel of love and acceptance, all the while knowing that those around you would disapprove of you if they knew you fully. It takes a certain spiritual wisdom to recognize this sham. Having seen the hypocrisy of mainstream churches, many gay men decide they want nothing at all to do with organized religion.

Fortunately, this same sensitivity is responsible for much spiritual searching on the part of gay men and women. Groups like Metropolitan Community Church, Dignity (gay and lesbian Catholics), Lutherans Concerned, Integrity (gay and lesbian Episcopalians), Beyt G'vurah (gay and lesbian Jews), and Friends (Quakers) for Lesbian and Gay Concerns provide settings for spiritual exploration and sharing. Some gay men find acceptance and growth in eastern or pre-Christian (pagan) religions. Yet others find more personal routes for expressing their relationship to the universe, such as music, poetry, or gardening. In fact, a spiritual revolution seems to be taking place in the gay community in part as a response to AIDS. In the face of adversity, gay men are once again demonstrating their capacity to dig deeper within themselves and transform pain into personal growth.

Last but not least, a number of courageous gay men and lesbians have decided to work within the mainstream churches, out of a personal conviction that they are called to bring about change from within. This requires great inner strength and an ability to acknowledge the good in these churches, while rejecting shaming messages about one's own sexual orientation.

What happens if you do not find a way to express your spirituality and continue to feel the condemnation of traditional religion? The most obvious result is lingering feelings of shame and unworthiness, which can have detrimental effects on close relationships. In the words of Dr. John McNeill, the gay priest who was expelled from the Jesuits because of his writings on homosexuality: ". . . to have a stable, healthy relationship, one needs to have a healthy self-love and acceptance, which is psychologically possible only when one can accept one's sexuality as morally good and . . . compatible with God's love (p. 245)."[4]

If you have no established spiritual outlet you may also feel empty and that life is without meaning. Several years ago one of us saw a suicidal gay man in a hospital emergency room. The son of a Baptist minister, he had rejected his religious upbringing and claimed to be a fervent atheist. Yet he told of wanting to kill himself because there was "something vibrant and beautiful inside" him that he "knew was there, but couldn't connect with." We believe this young man's despair was the result of feeling cut off from his spirituality, that vibrant, beautiful part of himself. Perhaps you long to connect with this part of you.

Yet another sign of spiritual barrenness is an emphasis on external factors in relationships and a lack of attention to deeper ties. This attitude, which we have called "all that glitters is gold," is certainly not peculiar to gay men. We see evidence of this idea every day in our wider culture. However, being rejected by organized religion certainly could set you up to believe that only tangible things are to be trusted. Our hope is that you can draw upon your experience in being different from the rest of society to reclaim genuine spiritual values and thereby invigorate your relationships. In doing this, it will be essential to cultivate forgiveness and to differentiate the baby (spirituality) from the bath water (religious practice).

Finally, analogous to the process in families, if you openly participate in a mainstream religious community, it is likely that all members of that community will benefit from your presence. Through their gay and lesbian members, traditional churches are currently given the opportunity to reexamine outdated moral precepts and to acknowledge "that of God in every person." Such an affirmation could greatly enhance the ministry of these churches and have profound effects on the lives of all members. Again quoting from John McNeill: "The gay . . . movement is . . . offering . . . churches a challenge and an opportunity to grow to the full stature of the human family." Our prayer is that traditional churches will grasp this opportunity, and experience the same spiritual healing that is taking place in the gay community.

THE GAY COMMUNITY

I remember the first time I walked into a gay bar. I was scared and had to be coaxed to go in. The bouncer joked with Tim, my first lover, about where he had found such a cute one, and I began to relax almost immediately. Then we rounded the corner and I spotted the dance floor: all these beautiful men were laughing and holding each other as they danced. Tim put his arm around me and kissed me. I was in shock. After years of thinking I was the only gay person in the world, I was surrounded by gay men. I felt so free and accepted. I was on a high all night. Tim and I danced until early morning and still I wouldn't leave. There was some kind of magic in that room and I wanted every bit of it I could get.

After coming out, many gay men begin to participate in the gay community. In fact, it is probably best to speak of gay communities, for there has never been a unified gay culture in this country. Although the stereotype of the urban gay clone definitely has some truth to it, even in the late 1970s, only a small number of gay men fit this description. Now, gay male culture is even more diverse, due to recent transformations. As described by Eric Rofes in his book, *Gay Life*:

> We are considering changes which have been evolving slowly over the past fifteen years; new and different ways in which a vast population of gay men conceptualize their homosexuality, structure their relationships, pursue careers and interests. We're talking about men who have survived the repression of the closet, worked through coming-out issues, grappled with contemporary gay male images and emerged intact, relatively satisfied with life and fully at peace with their whole selves (p. 1).

Writing about gay male culture today is like photographing a model who is constantly in motion. We have the urge to insist, "Please stay still—don't move," all the time aware that the movement is part of what we must capture in our description.

Several important things happen to you when you participate in gay society. First, healing starts to take place. You cannot learn self-acceptance in a vacuum, and the gay community can help you overcome your hurts and shame. After years of loneliness and pain, you may find joy and a renewed pride through gay bars, organizations, and relationships. Instead of thinking, "No one could possibly love me," you may begin to believe, "Maybe I'm okay the way I am."

Given the deep connection between anger and shame, it is not surprising that one way the gay community heals is by helping you to identify and express your anger. "I'm not going to stand for this anymore!" may sum up this part of your journey. During this period, you may discover old resentments toward family members and begin to empty the reservoirs of rage that you stored within from years of disrespectful treatment by society. Although this process may be frightening for friends and family, remember, it's an important part of your healing. Don't be scared by your anger. The ability to express anger respectfully is essential in close relationships. By helping you discover and express your anger, the gay community is preparing you for intimacy.

As you participate in gay culture, you also develop your identity as a gay man. This may sound insignificant, but it's not. It's very important to belong to some supportive group of people who share your characteristics and heritage. If you never find such a group, you may feel lonely, unfulfilled, and confused about who you are. Such feelings may affect adult intimacy by leading to a "Tell me who you want me to be" pattern in relationships; instead of determining who you are, you become whatever your latest partner is looking for, even if it isn't what you're like at all. For years, many gay men and adolescents struggled with these issues because they had no models of what it means to be gay.

Today, gay boys and men have a much easier time than ever before in obtaining information about gay culture. If you are a gay adolescent, you probably have access to gay culture through friends, movies, and books (like ours). Gay men now have many ways of locating each other. Once you come to the realization that you are gay, the chances that you will remain confused and isolated have greatly decreased. You can now explore your personal identity with much less fear than before. Because a firm identity is essential to intimacy, whatever you do to strengthen your own identity will better equip you to form close relationships. Gay culture, with its relatively consistent set of values and traditions, provides a model and a mirror through which you can discover who you are.

So what is the relatively consistent set of values that comprises contemporary gay culture? Actually, there have been several stages in the development of these values. In the early 1970s, at the beginning of modern gay liberation, gay male culture was antiauthoritarian and emphasized individuality and personal freedom. Lots of energy went into politics, for gay men were establishing their rights to live as they wished. The mottos then were "Gay is good!" and "Nobody is going to tell us what to do anymore!" Intimate relationships were desired but not emphasized; everyone was having too much fun to settle down.

In the late 1970s and early 1980s, there was a shift away from political values in the gay male community, although some individuals courageously continued to work for gay rights. The new emphasis was on beauty, excitement, romance, and material possessions. It's as if, having come out en masse, gay men were now determined to treat themselves well and realize their dreams. "All that glitters is gold" sums up this period, and although many gay men were interested in close relationships, there was much searching for how to bring these about.

During this period of celebration and exploration, several aspects of the gay community may actually have worked against intimate relationships. First, there were staggeringly high rates of alcohol and drug abuse among gay men, which are certainly detrimental to close relationships. Second, in many ways the gay male community supported "tricking," that is, anonymous sex. As we elaborate in Chapter 4, repeated experiences of separating sexuality and intimacy can make it difficult to unite them in one relationship when you later want to.

But change is afoot. Gay men today seem more interested in health than beauty and more intent on fulfillment and joy than excitement. Materialism is being replaced by spiritual searching, and there is intense concern about how to establish quality relationships. This quote from the book *Gay Life*, from an essay by Paul Reed entitled "Serenity," reflects the current trend in gay male values:

> Gay men continue to come out of their closets, migrate to gay urban centers and lead lives in that legendary pursuit of happiness. An edge has been lost, a certain tension is now gone, but it is being replaced by the deeply enriching experience of serenity which blankets our community. We are growing strong in mind, spirit, and body, and at long last we're becoming truly fit. We are on the verge of tremendous success. Serenity is at hand (p. 14).

Some of the gay men in our groups tell stories of the gay community with yet another theme, which we call the "oppressed-oppressor" phenomenon. For fifteen to twenty years you feel different and ashamed because you're gay, all the while longing to find a group of people like yourself who will accept you. Finally, you go through the difficult process of coming out and discover that you're not alone. You are exhilarated at first: there *are* other gay men out there and you're not condemned to the life of a monk! But this joy is short lived. You rapidly find out that you don't fit into this new group of people either: you're not good-looking enough, don't dance well, have no Polo shirts, and don't drink. At first, you try to fit in, but no one gives you the time of day. Then you give up. It's hopeless. The oppressed have become the oppressors. You're an outsider all over again.

This is a situation where the power of community backfires. In establishing a coherent and solid identity for certain gay men, some gay communities exclude many others. These other men do not fit into the prevailing set of values because of some personal difference. Instead of healing and identity, they find scorn and rejection in the gay community.

The oppressed-oppressor phenomenon is not found only in the gay community. A similar process can occur when any oppressed group constructs its own identity. The oppressed-oppressor phenomenon stems from the shaming message internalized from society, "Differences will not be tolerated." This message is simply applied in a new context: we may be different than they are, but you have to be the same as us, or not belong. Although not peculiarly gay, this dynamic concerns us because it is so destructive to intimacy.

Gay men who have faced this type of double rejection are often extremely cynical about gay male relationships. They can be very homophobic and may believe that all gay men are shallow, hypocritical, and incapable of intimacy. Such attitudes can lead to the "I can't say yes" pattern, in which, having been hurt, you find no one safe enough to trust yourself with in a close relationship. No one is good enough for you. Actually, your harsh exterior covers a deep sense of despair and isolation. When your family and your adopted family have both betrayed you, where else can you go?

In fact, the solution for the gay oppressed-oppressor phenomenon is already being worked out. As the gay community becomes more established, more sure of itself, and more mature, there is an increasing breadth of models for gay men. It's as if we all, in a group, are growing out of the stage of pseudo-intimacy—in which differences are seen as threatening and everyone tries to be the same—into a new level of development, where individual differences are accepted and even celebrated. This maturation is likely to bring new vitality to the relationships of gay men.

THE IMPACT OF AIDS

I feel like a cad, but ever since Jon was diagnosed with AIDS, I haven't wanted to have sex with him.

Oh, he's ready and willing since he got out of the hospital, but every time I unzip my fly I think about how he's going to die. That makes it hard to get hard, if you know what I mean. So far, he's acted pretty understanding, but I think it pisses him off. And it's frustrating for me too. Here I am, 28 and at the height of my career, and I have to think about my lover dying. It's fucking unfair, that's what I say.

■ ■ ■

It's a small thing—getting a dog—but I couldn't make up my mind about it for months. Ever since finding out I was HIV positive, I didn't want to start anything new. I barely had the energy to take care of myself, let alone another living thing. And I kept asking myself, "Do I really want to get attached again, knowing that I could be dead in a year?" In the end, I went ahead with it, and now I'm really glad. Sure, I could go anytime, but that was always true. I'm just more aware of it these days. I'm taking one day at a time and enjoying what I can. And I tell you, I've been enjoying Midge! I've gotten more from her than from any other pet. Sometimes when we go out running, I cry just seeing how happy she is. Midge lives so much in the moment—just like I want to live—and I guess the feeling is rubbing off on me a bit. This is strange to say, but even though I never wished for the positive test result, it's helped me appreciate life more. Now, each day feels like a gift.

In recent years, AIDS has become a part of all our lives. At this writing, in the United States alone, there have been 136,204 recorded cases of AIDS and 83,145 recorded fatalities.[5] Whether you know someone who has died from an AIDS-related illness, have gone through the anxiety of taking the HIV test and waiting for the results, have examined your sexual practices to see if they are "safe," or are yourself a person with AIDS, AIDS is likely to have touched your life. If you are one of the lucky few whose life has not been greatly affected by AIDS, you still cannot afford to ignore this condition. AIDS has become an undeniable reality for all of us.

For these reasons, it's important to look at how AIDS has changed intimacy building among gay men. At the very least, AIDS has complicated the task of forming intimate relationships for gay men. At most, AIDS has made relationship building a formidable task, and there is increased frustration and despair among gay men who are searching for closeness. Conversely, the response to AIDS by gay men and others has also led to an increased valuing of intimate relationships. A balanced portrayal of AIDS must examine both of these processes.

In what ways has AIDS made intimacy building among gay men more difficult? Understandably, it has accentuated fear and distrust, for the possible hurts in relationships are no longer just emotional. Intimacy (at least sexual intimacy) is literally a life-threatening act that requires great courage, good judgment, and trust in your partner. While these factors have always been necessary for intimacy, now they are vital.

As the risks of trusting others have increased, people have reacted as one might expect. Some gay men have become more isolated, fearing to open up to any partner, and have given up all hopes of establishing an intimate relationship ("I can never say yes"). Some men have given up physical relationships with others entirely, in favor of repeatedly masturbating in front of video recorders or with anonymous partners on conference-call phone lines. Other men have used the threat of AIDS as an opportunity to improve communication with friends and sexual partners and to reexamine their commitment to their own health. Finally, some gay men sadly persist in their denial of AIDS and of the possible consequences of indiscriminate sexual activity. This latter response is tragic, in that it is potentially fatal.

The response you exhibit to AIDS is often tied closely to your attitude about intimacy before AIDS became a factor. If you were scared and distrustful of others before AIDS, you may be even more so now. If you were ready to sacrifice your life and well-being for a lover, AIDS is unlikely to alter that. If you preferred fantasy lovers to real ones, your video recorder may get even more use these days. Similarly, AIDS may accentuate the way you and your family relate. Those family members who've come to terms with their grief are likely to respond with support and concern. And family members hiding feelings of disapproval now may feel justified condemning you for your sexuality. Certainly you and your family can continue to grow out of emotionally unhealthy patterns. But a healthy response to AIDS requires a mature view of intimacy.

Apart from concerns about your own health, you also face the ever present threat of serious illness or death in your friends. It's hard to get close to others when you're aware that either you or they may be gone in five years. And the commitment to stay with a lover through a painful and financially taxing illness is understandably difficult to make. These challenges are clearest for those gay men already diagnosed with AIDS and for their friends and family. Of those men described at the beginning of this section, the one who got a pet eventually broke through his fear, while Jon's lover is still struggling. How would you react in such a situation? Again, there is a range of possibilities, and your choice is likely to reflect your feelings about intimacy in general.

One result of the threat of loss is depicted in a cartoon: As a puzzled marriage counselor looks on, one partner in a couple explains: "It seems that the only thing keeping us together is that neither of us has AIDS." Although exaggerated, the point is clear: AIDS can be an excuse to prolong unsatisfactory relationships. This is especially likely if you have difficulty believing that you deserve a good relationship.

This brings us back to the topic of shame. Shame among gay men has been intensified by AIDS. In our work as psychotherapists, we find that many of our gay male clients have at least partially (and sometimes unknowingly) accepted the message of fundamentalist preachers: AIDS is a divine punishment deserved by gay men because of the sinfulness of their sexual practices. Believing this can drive you back in the closet, or at the least, keep you from ever coming out. Furthermore, you may find it difficult to completely reject this dehumanizing message while accepting a related but healthy message: you must take responsiblity for your sexual practices and safeguard your life. We encourage you to separate shame and responsibility, accept safer sex practices, and reject shame.

Have you ever thought about how your family and friends are affected by AIDS? Often, the families of gay men must deal with the irrational fears of others about AIDS. They may be harassed by co-workers, shunned by friends, and even ignored by relatives who fear that they are contaminated. Being subjected to such treatment can reawaken old feelings of guilt and responsibility for your gayness (e.g., "How did I fail as a parent?). And of course, these feelings only intensify the grief of those whose loved ones have AIDS.

What happens to you and your family when you are subjected to the shaming messages of fundamentalists and others like them? Feelings of unworthiness increase, make it difficult for you to open up to others, and often lead you to expect less from close relationships. By making intimacy less possible, shame actually perpetuates unsafe sexual behaviors that make AIDS more likely: "The baths are the best I can hope for. What does a jerk like me have to lose anyway?" Finally, shame often has a direct tie to anger in relationships. Many gay men with AIDS are understandably enraged about society's treatment of people with AIDS. This increased frustration can place severe strains on close relationships. For these reasons, the healing of shame is an essential part of the fight against AIDS.

There is one bright spot in an unfortunate turn of events. The spread of AIDS to heterosexuals is tragic. One positive result, however, may be less blame being placed on gay men and their families. As AIDS is no longer viewed as a gay plague and the circle of concern broadens, perhaps the shame associated with AIDS will decrease.

Fortunately, many gay men have responded to AIDS in positive ways. For example, many men are taking better care of themselves physically and emotionally. Rates of gonorrhea and syphilis are decreasing in many parts of the country. Drinking, smoking, drug use, and overworking are down; taking vitamins, exercising, and enjoying clean fun arc on the rise. In the face of the current crisis, gay men have come to cherish themselves more and are expressing this feeling in concrete ways. Apart from increasing individual health, these steps are likely to yield stronger relationships and a healthier gay community.

An awareness of AIDS may also help you appreciate life more. Like the man quoted at the beginning of this section, your days may seem more precious, your friendships more valued, and material things less significant. You may let go of grudges and be more anxious to reconcile with your family. Your love may flow more freely and you may take more emotional risks. A well-known piece of advice is, "Live every day as if it were your last." AIDS brings this message home to all of us in a very real way.

Many families and friends of gay men are also showing their love in response to AIDS. They aid in nursing sick sons and brothers, have donated money for AIDS research, and are joining the ranks of people pressuring the federal government for increased attention to AIDS. We have witnessed several instances of fathers and mothers who have put aside their doubts and reservations about their gay son's sexuality, in order to support them during a health crisis. Such actions have positive effects on whole families, as well as on the individuals involved, because they communicate the healing message, "Our love for each other is more important than any differences we may have."

AIDS is also changing the value structure of the gay community. There is less focus on the externals of beauty and money, and more attention to deeper qualities of commitment, involvement, and compassion. Pettiness seems to be falling out of fashion, and there is increased tolerance for a diversity of lifestyles and individuals. Obviously, these changes do not occur overnight, and there still are many places where "all that glitters is gold." But a fresh, new spirit is in the wind that bodes well for close relationships among gay men.

In fact, one of the most striking effects of AIDS is that gay men are giving more attention to close relationships than ever before. Many men who were once confirmed cruisers are now struggling in the throes of their first monogamous relationship. Gay male couples are expressing their affection in ways that they never have before. And many men across the country, who help care for people with AIDS, are learning how to love in the face of death and illness. In fact, everywhere we go we see a thirst among gay men for intimacy. This could radically transform the gay male community, and we are more convinced than ever before of the relevance of personal introspection and spirituality.

In many respects, AIDS has created a spiritual crisis. Questions of life, death, and the meaning of relationships may be more prominent for you now. Material possessions and superficial friendships, which once seemed to satisfy, may have lost their comfort and their value. And as grief and sorrow sweep through your life, you may despair or be full of rage at a God who would allow such a tragedy to happen. Such feelings are understandable. You may also view AIDS as a challenge requiring courage and personal growth, deeper ways of expressing your spirituality, and more fulfilling relationships. Although we cannot, like some, call AIDS a blessing, we are moved and encouraged by the responses of gay men and others to AIDS. As we look around us, each day seems to echo the phrase, "See how much we love one another!"

> *Sometimes I still think about what I would do if I could choose to be gay or straight. Twenty years ago I would have answered immediately, "Make me straight!" But now I'm not so sure. I mean, yeah, we put up with a lot of crap. And, in some ways, AIDS has made things worse. But other times, when I'm in a group of gay people, I find my heart in my throat from the courage and strength that I see. Last year, my father saw it too. I took him to our Dignity Mass, and afterwards I found him in the hall crying. "It was so beautiful," he said, "to see the community you have. The rest of us are missing out on that feeling." I still don't know, but sometimes I wonder if we gay people fit into God's plan for the world in a special way, to inspire and to challenge others. If only I could hang on to that vision all the time.*

These then are the experiences that shape gay men: being different, feeling secrecy and shame, coming out, male socialization, living with our families, our religions, the gay community, and AIDS. Perhaps in reading this chapter, you saw these forces as working against you in being intimate. Perhaps you had the opposite reaction, and believe that you should have an easier time in close relationships than heterosexuals or lesbians. In fact, neither of these is true; gay men are neither better nor worse at intimacy. Gay men approach relationships in a unique way, and this is, in part, determined by the many forces described here. Understanding this cultural heritage can be an incredible asset to you in relationships.

We have stressed common themes and patterns, but

there are many differences between individual gay men, which also affect intimacy. Also, our view of gay male socialization is necessarily incomplete and limited by our own vision. We have drawn upon scientific research when it was available, but much of this chapter is based on our own experiences and observations. Our insights have come through listening with our hearts to our lives and the lives of those around us. Nevertheless, our views may differ from yours, and there is no way to prove much of what we have said. We offer our ideas unabashedly, as a starting point for discussion, and as a framework for you to understand the rest of this book. We will continue to learn by hearing the ways that your experience differs from ours.

We hope this chapter has personal significance for you. You may have relived past relationships with family members and others. Pause and notice your reactions to being reminded of these parts of your life. You may feel sad or bitter about losses that cannot be undone, or cynical about the value of connecting with others in the future. Or you may have fond memories of the awkward and unique unfolding of your gay identity. Perhaps you feel emotionally flat from reading this chapter: "It had no effect on me one way or another." These and other reactions are all part of your personal journey.

To assist you in your growth, and as a preparation for the following chapter on sexuality, we encourage you to reflect again on your life. This time, we invite you to work a very special miracle: forgiveness. Sometimes the cruelest hurts are those that we impose on ourselves. But you can free yourself from this pain. You already know how to do it.

> *We perform a miracle that hardly anyone notices.*
> *We do it alone; other people can help us, but when we finally do it we perform the miracle in the private places of our inner selves.*
> *We do it silently, no one can record our miracle on tape.*
> *We do it invisibly, no one can record our miracle on film.*
> *We do it freely, no one can ever trick us into forgiving someone.*
> *It is outrageous: when we do it we commit an outrage against the strict morality that will not rest with anything short of an even score.*
> *It is creative: when we forgive we come as close as any*

human being to the essentially divine act of cre-
ation. For we create a new beginning out of the past
pain that never had a right to exist in the first place.
We create healing for the future by changing a past
that had no possibility in it for anything but sickness
and death.
When we forgive we ride the crest of love's cosmic wave;
we walk in stride with God.
And we heal the hurt we never deserved.[6]

NOTES TO CHAPTER 3

[1]Numerous studies have shown a relationship between boyhood effeminacy and adult male homosexuality. Bell, Weinberg, and Hammersmith
(1981) found that childhood effeminacy best distinguished gay men from
heterosexual men. Whitam (1980) and Saghir and Robin (1973) respectively found that 85 percent and 67 percent of the gay men they surveyed
report histories of childhood effeminacy. McWhirter and Mattison (1984)
reported that 77 percent of their gay male sample remember being
"sissies" in childhood. Finally, Green (1987) found that 75 percent of
effeminate boys were homosexual or bisexual as adults.
[2]An elaboration of these dynamics may be found in N. Chodorow, *The*
Reproduction of Mothering: Psychoanalysis and the Sociology of Gender
(Berkeley: University of California Press, 1978); and C. Gilligan, *In a*
Different Voice (Cambridge: Harvard University Press, 1982).
[3]M. Thompson, *Gay Spirit: Myth and Meaning* (New York: St. Martin's
Press, 1987).
[4]J. J. McNeill, "Homosexuality: Challenging the church to grow." *The*
Christian Century (March 11, 1987), pp. 242–246.
[5]These are official figures from the Center for Disease Control for cases to
May 1990. These figures certainly underestimate the incidence of AIDS.
[6]L. B. Smedes, *Forgive and Forget* (New York: Pocket Books, 1984), pp.
191–192.

GAY MALE SEXUALITY
AND INTIMACY

The challenge facing you and other gay men today is to embrace the joys of sexuality while grieving losses due to AIDS. This is a difficult task and, once again, the gay community is pioneering in an area that is crucial for everyone's survival. Others have begun to perceive that they too are affected by the epidemic of AIDS. We hope this chapter will aid you in this challenge, and we dedicate our message to those who have left us, to those who stand and wait, and to all who struggle with sexuality and intimacy.

There are many ways of talking about sexuality. Sexuality involves considerations of health, personal safety, politics, ethics and law, and questions regarding the meaning of life. This chapter touches on many of these topics, drawing on research, the heartfelt struggles of gay men in psychotherapy, and on our own growing pains as men. Through the experiences of the many gay men speaking in this chapter, you can reach a greater appreciation of your sexuality. Open yourself to these experiences. Put aside superficial differences and listen with your heart.

WHAT IS SEXUALITY?

Sexuality means different things to different people. If you are cruising the bars, it may be a way of seeing how you rate. Or being sexual may mean that you are just lonely. Psychotherapists may tell you that sexuality is a way to express anger or work out internal conflicts. Sometimes you consummate the intimacy in a relationship with ecstatic sex. Religious fundamentalists believe that sexuality invites God's wrath. Your new male acquaintance may see sex as out of the question. We won't mention how your mother and father view sexuality. There are as many ways of defining sexuality as there are people.

Here's what we mean by sexuality.

Sexuality is a lifelong process involving feelings, fantasies, and behaviors that promotes an adaptive, pleasurable, and competent use of your body to experience affection and intimacy and to build personal identity.

Sexuality occurs from the time you are in the womb until death. It involves an unfolding of identity. Sexuality is carried out in various ways, from sexual daydreaming to passionate intercourse, and it has many aims, from simple pleasure to procreation. Sexuality involves all of you, all of who you are: erotic dreams, tender massages, exotic perfumes, fantasized lovemaking, physical health, safer sex, and deep embraces. No way of expressing sexuality is better or worse than any other, although some ways of being sexual may be more arousing than others.

You may object to our definition of sexuality: "According to you, nearly everything is sexual." To some extent, that is our belief! Passionate feelings about your body are not limited to what you do in bed. In our view, sexuality is a gift that you can enjoy each moment you live.

Also, by our definition, sexuality is more than what you do; it is who you are. Through the development of your sexuality, you define your identity: gender, gender identity, sexual orientation, and sex-role identity. As you develop your sexuality in all its facets, you have more ways of interacting with other people and of feeling good about yourself. When your sexual development is hindered, you feel less worthwhile. Gay men encounter particularly challenging hurdles in developing their sexual identities.

DEVELOPING A SEXUAL IDENTITY

How do gay men develop a sexual identity? Clearly we cannot fully answer this question here, but we will share some basic perspectives. First, we examine the components of sexual identity and discuss their relevance to gay men. Second, we discuss the development of a gay sexual identity from adolescence to adulthood. Our aim is to help you appreciate the mystery and magic of your sexual being and your finesse in juggling same-sex feelings in a heterosexual culture.

While in the womb, your *gender*, your physical maleness or femaleness, is biologically established through a variety of factors, including hormones. By the eighth week of pregnancy external sexual organs begin to appear; male and female fetuses are clearly distinguishable by the third or fourth month. In males, the testes descend between the seventh and ninth months, moving from the abdominal cavity into the scrotum. The finishing touches on sexual anatomy are completed during the last months of fetal development. The development of gender is no different for gay men than other men.

As soon as you were born, your parents and other family members probably treated you in special ways because of your gender. You already know the custom of dressing boys in blue and girls in pink. But did you know that during infancy, girls are generally pampered and boys treated more aggressively by adults? From early on, boys are given different toys than girls and are allowed to explore their surroundings more. From earliest childhood you began to learn what it means to be male or female. Your sense of yourself as male or female is called your *gender identity*. By twenty-four months of age, most children can identify differences between boys and girls, noticing that boys and girls are dressed differently, have different physical characteristics, and act differently. Generally between thirty and thirty-six months, children are able to identify their own gender—"I am a boy." Also, by their third birthday most children know that their gender is permanent—"I will always be a boy." Gender identity, besides being shaped by society, family, and parental messages about gender, can also be directly influenced by biological factors such as hormones.

Because it is established at such an early age, gender identity has enormous influence on personality and later sexual functioning. It is especially important if you were considered effeminate as a boy, because boys like this develop distorted gender identities. You may have told yourself, "I know I'm not a girl, but I'm too much of a sissy to be a boy." Such confusion can affect you in several ways, from insecurity about your maleness to the feeling that your gender is a biological mistake. Either of these outcomes strongly affects adult relationships. Gay men who have residual doubts about their gender identities often use sex as a way to reassure themselves about their maleness—"If I'm with a macho man, then my identity worries are over." Or, they may act supermasculine to cover up their insecurity. Such strategies never really relieve the basic conflict about gender identity.

Another important aspect of sexual identity is *sexual orientation*, the sense of being sexually attracted to partners of the other sex, the same sex, or both sexes. The origins of sexual orientation are very complex, and there is increasing evidence that it is influenced by biological factors. A well-known sexologist, John Money, claims that in the womb, hormones lay down a blueprint for the later development of sexual orientation. Although biology may be important, sexual orientation can also be significantly affected by experiences after birth with family and peers. [1]

What are implications of this current theory for you as a gay man? First, no one factor is responsible for your sexual orientation; it probably depends on several factors. Second, the origins of your sexual orientation may be different from those of other people. Perhaps for you, biology was the primary determinant of your sexual orientation. Or perhaps you began with a broad potential for sexual expression, which was then crucially shaped by your family and early life experiences. You may never know for sure why you are gay. Third, your gay sexual orientation probably was not a choice that you made, no more than you chose being a boy rather than a girl or speaking English rather than French as your native language. Finally, it is unlikely that your sexual orientation can be altered after adolescence.

The earliest manifestations of sexual orientation can occur during school-age years, in flirtatious play with other children or a crush on a particular teacher. The private awareness of sexual orientation generally occurs by adolescence; however, some gay men postpone this realization until much later.

Gender identity and sexual orientation are both shaped by biology and family. Besides these influences, the larger culture also played an incredibly significant role in your sexual development. From the first moments of birth, a child is taught to behave according to cultural standards for its gender. These standards are internalized to produce a *sex-role identity*, the awareness of how boys and girls are supposed to act. Typically, boys are masculinized to show aggressiveness, competitiveness, and ruggedness and girls feminized to show passivity, cooperation, and vulnerability.

Preschool children often have flexible sex-role identities. They revel in dressing up in adult clothes, sometimes of either gender, and playing adult roles, again of either gender. In contrast, during school-age years, sex-role learning is particularly intense, and children try to fit in with peers. They often take their cues from parents, teachers, peers, and the media about what it means to be a boy or girl. The lessons that boys learn about male identity during this period strongly affect their relationships and self-image for their entire lives. When internalized, messages such as "intimacy is dangerous," "real men are always on the make," and "queers are freaks" are part of the sex-role identity of both gay and heterosexual men.

SEXUAL DEVELOPMENT IN ADOLESCENCE AND ADULTHOOD

For most boys, the basic components of sexual identity are in place by the beginning of adolescence. However, your sexual development continues throughout your life span.

Adolescence. Adolescence is a crucial time for sexual development. Your experiences during this period strongly affect your relationships for years to come. Male secondary sexual characteristics—lower voice, more body hair, increased size of the penis and scrotum, large muscle development, and "wet dreams"—begin to appear and continue into young adulthood. Frequently there are periods of rapid physical growth in which a boy's body appears to be out of proportion. All these changes, combined with acne, unpredictable erections, and physical awkwardness, can lead to feelings of shame about your body. Many adolescents feel that their bodies are their worst enemies. Such feelings are normal, but if not recognized and resolved may result in body shame as an adult.

Total reliance on others for identity comes to a screeching halt during adolescence. During teenage years, the adolescent reviews his entire sexual and psychological development and begins to redefine his own identity. Sometimes teenage boys brazenly exaggerate clothes, hairstyles, affectations, and provocative behavior with the expectation that others will be totally accepting. By alternately experimenting with these new behaviors and then retreating to childhood expectations, a boy explores his personal sexual lifestyle. For example, he may decide that he can be sexual on the first date, that his partner had better appreciate his mix-and-match taste in clothes, and that he likes to be caressed in certain places and not in others. When dating becomes too stressful, he may lie around at home to be taken care of like a child.

Peer influence is strong during adolescence. Teenage boys use friends to develop social skills and gather information about the ABC's of sex. They also look to friends to find values that are different from those of their families. By identifying with peers, boys break away from their families and leap into young adulthood.

Adolescence is also a period of intense sexual experimentation, which serves several purposes: a boy learns that his body is a source of pleasure, becomes aware of the needs and feelings of others, and is drawn into his peer group. Teenage boys frequently don't separate friendship and sexuality; unwanted pregnancy and venereal disease are perils of this period.

Gay boys have a particularly difficult time in adolescence. When they recognize that they are sexually attracted to boys, gay adolescents follow a radically different path of sexual development from their heterosexual peers. Many of the typical experiences of adolescence—dating, going to proms, displaying affection, sharing stories of sexual exploits with friends—are not easily available to gay boys. This can leave them feeling like incredible misfits. Because they don't fit into their peer group, many gay adolescents isolate themselves and miss out on learning social skills and solidifying values. They also face a greater challenge than heterosexual peers in separating from their families. Heterosexual boys often distinguish themselves from their families through dress and taste in music. For gay adolescents the differences are much more fundamental and difficult for families to accept. Parents of gay adolescents often lack the words to explain their son's gay identity. In response to their lingering sense that something is wrong, they may cling to their son in an attempt to protect him.

The normal adolescent feelings of shame and confusion are intensified for many gay boys, for their same-sex feelings give them another reason to believe that their bodies have betrayed them. They may conclude, "I hate my body; it's ruining me!" Generally, gay adolescents have fewer opportunities than heterosexual adolescents for sexual exploration. This can leave them feeling isolated, emotionally distant, and distrustful of their bodies. Some gay youths find outlets for sexual exploration in the adult gay community. However, this leaves them vulnerable to exploitation, physical violence, and sexually transmitted diseases.

As a result of the difficulties they face, many gay adolescents put their sexuality on hold and go into hiding rather than engage in the sexual experimentation normal to adolescence. Consequently, the tasks of adolescence are held over for many gay men into adulthood. This delay in maturity can cause considerable stress in later years.

Young Adulthood. The end of adolescence signals the beginning of young adulthood, when most young men begin to feel a need for more meaning in their sexual behavior. Although there may be no decrease in the frequency of sexual activity, casual sex may have lost some of its appeal. Young adults begin looking for more quality and depth in their sexual relationships. Intimacy and sexuality begin to be seen as distinct choices, and young adults sometimes despair about integrating the two processes. They may seek healthy models of intimate relationships and ask advice from adults. They often feel troubled over ethical decisions, fidelity, trust issues, and future goals. Through trial and error, introspection, and peer support, some harmony of intimacy and sexuality is eventually achieved.

Many gay men only begin to explore sex in their young adult years. Having been sexually repressed during adolescence, young gay adults are often very sexually active, more

so than any other group. Through their sexual experimentation, these men are doing more than just being sexual. They
are defining their identities, learning to feel good about their
bodies, and establishing connections with others. You will
recall that these are the normal tasks of adolescence and are
better done late than never. These gay men may pressure
themselves to make up for lost time, as if they believed, "I
better get as much sex as I can; it may be taken away from me
again." Some gay men use sex to counteract years of anguish
and shame. During this period, questions about when to be
sexual are frequently decided by looking to the gay community for answers, rather than by listening to one's own feelings. Unfortunately, models of committed gay relationships
are often difficult to find, leaving many young adult gay men
feeling cynical and hopeless.

Adulthood. The next stage of sexual development is
adulthood, primarily devoted to generativity: the bringing
forth of some offspring, in the form of a child, creative
project, or career accomplishment.[2] Generally, during this
time, men desire to leave a legacy to the world. Noticing the
passing of time and having achieved some integration of
sexuality and intimacy, adult men yearn for validation of
their own internal growth.

Signs of aging begin to appear during this period: weight
gain, graying and loss of hair, wrinkles, and less physical
agility. There may be jealousy of youth, pretense about being
young, and fear of physical incapacity. The pressure to be-
queath something to the world can leave less time to relax
and be sexual. Thus, intimate relationships can be severely
tested during this period, as people in committed relationships are challenged to balance individual needs with the
demands of their partners.

What are the sexual tasks of adult gay men who have
attained some degree of intimacy? Clearly, the task of
generativity is uniquely challenging to gay men, because they
often do not have children and yet may yearn, like heterosexual men, to give something to the world. To resolve this
dilemma, some gay men adopt children or assume the responsibility of raising children from a prior heterosexual relationship. Often, gay men in a partnership decide to be parents in a symbolic way, by working on a creative project
together, having their relationship serve as a model for other

gay men, and devoting their creative energies to community and spiritual development.

Gay men in this age group often face a greater challenge than heterosexual men in coming to terms with the physical signs of aging, perhaps because of the gay community's emphasis on youthful beauty and thinness. Those men who relied on their physical attractiveness to make sexual connections in young adulthood may have the greatest difficulties during this period.

Late Adulthood. The middle and late years, generally starting around age fifty, represent the final stage of sexual fulfillment. The principal task during these years is reliving one's entire sexual and emotional life, by witnessing the blossoming of past accomplishments and through reminiscing. Decreases in height, muscle mass, strength, and cardiac power may become noticeable during this phase and remind you that death is coming closer. While sexual interest may continue to thrive, it takes men longer to reach orgasm. Changes in sexual functioning challenge older men to develop a broader view of sexuality. Partners in committed relationships may need new flexibility to respond to illness and death. Some older couples report that they have fallen back in love with each other and have a deeper appreciation of the value of intimacy. For other couples, there may be feelings of monotony and fears of anticipated sexual difficulties in their relationships. Those who are single, or alone because of the death of a partner, face isolation and loneliness during this time of life. Such feelings can be alleviated by intimate relationships with peers. These are the years when the last sensuous waltz can linger with dignity, warmth, and meaning.

The sexual development of older gay men is currently one of the best-kept secrets. When our generation reaches this period of life, much more will be known about this subject. Currently, many older gay men express strong feelings of alienation and isolation. In part, this may be because older gay men lack the same options as heterosexual men for peer support. Older gay men often have difficulty locating each other due to their small numbers, and because of the greater shame surrounding homosexuality when they grew up. There is one thing definitely known about late adulthood: as you sow, so shall you reap. The work that you do now to develop intimate relationships and feel pride in your identity will have special rewards in the future.

BICULTURALITY AND GAY SEXUAL DEVELOPMENT

You faced a special challenge in your sexual development that you may not be aware of: biculturality. Much as Chicanos learn to survive among Anglos, gay men must master the sex role expectations of heterosexual society, while also acculturating as gay men. These two cultures have important differences in dress, slang, aesthetic tastes, sexual values, and expectations of men, which makes sexual development especially challenging for gay men. Some gay men are more fluent in gay culture, some in mainstream culture, and others show a reasonable degree of comfort in both.

You may be familiar with some of the difficulties other bicultural groups face.[3] For example, you may feel behind in establishing your sexual identity and developing relationship skills. Such delays are common in bicultural individuals; after all, you had to learn two languages, traditions, and sets of values, while the rest of the world only had to learn one. Many gay men feel confused and distressed about their identities and torn by their loyalties to different sets of values. Such anguish is common when you are trying to fit into two societies at the same time. And gay men who fit both gay and heterosexual cultures often feel lost and alienated. No matter where they go they may feel different and have difficulties establishing deep ties. People who have two other cultures report these same feelings. Recognize the difficulties you face by living in two worlds; these are not your fault, but simply the result of your biculturality.

Like other bicultural people, you may find several ways to alleviate the stresses of biculturality. One way is to gradually withdraw from one of the cultures. You may live in a gay ghetto, work in a gay business, and have only gay friends. These days you can even have a gay dentist, doctor, stockbroker, and plumber! Other gay men opt for heterosexual culture. They maintain marriages, socialize mainly with heterosexual couples, and join the predominantly heterosexual country club. Yet another solution is to look for other bicultural individuals. Some social groups, such as Gay Fathers, include men who are trying to fit into both heterosexual and gay cultures. In groups like this you can discuss your bicultural experiences and get support. Our hunch is that if you can accept your biculturality and maintain ties to both cultures, you'll have a fuller sense of your identity, which will allow you to be more honest and intimate with other men.

Clearly, you also possess strengths as a result of your struggle with biculturality. Bicultural persons often understand the relative nature of social rules and values. It's as if they learn, through their ties to two cultures, that societal norms are not written in granite. This can give you the wisdom to develop your own tastes and values. Gay men often deeply comprehend the value of sexual diversity and the great impact of sexual development. How could you not? It's in your soul!

It is not only gay men who benefit from their biculturality, but society as well. In their crossing back and forth between gay male and mainstream cultures, gay men often bring the treasures of their development to heterosexual society: flexibility about male identity, an appreciation of art and music, humor and playfulness, compassion for the pain of others, a respect for varied expressions of sexuality, and a deep awareness of how the spirit moves in all people.

Forming a sexual identity is a complex human process, and you can be proud of your bicultural sexual development. The challenge to you and other gay men is to accept your internalized heterosexual and homosexual identities. As you comprehend the depth and richness of your sexual development, you'll recognize what a miracle you are and your connection to all humanity.

SEXUALITY AND INTIMACY

What's the one thing that comes to mind when you hear that two gay men are intimate? *Sex*, of course! Failing to see the differences between sex and intimacy may be the one and only thing that fundamentalists and some gay men have in common. At one extreme are those men who confuse sexuality with intimacy and believe that the only way to be close to another man is to get into his pants. At the other extreme are people who feel that getting turned on means that you need to get married to a partner. Either extreme restricts opportunities, impedes personal growth, and results in disillusionment. You deserve to recognize a range of choices encompassing sexuality and intimacy.

A COMPARISON OF SEXUALITY AND INTIMACY

First, let's look at the similarities between sexuality and intimacy. Both processes are pleasurable, as well as anxiety producing. Both processes require skills that need to be learned throughout one's lifetime. Generally, you share intimacy and sexuality with other people when you take a special liking to them. The physiological responses of intimacy and sexuality are quite similar: your breathing becomes more rapid, your heart beats faster, and your pupils dilate. And being intimate may evoke the same feelings as being sexual: excitement, elation, passion, and longing for the other person. Both ways of connecting are intense and meaningful. It's easy to see how the two processes get blurred.

Sexuality and intimacy are different, however. Most people learn to be sexual before they learn to be intimate. Also, sexuality primarily involves an awareness and confidence in your body. In contrast, intimacy enhances your total emotional growth. When two men are sexual together, their main desire is to give pleasure to each other. When two men are intimate, they sometimes tell each other things they don't want to hear, which may be distressing. Being sexual often brings about intimate feelings, but not necessarily. Finally, sexuality may draw you toward the challenge of intimacy, but it doesn't guarantee that you will attain it.

Neither intimacy nor sexuality is better than the other. They are simply different.

Intellectually this may all make sense. But as you may know, it's another thing to make such distinctions when you have a good-looking man on your couch. Trying to sort out when to be intimate, when to be sexual, and when to combine the two processes can lead to so many questions that your head will swim. "How do I know if he loves me? How do I know if I love him? Why can't we just be friends? Why can't we just be lovers? Why are my feelings so strong? Why are my feelings going away? Am I really attracted to him? Is he really attracted to me?" Erik expresses the "storm and stress" of this situation:

> Ever since I turned thirty, I need more than a trick. Maybe AIDS has something to do with it. So there I was last night on my third date with Steve, a gorgeous medical student. He's the first man I've ever been serious about. And does he ever have the hots for me! Can you believe it, all we did was kiss? Wanting more than sex is a whole new ball game. What are the rules? I can't just jump in the sack with him. I need time to understand my feelings. Maybe I'm kidding myself about loving him. You know, maybe he is some sort of father figure. Maybe he's not serious about me. I don't need to have a fling. But God, how long is he going to wait around while I am acting like a prude? I guess I'm scared that sex will ruin it all. I just don't know where sex fits in.

Erik is confused; remember that confusion is a normal part of adult development. There is a period in young adulthood when you distinguish intimacy needs from sexual needs. At this point, you may feel you have had all the sexual experiences you require to feel assured about your sexual lifestyle. Something within you, quiet and unexpected, announces that you want more commitment in relationships. Being sexual may feel less important, the need for intimacy more urgent. (Don't worry, you will not have this calling until you are ready for it. You will not catch it from this book!)

Typically, when you reach this stage of development, your first response is intense ambivalence. At this point in your life, you are torn between emotional involvement and immediate sexual gratification. Because many gay men must postpone their explorations of sex and relationships, they often deal with this ambivalence into middle age and beyond.

Most commonly, gay men who have trouble balancing their ambivalence about sexuality and intimacy err in one of two directions, although some show both patterns. Most frequently you try to divorce the two processes and never let them come together in the same relationship. You could be

active sexually, but restrict your sexual contacts to anonymous encounters or to men obviously unsuited for intimacy.
You may even be capable of intimacy in other situations, and
may have close women friends, gay male buddies, and even
live-in companions with whom you are never sexual. The
difficulty lies not in sexuality or intimacy alone, but in joining sexuality with intimacy.

This pattern is not restricted to gay men, and appears
frequently among men in general. There is much speculation
on why this is so. Some scientists believe that men are
biologically equipped to separate sexuality and closeness to
allow greater genetic diversity in the population and thereby
benefit the human species. It is also possible that male socialization contributes to the ease with which men separate sexuality and intimacy. For example, "boys will be boys"—with
its double standard, encouraging males to be sexually active—
and "intimacy is dangerous" are two messages given to men
by society and families. Neither of these standards helps men
integrate sexuality and intimacy.

There are other reasons why some gay men may choose
to separate sexuality and intimacy. First, combining sexuality
and intimacy raises the emotional ante. Being both sexual
and close to another person intensifies the experience. You
may feel angrier, sadder, more joyful, or more jealous than
you ever remember being before. Such intense feelings can
be frightening, especially if they are not what you expected.

A related point is that intimate sexual relationships often
bring up unfinished emotional business. New feelings loosen
up old feelings, which then may rise to the surface of awareness. This can be perplexing, for the feelings may seem
entirely inappropriate. A client, Michael, poignantly expressed
this quandary:

> *Oh, God. I am just sick of these tears. I don't know
> why I'm like this. My job is going well. Mark is a
> darling. If things are so good why do I feel so bad?
> All my life I wanted to be close to another man. My
> dad never hugged me. We never talked about per-
> sonal things. He probably was upset because he
> suspected I was gay. Now when Mark tries to be
> tender with me, I can't trust him. Sometimes I just
> can't stand his being so nice to me. It makes my skin*

crawl. How can he stand being with me? Why am I
always crying? You would think that I'd be grateful
for where I am. I hate these tears. Am I going crazy?

Michael's pain is not a sign of his failure but of emerging
self-awareness. By letting himself experience sexuality and
intimacy in a caring relationship, he is learning that his
sexuality was not the cause of his father's aloofness. He can
no longer blame himself for his father's failure to show affection. Such a realization is monumental! Intimacy leads us
down many paths we would otherwise never have discovered.
Separating sexuality and intimacy postpones the pain that
comes with self-discovery.

Men who separate sexuality and intimacy often come
from families that believe sex is dirty and that you should
never be sexual with a person you love and respect. There is
often great concern in families like this about nudity and
overly restrictive rules regarding dating. By failing to recognize sexuality as a healthy and joyful part of life, such families play a role in separating sexuality and intimacy.

Many gay men are rightfully angry about oppressive
traditions in their families and in society that caused them
anguish for so many years. This anger can lead gay men to be
skeptical about the traditional value that restricts sex to committed relationships. You may feel that uniting intimacy and
sexuality is selling out to a heterosexual culture, on a cultural
as well as personal level. Not so long ago, monogamy was
seen in some gay circles as politically incorrect, and some of
our clients who disliked anonymous sex complained that they
were viewed as old fashioned by gay male friends.

The mainstream gay male community has often been
criticized for its lack of support for intimate sexual relationships, and gay male culture, perhaps more than any other,
provides numerous opportunities for sexual encounters that
do not require emotional intimacy. Such encounters may
contribute to the separation of sexuality and intimacy, or they
may simply reflect a tendency that already exists. In either
case, opportunties for anonymous sex are now viewed with
much less favor in the gay male community.

AIDS has created a revolution in the way gay men view
sexuality and intimacy. Many gay men who were once firmly
intent on keeping their sexual and intimate relationships com-

pletely divorced are now beginning to look for long-term intimate relationships. This is a courageous and wondrous act of self-love, or at least good common sense. However, the desire to unite sexuality and intimacy does not always translate into the ability to do so. This is especially true if you have kept these processes separate for many years.

Imagine that sexuality and intimacy are like two rivers in a wide plain. For most of us, these rivers sometimes join and flow together, and at other times diverge and move in separate riverbeds. If the rivers are not allowed to come together for a long time, they dig deeper channels of their own. You may still be able to unite them, but it will become more difficult the longer you wait.

This metaphor helps explain the despair that some gay men feel about uniting sexuality and intimacy in their lives. Sensing the difficulty of the task, and yet knowing the dangers of anonymous sex, these men resign themselves to making love to video recorders or anonymous phone partners, or risk their lives to find the human contact they so greatly need. These are not the only options for men who are struggling to unite sexuality and intimacy.

At the opposite end of the continuum are those men who can't tell sexuality and intimacy apart. This pattern is less common among gay men than keeping the two processes separate, but occurs often enough to warrant description. David, a 31-year-old client, provides an example of this pattern:

> Sure, if a friend wants to sleep with me, I do it. Why not? After all, I want to show him that I care about him. The important thing is for people not to take sex so seriously. That's what causes all this jealousy. Take my friend Alan, for example. Alan was out of town last month and his lover, Charles, and I had dinner at my place. Charles kept talking about how much he missed Alan and, well, one thing led to another and he ended up staying the night. When Alan found out, he was furious. Imagine! As I explained to him, it was no big deal, just my way of making Charles feel less lonely.

David's naïveté about Alan's feelings is a telling sign that he has never learned to distinguish sexual and affectionate feelings. This confusion is quite normal during adolescence, when you often confuse sex and closeness and use sex as a way of connecting to others. This confusion typically goes away in young adulthood, as sexual needs become distinguished from the need for affection. In an adult gay man, a lack of differentiation between sexuality and intimacy is cause for real concern.

If you're like David, you have few or no rules about when you will be sexual. Sex is simply a sign of liking someone. You see sexuality as a cure for all types of distress in others. When confronted with someone who is angry, lonely, depressed, or anxious, your solution is to offer your body as solace and distraction. Because you have difficulty saying no to potential sex partners, you may engage in sexual practices that are dangerous to your health, rather than set limits in a sexual relationship.

As you might imagine, this view of sexuality and intimacy can create major problems in your life. If you're like David, you are often taken advantage of by others and can suffer severe physical as well as emotional hurts. And because so many of your relationships are sexualized, you tend to have few nonsexual friendships for support. You underestimate the significance of sexuality in relationships, and often are severely hurt as a result. Sadly, when the rose-colored glasses are knocked off your nose and you realize that something bad can happen to you, you can end up bitter and full of despair.

What causes you to confuse sexuality and intimacy? Men who show this pattern come from families in which sexual boundaries were nonexistent or loosely applied. Nudity was treated casually and, frequently, no attempt was made to teach family members to make sexual decisions carefully. Some men who blur sexuality and intimacy have histories of sexual contact with family members.

Some men are guided by norms in the gay community that encourage their confusion of sexuality with intimacy. The availability of casual sex has convinced some men that sex is unimportant and that there is no reason to think before you jump into bed. Fortunately, AIDS is challenging this attitude.

The two patterns of imbalance we have described are prototypes. You may see features of each of these patterns at some time in your life, and you may alternate back and forth between the two. Each of these patterns is developmentally appropriate at certain life stages. Ironic as it seems, our task as humans is first to separate sexual from intimate feelings, and then to reunite them in our relationships.

Trying to connect sexually and intimately with another man can be exasperating. At times you may feel that you are waiting for something that will never happen. While we ourselves are still learning this balancing act, we offer you a few words of encouragement and some guidelines. In general, however, learn from your blunders. Orchestrating sexuality and intimacy in your life is a cyclical process: you take risks, you make mistakes, you gain wisdom, and you take new risks.

Is it worth continuing your struggle to integrate and balance sexuality and intimacy? Before you decide to invest in a second video recorder and spend your nights at home alone, let us tell you clearly, "Yes, it's worth it!"

Combining sexuality and intimacy in one relationship is a powerful experience, and these processes can enhance each other. If you think you've had great sex before, wait until you try it with a partner who has been angry with you and then forgiven you, held you when you cried, and cleaned up after you when you were sick. The trust and depth of such a connection can bring new heights of sexual ecstasy. Furthermore, the experience of having a partner accept you even when things are not going well sexually can provide a timeless feeling of being cherished. You may pride yourself on the ability to make deep and meaningful connections with others, to listen, and to be a good friend. But the intimacy that can develop in a sexual relationship is special.

Another reason to struggle to integrate sexuality and intimacy is that joining them will further your emotional growth. As was so clear in Michael's case, intimate sexual relationships present you with personal quandaries that don't exist in nonsexual friendships or in sexual encounters that occur without intimacy. Confronting and resolving these dilemmas provides a way to learn about yourself, discover new strengths, and reach your full potential as a human being. You can choose how much you wish to grow in this lifetime, but we encourage you to grow as much as you can.

Finally, as with intimacy in general, successfully balancing sexuality and intimacy provides a wider range of choices in your life. Do you want an affectionate dinner with a nonsexual friend, a passionate night with an intimate lover, or a quiet evening at home alone? If all your relationships are sexualized or all are nonsexual, you have fewer options. By separating and seeking a balance between sexuality and intimacy, you enrich your life and build security for yourself.

Let us also assure you, you *can* integrate sexuality and intimacy. You may have gotten the idea from what we said so far that gay men are at a disadvantage in this area. In fact, there a number of factors working in your favor as you try to achieve intimate sexual relationships.

Most men are very good at separating sexual feelings from those of intimacy, and thus are unlikely to confuse the two. This may explain why so few gay men allow all their relationships to become sexualized. Women seem to have more difficulty in this particular area: they often want to make others happy, and show a greater tendency to consent to sex out of a sense of obligation or desire to please. Gay men seem to have an easier time saying no.

Probably the greatest asset you have in approaching intimate sexual relationships is that you have more role flexibility than heterosexual men. Because of your bicultural socialization, you probably have a sense of the relative nature of social rules and are likely to take cultural stereotypes less seriously than heterosexual men. Thus, you may reject the traditional male fear of intimacy, or the view that a man's worth is determined by the amount of sexual experience he has. By paying attention to your heart, rather than to role stereotypes, you as a gay man have an enhanced capacity to be intimate in sexual relationships.

Another important advantage you have is *intragender empathy*, the ability of people of the same sex to understand each other better than people of different sexes. The implications of this are monumental for the integration of sexuality and intimacy among gay men. Two gay men are more likely to be similar in their interests, their social histories, and their sexual interests than are most heterosexual men and women. The gender gap is large, and heterosexuals have to cope with this in seeking to unite sexuality and intimacy. Gay men and lesbians start out a bit ahead of the game.

Finally, AIDS has increased the desire of many gay men to successfully balance sexuality and intimacy. It may be hard to see this as an advantage; you're more likely to experience it as having to learn something new while a gun is pointed at your head. Nevertheless, there has been a shift in values in the gay community, and it's no longer old fashioned to hope for a sexual intimate relationship.

Whatever your reasons for seeking to unite sexuality and intimacy, we wish you a fruitful search.

Let's suppose you're going to make a giant leap in your life to be intimate and sexual with a special person. What things should you keep in mind?

First, we can't emphasize enough the importance of maintaining nonsexual friendships in which you can get support and practice closeness. Intimacy requires a lot of skill. You'll need to constantly juggle two questions: "When should I invest myself emotionally?" and "When should I keep my distance?" Because the stakes feel so high in relationships that are both intimate and sexual, it's easy to agonize over these decisions. Nonsexual friendships allow you to explore, test decisions, and make mistakes with less pain.

Second, as we have repeatedly advised, move slowly. Sex is never an emergency, no matter how much it feels like one. Generally it helps to allow sexual intensity to escalate gradually according to how well a relationship is going. Opening yourself to deeper feelings in order to build intimacy is a large self-investment. You owe it to yourself to approach relationships thoughtfully and with a bit of caution. As an old mentor once said, "Now you must cast your pearls more wisely."

Third, use your feelings as a guide. Never be sexual with someone when you are not sexually attracted to them, and do not agree to sex out of a sense of obligation or concern. If you feel unsure about your sexual feelings, postpone sexuality until you are more sure of the relationship. These rules apply to established relationships as well as new ones. If your sexual feelings for a lover decline, pause and ask yourself, "What is going on here that we need to deal with?" Forcing yourself to have sex in such a situation is not conducive to intimacy.

Above all, expect and learn from mistakes. We believe that even if Mr. Right turns out to be Mr. Wrong, the struggle to integrate sexuality and intimacy is itself worthwhile. As John Lennon once said, "Life is what is happening when we are planning for it to happen."

Developing a committed love relationship can be reminiscent of Charles Dickens's declaration in A *Tale of Two Cities*, "It was the best of times. It was the worst of times." But with thought and care, both you and your partner can escape the guillotine and reap incredible rewards.

COMMON SEXUAL CONCERNS

Attaining sexual well-being isn't a cinch. Coming out, making love, and developing pride in same-sex feelings are good starting points; however, to feel sexually adequate, you also need to face sexual issues that concern you personally. There is no way around it. Yet you are not alone. Many gay men have wounds from the struggle to come out that affect their sexuality. Victories are not won without battle scars. But old wounds can be healed. We encourage you to honestly face your sexual concerns by reading this section and seeing how it applies to you.

"IS THERE LIFE WITHOUT SEX?": CELIBACY

I feel doubly blessed. Each morning I say to myself, "Rafael, you are a gifted artista and you are loved by many friends." A year ago I would rise and say, "Rafael, your life is a mess! You gave up all your friends for one lousy lover." Can you believe a hot-blooded man like me not having a lover for a whole year? Neither could I, before now. I don't know how much longer I will be without a man. But today, when I think about this time alone, I say, "Gracias a Diós!" Now, I have my art, my friends, and my soul.

Perhaps you thought that you'd never see the day when celibacy was a viable option for gay men. There is a first time for everything! Periods of celibacy play an important role in healthy sexuality, and this applies to gay men as well as to others. This may make as much sense to you as saying that starvation is a part of healthy nutrition. Bear with us.

Celibacy allows you to pause and take stock of your sexual development. During periods of celibacy, you can find your bearings before setting out again on the challenging path of sexual relationships. By reflecting on what you have learned while remaining sexually inactive, you may better determine what your needs are at the time and gather strength.

Celibacy may naturally occur in the interludes between sexual relationships. Although you may feel lonely and sexually frustrated, you may also feel the joy of reclaiming parts of yourself that you ignored. Like Rafael, you can renew non-sexual friendships, be very productive in your work, and revise your self-concepts. The energy you would normally put into sexual relationships, you now turn to self-healing.

It's possible to undervalue celibacy if you fear that it will lead you back into the closet. After many years of having to refrain from sex, the idea of choosing to go without may seem ludicrous. However, having freedom about your sexuality means choosing to be sexual or celibate. Don't rule out celibacy before exploring how it feels to you.

Unfortunately, celibacy can also be a sign that you've been hurt sexually again and again. If this happens to you, you may swear off all sexual relationships out of fear and bitterness and cling to celibacy for an extensive period of time, the "I can never say yes" syndrome. This strategy may make you feel safer, but it may also impede your growth. Don't get us wrong. We are not saying that if you're scared, you should plow ahead and ignore your feelings. But as the saying goes, There is a season for all things. After you have licked your wounds and reconsidered your choices, it may be time to try again. If you find yourself unable to move ahead, you may need more intensive support, from friends, a minister, or a psychotherapist.

Sometimes celibacy is a sign that your development has been stifled, perhaps at a preadolescent stage of sexuality. If you have little awareness of sexual feelings, are threatened by the possibility of sexual experiences with adults, and feel a strong sense of obligation to your family, your problem may be arrested development. Commonly, gay men with this type of pattern come from families that were overly protective. These men are often extremely closeted about their gayness, partly out of fear of offending their families. Celibacy related to sexual underdevelopment is extremely difficult to overcome on your own; typically you will require professional assistance.

Of course, you might choose long periods of celibacy, often for a lifetime, out of a commitment to spiritual or humanitarian work. If you do, you often find that by refraining from sexual relationships, you are able to direct more energy to your chosen task. You may have intimate nonsexual relationships, which support you and further your personal growth. Gay men in this group are often very open about their gayness, exude joy about their sexuality, and bring out the best in others. What might seem to be a personal loss and sacrifice for others is for these people an opportunity for celebration.

So you see that celibacy is a valid option in healthy sexual development. But always ask yourself, "Is my decision not to have sex with others freely made or based on fear and hopelessness?" Only you yourself can know by paying attention to your feelings. When celibacy is right it will probably seem liberating and self-nurturing to refrain from sexual relationships, even though your sexual needs may not disappear. If you find celibacy constraining and depressing, ask yourself if it's time to come out of hiding. It may be easy to intellectually justify celibacy without ever facing the hurt or fears underlying it. If you are celibate out of fear or trauma, recognize your loss. This is the first step toward reclaiming your sexuality. And remember, even if you decide not to be sexual with other people, for a short or a long period of time, your sexuality is a vital part of you that deserves to be acknowledged and honored.

"I HATE MY BODY": BODY SHAME

You know, there are things I'll never be able to change about myself. How can talking help? Look how fat I am. I don't care what other people say. Who's going to love me? I'm all out of proportion. My head is too small, my legs are too skinny, and my trunk is too broad. Why do you think I wear these baggy clothes? Exercise is out of the question. How could I go to an aerobics class? They would laugh me out of there, just like in high school gym class. When I look in the mirror I feel like screaming, "Daniel, life is unfair." I'm so ready for a relationship, yet so far away.

Body shame is a rejection of some or all aspects of your body. It is similar to other forms of shame discussed in Chapter 3. For example, the roots of body shame often occur early in childhood. Also, families play an important role in the development of body shame, and it can profoundly affect your close relationships. In spite of what it has in common with other forms of shame, body shame has a unique relationship to sexuality.

Although you may seem emotionally available for relationships, if you have severe body shame, you are unable to sustain a deep connection with other men because you believe your body is irreparably flawed. You may see yourself as too fat, too thin, not properly proportioned, scrawny, too hairy, or not hairy enough. You may feel self-conscious about the way you talk, walk, run, or throw a ball. You might even believe it is impossible for you to dance or participate in energetic games. Such feelings also interfere with physical expressions of affection or with having fun in bed. It is difficult to relax sexually when you continually ridicule yourself or expect your partner to become disgusted with your body at any moment.

Remarkably, men with severe body shame may be the very men who are the objects of hot pursuit by many potential lovers! When this happens, body shame can seem like a cruel paradox that leaves you hopelessly stuck: "Why do I feel so bad about my body when everybody else tells me I look so good?" The key to this puzzle is to realize that body shame is often a metaphor for other, deeper feelings. Thus, even the most gorgeous hunk may feel shame about his body, if he feels worthless.

Although the manifestations of body shame are endless, the results are typically the same: You may shy away from deep sharing of yourself because you believe that no one will accept your body as it is. Body shame may also result in more than loneliness. If you feel severe body shame, you often express your hate and rage at your body by ignoring your physical health. You may abuse drugs or alcohol, refuse to exercise, and pay no attention to safer sex guidelines, as if believing, "What the hell, I'm cursed anyway." For these reasons, body shame can make you more vulnerable to AIDS.

Gay men often have particular difficulties with body shame. To illustrate this point, contrast Daniel's statement with remarks by Tim:

> *It's funny. I don't think a whole lot about my body.*
> *I played sports in high school—gymnastics, swim-*
> *ming, and track—and have always stayed in shape.*
> *I can protect myself and anybody I'm with. Yeah, I*
> *know, guys are supposed to look terrific these days.*
> *I'm all right to look at. So what's the big deal?*

Notice that Tim exudes an assurance about his body that seems too good to be true. Doesn't he feel insecure too? What makes Daniel and Tim so different? Well, read on as Tim explains:

> *Now if you ask about my partner, that's a whole*
> *different story. The lady I'm with had better turn a*
> *few heads. How else could I face all the guys?*

Of course, Tim is heterosexual. Clearly, he has body issues too, but they are more covert than Daniel's. Why do so many gay men dislike their bodies?

If you were seen as effeminate in childhood, you were often subjected to insults about your body. "You wiggle like a girl," "Why can't you throw a ball?" and "You look like a faggot" are just a few of the taunts that you might have heard. This type of negative feedback can lead to deep feelings of body shame. When these remarks come from family members, they can devastate your image of your body as a boy and cause deep scars for years to come.

Not all the taunting of effeminate boys is directed at their bodies. You may have been shamed in other ways; for example, "Why can't you be like your brother?" or "What do you mean, you want a doll? No, you can't have one. That's for girls. What's the matter with you?" Unfortunately, young children think concretely; when they feel unloved (for whatever reason) they may decide that their bodies are the reason for their unhappiness. For example, a five-year-old client, whose parents were going through a painful divorce, believed, "My parents are breaking up because I am ugly." While this reasoning may seem unrealistic to us, it makes sense to a young child. Effeminate boys who are ridiculed may conclude that they are unattractive, even if no comments are made about their bodies.

Most people who feel good about their bodies see them as a source of pleasure and enjoyment. As a gay man you were at a disadvantage at crucial points in your life in learning to appreciate your body. First, as a child, you may have steered clear of sports or other types of vigorous play, have been less interested in rough-and-tumble activities, and lacked other options for creative exploration of your body. You may have been afraid of being ridiculed by other children if you took part in vigorous play, a fear that is often well-grounded in past experience. Often there is a vicious cycle between body shame and physical awkwardness—the less you participate in physical activities, the less skilled you are, the more taunting you receive, and the more ashamed you feel. When the next opportunity to play baseball, hockey, or volleyball came along, you were understandably reluctant to get involved.

During the teenage years it is quite common to feel self-conscious and ashamed of your body. However, while heterosexual peers are engaging in extensive sexual exploration, getting over their awkwardness, and learning to enjoy their bodies, as a gay adolescent you have much more limited sexual opportunities. Without this experimentation, you feel doubtful and embarrassed about your body. Once again, the cycle of shame plays a role: some gay men had opportunities during adolescence to be sexual with other boys, but were too frightened and ashamed of their bodies to take advantage of these opportunities. Those who would most benefit from exploring their bodies are often those who are least likely to do it.

It is possible that sex-role learning also plays a part in the body shame of gay men. Some gay men adopt stereotypical notions of physical perfectionism that are commonly seen in women who wish to attract men: "I must be thin," "My body must be perfect," and "Men only love me for my beauty." If you, like women, view yourself primarily as attracting men, you may endlessly obsess about your physical desirability. In the example, Tim, in contrast to Daniel, sees himself as a pursuer. Being the one who does the chasing allows him to worry less about his attractiveness. Another message given to women is, "You're too delicate to exert yourself." If you identify with this stereotype, it can undermine confidence in your body and you may avoid physical challenges.

Tragically, the gay community often reinforces the body shame of gay men. The ideals of thinness, youth, masculine looks, and perfection in body appearance are yardsticks to which few men can measure up. In comparison with such standards, most people have defective bodies. Again, a cyclical pattern occurs: You feel insecure about your looks so you seek to raise your self-image through connections with beautiful partners. But by rejecting less physically attractive men, you perpetuate the standard that hurt you in the first place.

The most prevalent cause of body shame is perhaps the most compelling but difficult to understand. Remember what we said earlier, that body shame is often a metaphor for other feelings? Some gay men harbor deep feelings of shame and unworthiness that get translated into body shame. It may sound absurd to you that if your parents had a disastrous sexual relationship, you may feel ashamed about your body, but this kind of association is common. Body shame is especially likely when your feelings of unworthiness pertain to sexuality, for sexuality has a profound connection with your body. "Symbolic body shame" is our term for body shame that is an expression of other types of shame.

Symbolic body shame is crucial for understanding the puzzle we presented at the beginning of this section, how you can be quite conventionally attractive and still despise your body. This situation is paradoxical only if you believe that the source of your anguish is your body. When you realize that body shame can symbolize other types of emotional pain, the puzzle is solved. Symbolic body shame makes you not only believe you are unattractive, you actually see in the mirror what you expect to see.

Perhaps now you can understand why body shame is such a persistent problem. Body shame is a self-fulfilling prophecy, which becomes deeply ingrained in your identity. It affects your view of yourself and your interpretation of many situations and can cause a spiral of physical neglect that produces further shame. Body shame snowballs over the lifetime, and trying to overcome body shame may feel like climbing a mountain during an avalanche.

You may ask, "How can I come to love my body?" Clearly, each of us must answer this question for himself. We suggest three clues to assist you. First, *accept your body as it is*. Sound too simple? It's not. Sometimes the more pressure you put on your body to be right, the more unrealistic your expectations become, and the harder it is to like anything about your body. Clearly, effort is required to have a physically fit body. However, body image is more than a matter of physique. Start improving your body image by identifying your assets and finding ways to see beauty in your flaws. Be creative. For example, gray hair could mean that you're over the hill or it could mean that you are wise and have had many life experiences. You have to start somewhere, so why not start where you are?

Second, *expand your conceptions of beauty*. Have you snubbed the nice man down the hall because he wasn't good-looking enough? Have a cup of coffee with him and look for something about him that you find attractive. We're not suggesting that you ignore your feelings and get sexually involved with men you find unappealing. But, sometimes, when you give someone a second chance, you'll find a sparkle that you overlooked. And this new awareness can translate into a new acceptance of yourself.

Finally, *take risks*. Develop your athleticism, creatively explore your body, and gain confidence in your ability to protect yourself. Feeling physically fit and skilled at some form of athletic expression can be as exhilarating as the best sexual experience you've ever had—sometimes it's better! A healthy sense of humor about past physical accomplishments, or lack thereof, coupled with a fierce determination to challenge your body physically, can allow you to enjoy your body on many levels. Be imaginative in choosing an activity. If you don't like it after a while, look for something else. You may find it easiest to begin with some kind of noncompetitive physical exercise. However, consider sharing your workout with others. Although you risk exposing yourself, you'll have much more fun. You may feel a lot of inertia as you begin to exert your body, but as you gain skill, confidence, and strength, it will get easier and your body will seem like a precious gift. This is one gift you will surely want to share with trusted friends!

"I ONLY WANT MEN WITH BIG COCKS": SEXUAL RIGIDITY

Suppose, at a party, you meet an attractive and approachable man who expresses himself well and has a promising career. You notice that his eyes sparkle when he talks to you. Sound promising? Like most of us, you might feel flattered, intrigued, and anxious to know more. Let's assume that later you discovered, through the grapevine, that he had recently placed an ad in the *Advocate* that read:

> *Hot Italian stallion wanted for my stable. Must be at least 8", uncut, and enjoy being worshipped and serviced. Olive complexion only. Prefer green eyes, but am flexible. Avid horse lover waits to rub you down.*

How do you feel now? Perhaps you fit the bill, but most of us wouldn't. Our guess is that you would feel deceived and turned off: "If I was a hot Italian stallion, I wouldn't let this guy sweep out my stall." Most of us would probably feel the rigidity of this man's requirements is just too much to deal with, even for a sexual liaison.

If you, like the man who placed the ad, experience the phenomenon of sexual rigidity, you have a narrow range of possible sexual partners: you prefer only black men, uncircumcised men, hairy men, blond men, men with big cocks or some other attributes. Or you may require specific and inflexible conditions in order to be sexually gratified: you must be anally receptive, have your partner tie you up, act out a specific script, or shower before sex. Also, there are different degrees of sexual rigidity. Almost everyone has sexual likes and dislikes, and at times, all of us get into certain sexual routines. However, most of us retain an ability to be flexible and curious with partners. Sexually rigid men have alternative ways of being sexual, but generally choose to ignore these options. In extreme cases, such men have only one means of obtaining orgasm and are called fetishists. Typically, the greater the sexual inflexibility, the more difficulty you have forming intimate sexual relationships.

Sexually rigid men often have a tough time finding partners with whom both sex and deep sharing is possible. To understand this difficulty, let's examine the preceding example. Clearly, there is nothing inherently wrong with this man's advertisement. If he can get a hot Italian lover, good for him! Like most sexually rigid men, however, he may discover that men who fit his qualifications are not necessarily cut out for intimacy. Even in ideal circumstances, it is difficult to find a compatible lover. The more nonessential attributes (eye color, hair color, national origin) you are willing to leave up to fate, the more likely you are to find a suitable partner. If you are sexually rigid, you often compromise by selecting partners who fit your sexual type, but who are unsuited for close relationships. This can lead to the block to intimacy described in Chapter 2, "All That Glitters Is Gold," in which you lose touch with your spirituality by focusing exclusively on appearances. Even when you find a partner, having rigid sexual patterns you frequently have a mechanical and impersonal approach to relationships: "As long as you fit my fantasy, it doesn't matter how much we care for each other." You may hide the source of your attraction for your partner (race, cock size, or hair color), and try to convince him that you value him for other attributes (intelligence, spiritual depth, or talent). This dishonesty essentially interferes with your self-respect and creates distrust. Because you are sexually rigid, you often treat your partner like a pet or a prized object, more than as an equal human being, which is understandable, since sexual rigidity causes you to essentially relate to body parts, not to the deeper personal qualities of your partner. For these reasons, sexual rigidity often destroys intimate relationships.

When you are the partner of a sexually rigid man and you begin to realize on what basis you were chosen, you often feel betrayed: "He only loves me because of my big cock, not for the reasons he told me." You may wonder if your partner really loves you, or is he simply using you to embody his shadowy fantasies. Such doubts can cause a relationship to feel unsafe: "If he only loves me because I'm black, couldn't I be replaced?" Unfortunately, your sexually rigid partner may not be able to console you with honest reassurance, particularly if a large part of the relationship has been based on falsehood.

Without judging or overly analyzing, let us simply say that if you have rigid sexual patterns, you restrict the depth of your sexual fulfillment. Often you are unaware of your full sexual potential, stuck in an attempt to find some inner healing. What is it that needs to be mended? Frequently, a narrow sexual focus symbolizes a deeper wound, although this often is unconscious. When a sexually rigid man says, "I only like men with big cocks," he may be describing how ashamed he is about his body and how insecure he feels as a man. Having sex with a well-endowed man may feel like a way of confirming or enhancing your own maleness. One client described the feeling this way: "When I am having sex with a man who has a big cock, I sometimes feel like I am him and I have a big cock." Sometimes, sexual rigidity is related to childhood trauma. Although sexual rigidity is not restricted to gay men, among gay men, it can be a sign of shame and pain about one's gay identity.

If you struggle with sexual rigidity, it is possible to increase your sexual options, although you may despair of doing so. You may require professional psychological assistance to deal with the anxiety of expanding your sexual preferences. But sometimes healing takes place on its own. For example, you may initially select a partner on the basis of skin color, and then come to love him for other reasons as well. The next time you look for a sexual partner, you may discover that your tastes have broadened slightly: you are attracted to men who resemble your former lover!

It may surprise you, but you can also expand your sexual horizons through any activity that helps you learn to love: volunteer work with the homeless, being a buddy to a person with AIDS, or taking an art class. How does this work? As you come to see beauty in places you formerly overlooked, you will find many more men attractive.

You may fear that if you grow out of your sexual rigidity, you will lose the excitement, vitality, and passion of your sexuality. Not so. You will find more of the world to be sexy and intriguing and will have more options for your relationships.

"I CAN'T GET ENOUGH SEX": SEXUAL ADDICTION

I'm Michael. First I lost my job. Then I lost my lover. At least I have my life. I'm starting all over again. It may sound crazy, like it can't happen to a gay man. But it can. I'm a recovering sex addict. I started realizing something was wrong when a trick tied me up, raped me, and tried to slit my throat. Sure I was fooling myself, but I wasn't asking to be killed. I used to think there is no such thing as too much sex for a gay man. I was wrong. You know, the worst part of my problem was that I didn't know I had a problem. I was the last to know. I was so out of control that even when I got fired for having sex in the company rest room, it didn't stop me. Sometimes I feel I should move away from this city or crawl under a rock. At least I am not covering up my problem now. If it weren't for my twelve-step SAA [Sex Addicts Anonymous] group, I wouldn't be alive today. I am doing more than surviving. With help, I am learning to love my gay feelings.

Michael's story is not uncommon. Some gay men relate to sexuality much like an alcoholic does with alcohol. Sexual behavior and thoughts become so out of control and so ritualized that they interfere with life functioning. This pattern is called sexual addiction. Sexual addiction is not a secret plot dreamed up by heterosexual mental health professionals to drive gay men back into the closet. It is not an attempt to take away your enjoyment of sex. Sexual addiction is a serious and often crippling problem with sexuality.

Sexual addiction is also different than adolescent sexual exploration. During adolescence, there is a need to explore sexuality and have many sexual experiences. As discussed earlier, this sexual exploration is often delayed until adult years for gay men. Adolescent sexual exploration, even when postponed, is of limited duration, clarifies personal preferences about sexuality and friendship, and builds your self-esteem. In contrast, sexual addiction is open-ended, aimed at impersonally relieving tension and depression, and has a negative effect on your personality. We are not inferring that gay men are promiscuous, or that sexual addiction is a problem restricted to gay men, nor are we preaching against casual sex. Casual sex doesn't make you a sex addict any more than social drinking makes you an alcoholic.

How do you distinguish sexual addiction from an enjoyment and love of sex? For an addict, sex is an obsession, much as a fix is for a junkie. Relationships are a means to one end—sex—and sex is used to avoid life's pain. For example, if you are sexually addicted and you're depressed about your job, you may go out to the bars to pick up men, rather than confront these feelings. Or you may spend a night at the baths when angry at your partner rather than dealing with him or your anger. The key element of sexual addiction is a persistent and unsuccessful struggle to get your sexual behavior or thoughts under control. Like Michael, sexually addicted men make repeated promises to limit their obsessive sexual behavior, but fail to live up to their resolutions. This loss of control is deeply humiliating and depressing, whether the behavior is public or private. Men who are compulsive masturbators are often just as devastated by a failure to limit their activity as men who compulsively go from lover to lover.

Sexual addiction can also occur in committed relationships. In this context, you can feel that sex has become too important in your relationship and that other ways of connecting, like holding each other and talking, are insignificant. It's common for lovers to have difficulties coordinating their sexual appetites. These differences, however, can often be resolved by open communication, respect for individual needs, and a recognition that sex is only one of many ways to share love. In contrast, sexual addiction often involves manipulation, constant pressuring and blaming, and a feeling that sex is the only thing holding your relationship together. Such ties are desperate and are far from intimate.

Although sexual addiction is not restricted to gay men, it can have particular significance in same-sex relationships. Some gay men try to make up as adults for time lost in adolesence and treat sex as a cure for all of life's ills. This can be a setup for sexual addiction. Many gay men develop their sexuality in a context of secrecy and shame, and these feelings can fuel the loss of control that is at the basis of sexual addiction. The availability of anonymous sex in gay male society makes it difficult for sexually addicted gay men to get control over their behavior.

When you get the feeling that sex has become too important in your life and is undermining your self-respect, you should get a professional evaluation for sex addiction. It is crucial that you see a professional who thoroughly understands sex addiction and the difficulties of gay male sexual development. A twelve-step SAA group can be an important adjunct to individual therapy, if one is available. You can find one in your area by calling the National Directory of SAA groups, at (818) 704-9854. Recovery from sexual addiction will allow you to reclaim the joys and pleasures of sexuality and of your gay identity.

"WHY CAN'T I PUT THE PAST OUT OF MY HEAD?": SEXUAL ABUSE

In a hesitant voice at an initial therapy meeting, Paul asked, "Are you gay?" The therapist replied, "Why does that matter to you, Paul?" At this question, Paul broke down in tears and blurted out that he had been molested by a male teacher at age eight. Later, he shared his anguish:

> *I hate my gay feelings and I want your help to get rid of them. Did that teacher make me feel this way? Or was I supposed to be gay? I despise myself for having a crush on him. I loved the ground he walked on. I was his favorite. I know I am supposed to hate him but I can't. I loved him. The only thing I can hate him for is picking somebody else. I feel like my whole life is a funeral waiting to happen. When I want sex I either pick men who abuse me, or if I am with decent men, I get scared and depressed. Sometimes I wish I could just tear my balls off.*

Some gay men tell of having had pleasurable sexual experiences with adults when they were children. Frequently they report that they, to some degree, initiated and cooperated with the sexual contact. It is possible that these men are now enjoying satisfying sexual and intimate relationships as adults although we encourage them to carefully consider the effects that their early sexual relationship had on them. As psychotherapists, however, we see many men, like Paul, whose early sexual experiences with adults were so damaging, in fact that we see them as victims of sexual abuse.

Boys who are sexually abused experience trauma as a result of being forced or tricked into sexual activity, either by an adult or someone they regard as family. Until recently, sexual abuse among boys was an unrecognized problem. Nowadays, there is increasing awareness that boys, as well as girls, can be hurt by sexual contact with adults and family members. Some studies show that one in eleven boys has had sexual contact with an adult by age eighteen.[4] This compares with a one-in-five ratio for girls. More recent studies show that boys and girls are molested at nearly the same rate, and that much more sexual abuse occurs than is reported.[5,6]

Despite the frequency with which boys are sexually abused, they often do not regard themselves as victims of abuse because they feel they were active participants who should have known better. Also, according to our cultural norms, boys are supposed to feel grateful for all sexual opportunities, not traumatized by them. Thus, sexually victimized boys anticipate that their distress about sexual encounters will not be taken seriously by adults. Many remain silent about the abuse for years. Furthermore, boys whose sexual contact was with men rarely admit to being victimized because they fear that others will see them as sissies or queers if they talk about the sexual encounter. This terror is even greater when these boys have same-sex feelings and begin to recognize them.

Children do not understand the emotional pressures of a sexual relationship. They may cooperate sexually as a way of getting affection and attention from others, making others happy, or satisfying their own curiosity about sexuality. For these reasons, sexual contact with others may feel pleasurable, and some children may even act sexy around adults, unaware of the full meaning of their behavior. This may be especially true for children who have been sexually abused already and who have learned to act sexy in order to get attention.

Often, even when children cooperate in sexual relationships, they experience deep feelings of shame, betrayal, and distrust afterwards. These emotions are made worse when the adult or relative asks them to keep the sexual activity secret. Sexually abused children frequently feel burdened by the responsibility they carry for another person's happiness. This burden reflects the obvious vulnerabilities of children: they do not have the cognitive resources to understand the complexities of sexual behavior, are dependent on adults and other family members for emotional and practical support, and are typically unaware of their right to say no to others who have power over them. Adolescents are better able to understand the implications than young children, but are still emotionally immature. Sexual abuse can be as devastating to them as to young children. Some research indicates that sexual abuse is particularly disturbing to adolescents because their sexuality is just awakening and they often feel at fault for the abusive sexual encounter.

Children and adolescents never fully consent to sex, for consent implies a mature understanding of what sexuality involves. We believe that even if a child initiates sexual activity, it is always and entirely the adult's responsibility not to be sexual with children. As adults, we need to know that children depend on us to provide an atmosphere of safety and trust in caring for their needs. Even if some children can handle sexual activity, it is impossible to know this beforehand. Paul's final statement about castration says it all.

If you were sexually abused as a child, how does it affect you as an adult? You may find it difficult to accept your same-sex attraction and establish a gay identity. You may confuse your shame about same-sex feelings with the humiliation of sexual abuse. You probably believe that the adult who abused you was gay, which is not always true, so you may equate being gay with sexually exploiting others. And if you believe that, as a boy you seduced the adult, your disgust with same-sex feelings may be even deeper. In short, those of you who were sexually abused may experience same-sex feelings as a disgraceful and corrupt link to the men who abused you.

Having been sexually abused often leads you to see yourself as a misfit in the gay community. You may feel that your same-sex feelings have developed illegitimately, and that you would have been heterosexual if you hadn't been abused. Seeing yourself as different from other gay men, but being aware of your same-sex feelings, may make you feel like you don't fit anywhere. The result is isolation and profound despair.

What happens when you attempt to be intimate with other men? Relationships often have a nightmarish quality. Typically, you feel that there is a hidden price to pay for attention, so you fear any gesture of affection or caring from your partner. If you were abused, you may disdain caring and approval because you see them as a sign of weakness in your partner. Mentally, you may tell yourself, "If he loves somebody like me, he must be a fool."

Some of you who were sexually abused will feel most

secure when your partner is being abusive; that, at least, is familiar and you can control your partner through sexual manipulation. In this case your partner usually feels there is no way to connect with you; cruelty is out of the question and tenderness only leads to rejection. Often your partner gets confused and feels that he is a failure. In his frustration, cruelty may even seem like a viable option. Clearly, the emotional turmoil of such relationships interferes with the safety that is necessary for intimacy to develop.

All is not lost, however. If you were sexually abused as a child, with qualified professional treatment you can recover and go on to have productive and enjoyable relationships. There are two important parts to your healing. First, you must realize that you are not to blame for your early sexual experiences, even if you were sexually curious or found the sexual contact to be pleasurable. Second, accepting your same-sex feelings, no matter how they were obtained, is essential to developing a positive identity. Both of these steps may require contact with other gay men who went through a similar experience.

After two years of therapy, Paul shared an important personal victory:

> *I know you'll think this is crazy, but yesterday I kissed a man for the first time and we didn't have sex. My knees were shaking. The earth was moving! I loved his tenderness and I didn't get disgusted with him. I never thought I could do it. In my mind, being affectionate always led to what the teacher did to me. Now I am free!*

"WHY WON'T MY BODY DO WHAT I WANT IT TO DO?": SEXUAL DYSFUNCTION

Scott, a twenty-year-old blond Adonis, blurted out at his first therapy session, "I don't understand what's wrong with me. Here I am with this gorgeous man. We spend a great evening together. He's even a nice guy and I can't get it up! Now that makes a lot of sense." Clearly it doesn't make sense. Although he had only two previous partners, Scott had no history of previous sexual difficulties, had successfully come out to a loving family during adolescence, and seemed well-adjusted. When one of us assured him that such wasted opportunities might reoccur throughout his lifetime, his face turned from shock to horror. Finally, hinting of a smile, he boasted, "Come to think of it, we really got to know each other on that first date." Scott returned a week later, after another date, with an expression on his face that showed he accepted another cruel fact of life: the irrationality of the penis.

Yes, despite what you were told by friends growing up, sex is not something you can just order up, like french fries. Because you've had no problems with virility in the past, you may expect your penis to be as faithful as Big Ben. Well, your penis works even better than Big Ben, because it is *not* as dependable. Although it seems irrational, your penis is smarter than you think. When you can't get it up, your penis may be telling you that you have been working too much, are angry with your lover, feel guilty about an affair, have been too much of a people-pleaser, have a physical health problem, or are passionately in love. As in Scott's case, overstimulation and performance expectations sometimes create an overload situation for your penis. Reassurance and a sense of humor often restore you to relaxation and pleasurable sex. Such qualities are essential for sexy, intimate relationships.

Some gay men do experience serious problems of sexual performance, including impotence, inhibited ejaculation, and other problems. Clearly there are causes for these dysfunctions beyond sexual inexperience. Such factors as physical ill health, early problematic sexual encounters, medications, life stress, homophobia, and relationship problems can contribute to sexual dysfunction. Also, sexual problems can be complicated by shame ("My body is hopelessly flawed"), misplaced romantic ideals ("Prince Charming never loses his erection"), and too-rigid views of masculinity ("Real men are always up"). Such beliefs often cause gay men to feel unrealistic pressure to perform sexually.

If you are disturbed by sexual dysfunction for more than six months, consult a sex therapist with good credentials and a reliable urologist. Most mental health centers and hospitals have information about such professionals. If you have a partner, include him in your treatment. In a relationship, sexual dysfunction is always a couple's issue. Both partners typically have a role in the difficulties, and both partners are certainly affected by the dysfunction.

Many men feel ashamed about difficulties with sexual performance and are reluctant to talk about such problems. The tendency is to put off consulting a professional and hope that the problems will go away on their own. You go to a doctor when you are sick; seek the advice of a sex therapist when your sexual performance is consistently problematic. Although you shouldn't make a mountain out of a molehill, how can you tell the difference unless you ask for help?

SAFER SEX

Phone Fantasies
24-hour service

Talk to our steamy men any time of the day or night!
Choose from: Hot cops, truckers, musclemen, sailors, S&M.
Ask about our specials
MC and VISA accepted

Times have changed. To be a gay man it used to be enough to be out of the closet, cruise, and trick. If you looked masculine and had announced your identity to family and friends, it was even more to your credit. Having a lover, a respectable job, and a permanent residence were long-term goals. If you played a minimally active role in the gay community, you could feel gay pride.

Something deeper and riskier is expected of gay men nowadays.

The intensity of these new expectations is expressed in the following dialogue:

DAVID: *I can't believe I'm hearing this. You're telling me that you don't want to have sex with me because you're afraid of AIDS. Haven't you ever heard of safe sex? Don't you believe me when I tell you that I've only slept with two men in the last three years? Can't you see that I'm clean? Come on, take a risk. You know, all of us are going to die someday.*

ANDRE: *Why shouldn't I be afraid of AIDS! We've only gone out twice. I'm not saying I don't trust you, David. You're a beautiful man. I've never met anybody like you. It's just that I don't want to have sex with anybody right now. I think there's a lesson here for all of us.*

DAVID: *Sure. And I suppose next you are going to tell me that God is trying to punish us.*

ANDRE: *No, I'm not! But that doesn't mean there isn't something for us to learn. All those years of sex, sex, sex. It's disgusting! Isn't there something more important than two men getting it on? Maybe God is trying to teach us something. Maybe God means for us to be celibate right now.*

DAVID: *Now I know I'm crazy, falling for a religious fanatic! You know what I think? You know what the real truth is? AIDS has nothing to do with your celibacy. You're just punishing yourself for being a faggot.*

ANDRE: *Maybe we both are.*

The argument between David and Andre may reflect some of your own conflicts about being sexual. Sex used to be simple fun. Now it's a matter of life and death. Not only do you have to struggle with if, how, and why, you are going to be sexual, but also with the meaning of being gay and living a full life.

Because AIDS is not strictly a disease of gays, all heterosexual men and women are challenged to go through a similar examination of their sexuality. The sexual lifestyle of gay men has always been subject to scrutiny and discredit; however, and AIDS as a disease has many parallels with how society views gay identity: sexually transmitted, uncontrollable, shameful, latent, deviant, reprehensible, and life threatening. As a result, you may believe the message of society that AIDS is your fault, same-sex feelings are sick, and you need to be in the closet. You may resign yourself to lonely phone fantasies, or even worse, to sexual self-destruction. *You do not have to accept this message! You do not have to accept AIDS as a gay disease!* There is an alternative.

You can be sexually responsible and enjoy sex. David and Andre represent parts of gay identity that can be integrated. David's strengths include the permission to sexually enjoy and risk, a commitment to honest introspection and gay pride, and a fighting spirit. Andre's forte includes a willingness to hesitate and reflect, a strong survival instinct, and a desire for intimacy. Alone, neither man could thrive. A blending of their respective strengths makes Andre's and David's relationship and their identities extremely fulfilling.

Obviously, finding this middle road is not easy and will only be possible through frank discussions and intimate personal sharing. How exciting that David and Andre could relate so passionately and openly! Whether or not they were aware of it, they were already connecting on a deep level. You can too!

Let's be clear. Intimacy is not a replacement or a prerequisite for sex. Far from it. But a commitment to be intimate and sexual involves integrating pleasure and responsibility, and this requires increased communication among gay men. Celibacy out of fear and shame is an endorsement of gay identity as sinful and AIDS as a punishment from God. The life-as-usual sexual mentality has never affirmed gay identity, AIDS notwithstanding. With fortitude and a willingness to make mistakes, you can make wise sexual decisions.

We invite you to hear the voices of two men who are successfully struggling with clarity about sexual behaviors. These examples may help you find your own voice:

DANIEL: *I'm 23. I know I am going to meet a lot of men yet. Safe sex is the way to go. I don't really mind. I mean sure, it's inconvenient. But my straight friends have to worry about sex just as much as I do. For me, safe sex is a way of doing whatever is necessary to be with a man I care about. Besides, I have a lot of passionate nights ahead of me, and I don't want to miss any of them.*

PETER: *When I was Daniel's age, I probably would have said the same thing. I've had more than my share of action. I know this may sound reactionary, but I've decided to be celibate for now until I can be in a long-term monogamous relationship. I don't want to risk wearing rubbers. I'm meeting some men now. We're affectionate, but not sexual. I can wait. If I meet somebody special, I'd be sexual. But first I*

*would want both of us to have a current AIDS test.
You may think I am wasting my time, but I really
am enjoying life now.*

Before closing this section, we present the safer sex guidelines.

SAFER SEX GUIDELINES

Considered Unsafe

Rimming
Fisting
Blood contact
Sharing IV needles
Semen or urine in mouth or on skin with sores or cuts
Anal intercourse without condom
Vaginal intercourse without condom
Sharing enema equipment, douching equipment, or sex toys

Considered Possibly Safe

French kissing (wet)
Anal intercourse with condom
Vaginal intercourse with condom
Sucking—stop before climax
Cunnilingus
Water sports—external only

Considered safe

Massage, hugging
Mutual masturbation
Social kissing (dry)
Body-to-body rubbing
Fantasy, voyeurism, exhibitionism
Sex toys (when used only on yourself)

These guidelines are lifesavers. Use them. But don't stop
there. It's dangerous to identify safer sex with any particular
list of behaviors. Be concerned about your total well-being,
emotional and physical, not just with avoiding the AIDS

virus. The only *truly* safe sex is sex that makes you feel good about yourself and enhances your self-esteem. Don't fool yourself into thinking that you can disregard your feelings and do anything you want, as long as you follow the preceding list of rules. Instead, pay close attention to your emotions. These can serve as a compass that will steer you through any perilous waters ahead.

SEXUALITY AND SPIRITUALITY

It may jar you to read the words *sexuality* and *spirituality* together. You may think, "These two topics don't have anything to do with each other," or "This is really far-fetched!" By the end of this section, we hope that you will see that sexuality and spirituality are closely related and that gay men have a special role to play in modern views of spirituality.

The apparent incompatibility of sexuality and spirituality comes from a false distinction between body and soul. In traditional Christian teachings, the soul is seen as the residence of all that is dignified, beautiful, and eternal in humans, whereas the body is viewed as "a sack of dung, food for worms, filthy, shameful, a source of nothing but temptation to bad men and humiliation to good ones."[7] Modern theologians are beginning to realize the basic fallacy in such a view: if the body (and sexuality) is so horrible, why did God create it? This question has led to some important revisions in religious views of sexuality. Today, many theologians endorse the idea that sexuality is part of the divine plan and plays an important role in spiritual development.[8]

This point of view has important implications for gay sexuality. As mentioned earlier, scientific evidence suggests that the majority of gay men do not choose to be gay, and that biological factors strongly influence sexual orientation. This gives support to what gay men have been saying all along, "It can't be wrong for me to be gay. God made me this way!" In our view, gay sexuality needs no apology. On the contrary, gay sexuality is a divine gift, a great blessing to gay men and to other people.

Again and again we have seen evidence of this blessing with our clients and friends. David, a client, said with tears in his eyes:

Three years ago, when I first started seeing you, I used to cry myself to sleep because I was so grateful for your help. Now, I know there was something more than you that helped me. If it hadn't been for how strong my gay feelings were, I would never have seen a therapist. I would never have left my marriage. I would never have learned all the things that I now know about myself. Through my gay feelings, I've grown beyond my wildest dreams.

If only we all felt the delight in our sexuality that David does. Can you imagine the serenity we would have? Do heterosexual men and women have the experience of feeling God in their own sexual development? In our experience they do not, perhaps because they take their sexuality for granted.

Being faced by gay sexuality is a blessing to us all. It is up to us, as brave and wise people, to accept the gift. We could fill another book with testimonials of gratitude from families of gay men who have learned to cherish this gift. Each time we hear the same story our hearts skip a beat:

When Ron first told us he was gay we didn't know what to say. I went out to the garage and wept. I couldn't let him see my tears. Martha cried alone as she couldn't let me see hers. He may as well have told us he was going to die. Then, none of us knew how to love, except for Ron. Through a lot of hard work over the past two years, and with the help of friends at PFLAG [Parents and Friends of Lesbians and Gays] and our son, we discovered that something was missing in our family: the freedom to be who we are with each other. I can't begin to tell you what this lesson has meant to us.

The blessings of sexuality go beyond appreciating gay identity. Sexuality, in a trusting relationship, can feel similar to devout prayer. You may find that sexuality is a way of drawing closer to your spirituality and experiencing it in a real way. The intensity of being held and soothed in the arms of another man can make you feel totally accepted. The sweat and passion of your sexual acts can be as fervent as the preaching of a devout prophet. The warm glow and fulfillment of orgasm is like a gift of grace within you. Sexuality can be a door through which you come into contact with the spiritual level of your existence.

Another way that sexuality may bless you is by giving you the motivation to struggle with relationships. How many gay men might have spent their lives in total isolation, except for sexuality? How many times have you sworn off relationships in discouragement and frustration, only to try again because of sexuality? Through sexuality, you may confront challenges you might never have attempted, compose music that might otherwise have gone unheard, and write books you might never have written. Sexuality is a gift, a lure, and a reward that spurs you to greater personal and spiritual growth.

One aspect of sexuality that is frightening to many people is that it remains largely a mystery. In our technologically advanced society, many of us have the illusion that we can totally control our lives. Sexuality belies this fantasy. After years of research and with all their accumulated knowledge of how the body works, still no scientist can say for sure why you are gay and your brother is not. Also, sexuality pops up in our lives at the most inconvenient times to surprise us, challenge us, inspire us, and perplex us. You may attempt to put shackles on it with logic and rationality, but typically, you will fail. Sexuality is a link to your primitive and distant past. It reminds you of the unknown and the unknowable. It underscores the necessity of faith.

Finally, let us share a discovery that may aid you in your struggles with sexuality. In some ways, this insight contrasts with everything we've said so far in this book. We've spent pages discussing the complexities of sexuality and intimacy. We've advised you how to delicately balance these two processes in your life. We've reviewed patterns of sexual problems and urged you to choose potential partners carefully. We've given fatherly counsel about safer sex practices and the dangers of indiscriminate sex. We've spoken of the relationship between sexuality and spirituality, and how each of us, through sexuality, seeks a beautiful man who can open us to the infinite in our lives.

Our insight is this: the beautiful man you are seeking lies within you, waiting to be discovered and cherished. When he is uncovered, many of the complexities we have spoken of become easy and natural. Perhaps in searching for the perfect partner, you've really been looking for the beautiful part inside of you. If you surrender yourself to this beautiful part, the possibilities for connection with others are endless.

One moon shows in every pool, in every pool, the one moon.
    —THE ZEN FOREST SAYINGS[9]

NOTES TO CHAPTER 4

[1]Money (1987) has likened the development of sexual orientation to "native language, programmed into the brain through the senses." What does this mean? All of us are biologically prepared to learn language, but the particular language we speak depends on where we are raised. Similarly, we begin with a biological predisposition to be sexual, which is shaped by the culture around us. After a certain age, it is difficult or even impossible to learn a new language perfectly fluently. It probably is equally difficult to change one's sexual orientation in adulthood.

[2]The stage of generativity is described by Erik Erikson in *Childhood and Society* (New York: W. W. Norton & Co., 1950).

[3]M. Ramirez, "Biculturalism/multiculturalism in the Americas." In R. Diaz-Guerrero (Ed.), *Cross-cultural and National Studies in Social Psychology* (Amsterdam: North-Holland, 1985).

[4]D. Finkelhor, *Sexually Victimized Children* (New York: Macmillan, 1979), p. 143.

[5]G. Fritz, K. Stoll, and N. Wagner, "A comparison of males and females who were sexually molested as children." *Journal of Sex and Marital Therapy* Vol 7 (1981), pp. 54–59.

[6]A random poll of thousands of Americans was done by the Los Angeles *Times* in 1985 (August 25–26), p. 1. Twenty-seven percent of women and 16 percent of men said that they had been sexually abused during childhood.

[7]C.S. Lewis, *The Four Loves* (New York: Harcourt Brace Jovanovich, 1960), p. 142.

[8]See, for example, J. E. Nelson, *Embodiment: An Approach to Sexuality and Christian Theology* (Minneapolis: Augsburg Press, 1978).

[9]R. Fields, R. Weyler, and R. Ingrasci, *Chop Wood, Carry Water* (New York: St. Martin's Press, 1984), p. 36.

5

GAY MALE COUPLES

You may strongly want to love and be loved by another man over an extended period of time. You are hardly alone. As we travel around the country and discuss our work, we find that gay men hunger for information about loving relationships. Most often, we are asked how gay male couples stay together or how they resolve key problems. In part, these questions reflect the lack of role models for gay couples. Also, there has been increased interest in close relationships in response to the AIDS epidemic. Many gay men fear that their relationships will not last and that gay men are incapable of intimacy, fears that can lead them to frantically seek guidance from others about establishing relationships.

But the stereotypes are not true. Gay men clearly can form enduring relationships, and there are many thriving gay male couples in this country. Many of these couples have turned potential handicaps into strengths, providing lessons for all types of relationships. By reviewing what is characteristic of gay male couples, we hope to convince you you have what it takes for intimacy.

RESEARCH ON GAY MALE COUPLES

Prior to 1980, there was little research on gay male couples, and what existed was of limited quality. In recent years, several excellent studies of gay male couples have been published. These studies shed light on the special characteristics of gay male relationships. Because we refer to these studies repeatedly in this chapter, first you may want to know some basic facts about how they were conducted.[1]

The first large study of gay male couples was part of a larger project involving gay male, lesbian, and heterosexual couples. It was conducted in the late 1970s by two sociologists, Philip Blumstein and Pepper Schwarz, who summarized their findings in a readable book, *American Couples*.

The 969 gay male couples in the study volunteered after seeing notices in gay publications or hearing about the study through friends. Both partners in a couple completed 40-page questionnaires about themselves and their current relationship. Approximately 100 gay male couples were also interviewed by the researchers. Eighteen months after they filled out the initial questionnaire, close to 550 gay male couples responded to a follow-up questionnaire about their relationships.

The majority of participants were well educated. Many came from New York, Seattle, and San Francisco, and about 30 percent were from other locations. Most of the gay men were fairly young (80 percent were under 40), and more than half the gay male couples had been together five years or less.

In 1984, David McWhirter and Andrew Mattison, themselves a gay male couple, published *The Male Couple*. This study differs in important ways from that of Blumstein and Schwarz. Fewer gay male couples were studied (156), and no other types of couples were investigated. McWhirter and Mattison interviewed all couples. Also, participants were located by the friendship network method; every couple was asked to find friends who would take part in the study. Almost all couples were from the San Diego area, and there were proportionally more older and less educated couples than in the study by Blumstein and Schwarz.

The major finding of McWhirter and Mattison was that gay male couples show phases in their relationships, depending on how long they are together. McWhirter and Mattison identified six of these stages, which they respectively called: Blending, Nesting, Maintaining, Building, Releasing, and Renewing.

We refer you to *The Male Couple* for a detailed description of these stages. As an example of how they relate to intimacy, however, consider one stage, blending. McWhirter and Mattison's description of blending shares many features with pseudo-intimacy: intense togetherness, with a merging of identities and a downplaying of differences. The prevalence of blending in gay male couples in their first year suggests that pseudo-intimacy is normal for young relationships. Pseudo-intimacy is a major concern only when a couple remains stuck in the blending stage, for then their relationship fails to progress.

You may be wondering, "But do these studies tell me about *my* current relationship?" Perhaps couples who volunteer for research projects are special in certain ways. Couples with severe relationship difficulties may not participate. Also, to take part in a study you must consent to be interviewed by strangers or have your name on a mailing list, so highly closeted couples may not be represented. We are not criticizing these two studies, only pointing out that their results most likely pertain to you if you and your lover resemble the couples who participated in the research. Even if you are not like these couples, however, it can be useful to see exactly how you compare.

A second issue is the timing of the two studies. Both *American Couples* and *The Male Couple* are based on research done before the AIDS epidemic. Many gay men have changed their lives in response to AIDS. So, some findings from these two studies may no longer apply, and we will tell you when we think this is so.

ADVANTAGES OF GAY MALE COUPLES

You may have never considered that two men in a loving relationship have advantages compared to other couples. The strengths of gay male couples are often overlooked and are important if you are to understand gay male intimacy.

Last year, a gay male couple we know visited one partner's family at Christmas. A five-year-old cousin was fascinated by the two men, and asked a number of questions at the dinner table. When her mother explained that the two men were in a committed relationship, the girl appeared perplexed. She pursed her brow and earnestly asked, "But how do they know who is the mommy and who is the daddy?!"

Although this young girl obviously felt that the two men were at a decided disadvantage, research consistently suggests that this is not true. Many studies have found that same-sex relationships benefit from a lack of stereotyped sex roles. While this is not difficult to understand, it may surprise you just the same. All of us are aware of the caricature of the "butch-femme" gay couple, and you may even know such couples. Also, many gay male couples do establish fixed roles about cooking, cleaning, and other aspects of their relationships. McWhirter and Mattison found that such roles commonly occurred during the Maintaining stage of gay male relationships (years four and five).

Research shows a difference between roles in gay and heterosexual couples. In gay couples, role division is typically based on personal preferences and abilities; in heterosexual couples it is based on gender-role stereotypes. For example, in a traditional heterosexual couple, both cooking and housecleaning are likely to be done by the woman. In a gay couple, each man will do the task he prefers or does best.

Why base role division on personal tastes and skills rather than on tradition? It promotes greater individual happiness and more efficient functioning in a couple. If cooking and cleaning do not have to go together, you and your partner may have better meals, cleaner surroundings, and be happier. Also it's more fulfilling to do something because you really want to do it, rather than because it's expected of you. Not surprisingly, whether one considers heterosexuals, lesbians, or gay men, couples with the least stereotyped role division are the most satisfied with their relationships.[2] Traditional roles may be convenient or seem comfortable, but over the long haul, such patterns are limiting.

Why are gay male couples less likely to get into traditional roles? Clearly there are no gender cues to trigger these behavior patterns. Have you ever seen a competent woman "forget" how to do something mechanical when a man was around? Or a traditional man who lost the ability to work an oven when a woman was present? When two men get together, they are less likely to fall into such habits.

Also, gay men have greater range in expressing themselves as men, with the result that they have practical and emotional skills rare in heterosexual men. For example, you may know how to cook, sew, and care for young children, as well as how to comfort others emotionally. Most likely, you also learned a number of skills expected of men. The same is probably true of your partner. As in the theater, when you have a broader repertoire, you don't get typecast in a single role. And if one of you gets sick, a stand-in is always available.

Finally, recall our earlier description of the bicultural socialization of gay men. Because of your experience in both gay and heterosexual cultures, you are more likely to realize that cultural norms are not absolute. This gives you a freedom to explore and discover new solutions to old problems in relationships, such as the division of labor in a household. The two of you are less likely to do things a fixed way, simply because "that's the way it's always been done." You are likely to leave more room for creative expression.

Freedom from sex roles has broader implications for a couple than who does the dishes. Gay male couples are required to be more introspective about their relationships, and introspection can produce healthier couples. As one man told us, "When I was married there were so many things I took for granted. Now that I've come out, my lover and I talk about so many things. I appreciate now what it means to be in a relationship." The need for reflection and negotiation can make your relationships stronger and more authentic. Flexible roles are a real bonus for gay couples.

INTRAGENDER EMPATHY

Intragender empathy means that, in general, two persons of the same sex find it easier to understand each other's needs, feelings, tastes, and desires. This may seem like common sense. And if you've never been in a heterosexual romantic relationship, you may not fully appreciate the importance of intragender empathy. Intragender empathy helps explain many special characteristics of same-sex couples.

For example, Blumstein and Schwarz compared same-sex and heterosexual couples on the amount of leisure time they spent together and how satisfied they were with that time. Partners in gay male and lesbian couples spent more free time with each other. Heterosexual men and women enjoyed being together but also felt a need to be with friends of the same sex. Some of the activities they liked to do with same-sex friends were disliked by their partners. The researchers concluded, "Gay men and lesbians . . . have an advantage in that their need for such [same-sex] camaraderie can be provided by their partners" (p. 183).

Blumstein and Schwarz also found that gay and lesbian couples were more compatible regarding the balance of work and leisure time in their relationships. In heterosexual couples, the men often felt pressured to give more time than they wanted to the relationship, while women wanted more time than their partners gave. Members of gay male couples were generally satisfied with the amount of time spent in work versus play, probably because of their similar tastes and needs.

Intragender empathy may also give you and your partner an advantage in your sexual relationship. Masters and Johnson, the famous sex researchers, observed committed heterosexual and homosexual couples in their sexual interactions. They concluded that gay men and lesbians were better at pleasuring their partners, communicated more openly about sex, and used more total body contact when having sex than did heterosexual men and women. Intragender empathy is important in explaining these findings. As the researchers state, "Men know quite specifically . . . what usually pleases men, and women are indeed the only experts on the subjective appreciation of women's sexual feelings."[3] After hearing for so many years that gay sex is not as good as heterosexual intercourse, you may be relieved to find out that generally this is not the case.

Apart from compatibility in the bedroom and when having fun, intragender empathy holds out the promise of deeper, more meaningful relationships for gay couples. Women and men have such different life experiences that it is difficult for them to speak the same language in relationships. How often have you heard heterosexual women complain, "Why can't my husband talk to me?" or heterosexual men say, "I'll never understand women!" You and your partner may have an instinctual appreciation for each other's history as men. Such familiarity and compassion gives a solid base on which to build intimacy.

FREEDOM FROM THE RESPONSIBILITIES OF CHILD REARING

Although more and more gay men are interested in becoming fathers or raising children, the vast majority of gay male couples do not participate in child rearing. For example, McWhirter and Mattison found that only 8 per cent of the gay men in their study had biological children, and not all of them had continuing contact with their sons and daughters. This figure is substantially lower than comparable rates reported by Blumstein and Schwarz for heterosexuals and lesbians. At most, it would appear that no more than 15 per cent of gay male couples have responsibility for child rearing.

Like many gay men, you may feel great sadness about not having children. Such feelings are understandable. Many gay men have fantasies of someday having children. They long for more liberal guidelines regarding adoption and foster placement. Some have gone so far as to hire surrogate mothers. As any couple with children will tell you, however, there are also benefits to being childless.

One of these benefits is more available money. In general, the pooled income of gay male couples is greater than that of lesbian or heterosexual couples. In addition, because few gay men have children, they can spend more on themselves, their partners, and community projects. This money means added opportunities, some of which may affect intimacy. For example, you and your partner may have more money to invest in a home, education, psychotherapy, and couples' enrichment workshops. You may take more vacations, eat out more, and give each other more gifts.

Freedom from child rearing also means that gay male couples have more time for themselves and their partners. Many couples with young children find it difficult to be alone. Even when the children are asleep, the parents are often too tired to pay attention to each other. Communication and lovemaking can suffer drastically, and a rare weekend alone together in a motel can be a treasured retreat. If you are part of a childless gay male couple, you have more energy for the work of intimacy: more time to talk, play, fight, and make love with your partner. These opportunities can substantially benefit your relationship.

DISADVANTAGES FACED BY GAY MALE COUPLES

Of course, silver linings often come with clouds attached. Perhaps in reading the advantages of gay couples, you found yourself seeing the dark side. The strengths of gay relationships deserve to be acknowledged with no "ifs," "ands," or "buts." So do the disadvantages.

LACK OF ROLE MODELS

Romeo and Juliet, Ozzie and Harriet, John and Yoko, Mom and Dad; everywhere one looks there are models for heterosexual couples. In contrast, if you are part of a gay male couple, you may have few examples on which to base your relationship. Although the absence of role models encourages ingenuity in solving problems with your partner, you may also feel that you are living out the motto from Star Trek: ". . . to venture where no man has gone before." Of course, like many gay couples, intellectually you may know that you are not alone. You may even have gay male couples as friends. But if you live in a small community, you may not know how to find other gay couples. You have nowhere to turn when problems arise—no one to ask, "How did you two deal with this?"

The lack of available models for successful gay male relationships can mean more work for each of you and more struggles for both of you together. Because you have so little precedent, you may have to negotiate issues that are taken for granted in heterosexual relationships. Should you pool your money? In whose name should the car be registered? What should you do when one of you makes a career move? Some of these questions can be answered by looking at heterosexual relationships. However, many gay male couples have a healthy skepticism about traditional heterosexual marriage. You may be unwilling to use marriage as a model because you see so many problems associated with it. In the absence of healthy role models, it can be exhausting and stressful for you and your lover to negotiate every issue.

Another consequence of the lack of models for gay couples can be hopelessness or cynicism that their relationships can succeed. One couple we know had been living together for five years but refused to plan vacations or projects together more than six months ahead, in case they should ever break up. The implicit message was, "Even after all this time, we can't trust our relationship." This is an extreme example, but the same attitude can be seen in milder form in a number of gay men. For example, last year, one of us was at a dinner party with several gay men. During the meal, one man reported that two friends, a male couple who had been together ten years, had recently separated. There was a long silence, and then much head nodding as one man said, "I thought these two might make it, but I guess it's just impossible for gay relationships to last." You may be personally familiar with such feelings.

McWhirter and Mattison and Blumstein and Schwarz found that there were many thriving gay male couples. Many men had been partners for as long as thirty or forty years. McWhirter and Mattison estimated that there are 2.5 million gay male couples living in the United States today.[4] You may plead, "Where are they?" And how does one explain the stereotype that gay male relationships never last? Obviously, many successful couples stay hidden out of fear of prejudice or because they see withdrawal as essential to their relationships. Some couples hide their relationships even in the gay community. Two men we know, who have been together many years, avoid gay community functions. They say that other gay men see them as a model couple and constantly ask for advice about how to make relationships work. The two men find this tiresome.

Consider also that our stereotypes shape our perceptions. If you believe gay relationships are inherently unstable, every breakup will confirm this idea and lasting relationships will be overlooked. Each of us sees what he expects to see.

How can you and other gay men come to believe that you can have enduring couple relationships? Obviously, one way is for gay male couples to come forward in their communities and be open about their relationships. And it is not just in heterosexual circles that such witness is needed but also in the gay community. For example, Steve and his lover, Jim, recently went to a gay conference and stayed in the home of a man who was in his first gay relationship. After they wrote to thank the man for his hospitality, Steve and Jim received these words in return:

> Dear Steve and Jim,
>   I've been receiving all sorts of thank you's from the folks that stayed here . . . but . . . one of the things I didn't thank you for was the fact of your existence together. Admittedly I haven't been around too many male couples, but you two are the first that really seem to have a mutuality in your relationship. . . . I don't know what brought this on, I suppose ruminations on my first serious relationship. . . . But this week I've been struck by the number of "lovers" so many of my friends have had. . . . I hope you don't mind being pedestal-ized for a while. It's so much easier imagining the perfect couple if one has a real couple in mind. . . . You two seem more nearly one than any other male couple I've met. For which, thank you.

LACK OF SOCIAL SUPPORT

The scarcity of models for gay male relationships is part of a larger problem: the lack of social support for gay couples. Our society is clearly oriented toward married heterosexual couples. Airlines offer discount tickets to businessmen and their wives but not to gay partners flying together. Numerous tax and insurance benefits are available to heterosexual married couples but not to gay couples. It is often impossible for gay male couples to be adoptive or foster parents. And many churches offer couples' enrichment seminars or couples' groups for heterosexual relationships but no such support for gay relationships. Some people may justify these exclusions by noting that unmarried heterosexual couples are in a similar situation to gay couples. However, gay couples do not have the option of getting legally married. In fact, the lack of formal recognition for gay partnerships is one of the best examples of the lack of social support for gay male couples.

How does this societal snubbing affect you as part of a gay male couple? As our client Gilbert can attest, such experiences can make you feel that your relationship doesn't count. When visiting his parents, Gilbert overheard his mother bragging to a friend. She claimed that she always remembered her children's anniversaries and always sent greetings to her sons-in-law and daughters-in-law on their birthdays. Gilbert was tempted to point out to his mother that she had never once done these things for him and his lover in their twelve years together. In the end, he kept quiet, but felt bitter, depressed, and unappreciated for some time thereafter.

The lack of support for gay male couples may be responsible for a premature end to some relationships. Who knows what difficulties could be overcome, or how often you might try again, if you felt that others wished the best for your relationship? In fact, there is a mixed blessing to this lack of social recognition of gay couples. Some heterosexual couples stay together long after intimacy has died, because they fear what "the Joneses" will think. Gay couples, who stay together in the face of terrible odds, are more likely to do so because they care for each other.

There are other reasons to hope. The gay community is becoming more nurturing of gay couples, and research suggests that such support is important. A study of more than 200 gay men in close relationships found that men who were well-integrated in the gay male community had more intimate emotional relationships and were more satisfied with their lover relationships.[5] If you and your lover are in contact with the gay community, your commitment to each other may be strengthened.

Support from the heterosexual community is also forthcoming, although slowly. For example, some mainstream churches have begun to recognize same-sex relationships as worthy of their blessing and support. In the Society of Friends (Quakers), several congregations have already conducted marriage ceremonies or ceremonies of commitment for lesbian and gay male couples. We hope that other traditional churches will make such ceremonies available to same-sex couples.

RELATIONSHIP ISOLATION

Two people in a couple may forget about the rest of the world and focus entirely on themselves. This narrowing of attention is common and healthy in the beginning stages of a romantic relationship. When this focus persists, however, it cuts a couple off from others. Although it occurs in heterosexual, lesbian, and gay male relationships, several factors make gay male couples especially prone to relationship isolation.

Relationship isolation can occur on several levels. You may segregate yourselves as a couple physically and rarely leave each other. In extreme cases, you two may work together and spend every evening in each other's company, doing jigsaw puzzles or working on your home. If someone invites you out, you may decline, saying, "We're just homebodies." If a friend asks for a favor that would disrupt your routine, you may say, "I'm sorry, we're busy tonight." It may seem that you two need no one else to be content and are not interested in helping others. You've found a comfortable niche and see no reason to leave it.

Sometimes relationship isolation is more subtle. As a couple you may be active socially and involved in many activities (often together). Nevertheless, your relationship is the entire focus of your passion and energy. If you're engaged in conversation, the topic always shifts back to what you and your partner are doing together. You are likely to make very few "I" statements; everything will be "we did this," "we hope," "we want." Such couples show a marked lack of perspective. With all the topics deserving of attention, you may go on and on about where you're headed on your next vacation.

You may wonder what's wrong with such a relationship. There are several problems. Relationship isolation is often tied to pseudo-intimacy. If you and your lover spend all your time together, it can discourage individual risk taking and block personal growth. Eventually, you may find that you show many of the signs of pseudo-intimacy that we described in Chapter 1. Furthermore, relationship isolation goes against one purpose of close relationships: to prepare us for being in the world. M. Scott Peck has drawn an analogy between intimate relationships and a base camp for mountain climbing: "If one wants to climb mountains one must have a good base camp, a place where there are shelter and provisions, where one may receive nurture and rest before one ventures forth again to seek another summit."[6] As with base camps, your relationship requires careful tending. But if you stay in the base camp, you overlook the purpose of your expedition, and you'll never have the satisfaction of reaching the summit.

Are there particular reasons why gay male couples might cut themselves off from others? Yes. Intragender empathy can be one factor leading to relationship isolation. To the extent that your partner knows exactly what you want and has similar tastes and desires, there is little reason for you to go outside that relationship. In heterosexual couples, the gender gap can be a major source of tension, but it can also encourage partners to include others in their lives. Maintaining outside friendships and support networks is more of a challenge for couples of the same sex.

Relationship isolation may also occur in gay relationships because same-sex friends are seen as threatening to the relationship. A heterosexual woman may complain if her husband spends too much time with male buddies, but such friendships do not jeopardize her marriage. Conversely, if you get close to one of your male friends, your lover may become jealous. Therefore, you may avoid male friendships.

Responsibility for raising children is one of the best ways for a couple to avoid relationship isolation, for children have a way of forcing parents to look outside themselves. When you raise children, you can no longer think only of yourself or your partner in making decisions. Rather, you must often put aside your own interests to do what is best for children. And having children often pushes parents out of isolation into the larger community through school and sports and religion. Gay male couples tend not to rear children. Without children to widen their focus, relationship isolation becomes more likely.

The lack of social support for gay male couples can also encourage isolation and secrecy. If you cannot hold hands without others threatening you, you will not feel comfortable together. If it is not safe to identify yourselves in public as a couple, you will stay at home. And unless you know other people with whom you can be open, you will not invite others into your home because it is awkward to explain who your lover is. Social disapproval of gay male couples is probably the primary cause of relationship isolation.

COMMON DILEMMAS OF GAY MALE COUPLES

The seven problems presented here clearly resemble those of heterosexual and lesbian couples, but they are particularly applicable to gay couples. Each time we discuss a problem, we offer guidelines for successfully resolving it. For more in-depth exploration of your relationship, see Chapter 7.

"HOW CAN I BE OUT, WHEN MY LOVER IS IN THE CLOSET?"

ANTHONY: *"How was I to know you'd be so upset? All I did was list my name as a contact person for the gay runners' group."*

GERRY: *"All you did . . . ! What do you mean, all you did?! All you did was let everyone in town know that the person I'm living with is queer. The people at my job are going to love this!"*

ANTHONY: *"Oh, come on, Gerry. The people at your work are never going to see the gay newspaper. And even if they do, it probably won't matter. If only you were a little more open about being gay, you'd discover that people really don't care."*

GERRY: *"That's easy for you to say, with your cushy academic job. Remember, I work with kids; it's a different thing. I won't put up with your coming out for me."*

ANTHONY: *"Gerry, I didn't come out for you, I came out for me. But I'm not going back in the closet for you, either."*

After the first glow of a relationship has begun to fade, many gay men experience conflict over how public they will be about being gay. Disagreements about this in your relationship could be caused by many factors: one of you may have come out more recently, one of you may be more involved with heterosexual culture through work or friends or have more to lose if you risk coming out, or have more shame about being gay. Whatever is at the root of the conflict, differences in your comfort with being openly gay can lead to heated arguments.

Of course, many gay men are careful to choose partners who feel the same as they do about being publicly gay. If you've had conflicts in past relationships over this issue, you are especially likely to look for a lover who is similar to you. Nevertheless, Gerry's and Anthony's situation is common, probably because people change while they are together. You and your partner may start out at the same level of openness, but over time, one of you may become more open about being gay. In part, this may happen because close relationships help heal shame. Another possibility is that early in your relationship, you were more open than you typically are. Being in love makes even the most timid people reckless and courageous for a while. It is only after the initial excitement has waned that we return to our usual way of being. When this happens, many partners react with hurt and anger: "You used to kiss me good-bye at the train station. Why won't you do it anymore?"

We believe that the concept of bicultural identity, introduced in Chapter 4, is useful in understanding and resolving difficulties such as those shown by Anthony and Gerry. When one partner is more integrated in gay culture and the other is more integrated in heterosexual culture, you have a cross-cultural relationship. Miscommunication and hurt feelings are likely, and are similar to those that might occur if the two of you were from different countries, each with its own customs and language.

This perspective helps explain why mismatches in coming out are so important in a relationship and why they are not easily resolved. Anthony is not just asking Gerry to be more open about his gayness; he is asking him to let go of habits and customs he has had for years and to which he feels tremendous loyalty. These behaviors are part of family traditions and friendships, and Gerry will have to struggle with these relationships if he decides to be more open about his gayness. If Gerry chooses this path, he will most likely experience the aloneness and lack of identity that are common among bicultural individuals. Furthermore, Anthony is asking Gerry to fundamentally change the way he thinks about himself.

Similarly, Anthony may be trying to maintain an identity and subculture that he adopted after years of feeling different. He is not willing to give up his gay identity and friends for Gerry and would probably feel that he had betrayed himself if he did so. If Anthony feels threatened by Gerry's secretiveness, he may become defiant and act flamboyantly gay until he is sure of his own identity. Listing his name in the paper may represent this kind of action. Conflicts over gay identity can cause gay couples to become locked in power struggles.

Viewing a mismatch in coming out as a cross-cultural problem may minimize conflict. Some lessons in foreign diplomacy may help. For example, "When in Rome, do as the Romans do." Your lover's office party is not the time to wear the makeup you've been dying to try, or to practice your campy phrases or attitudes. Similarly, don't tell the latest AIDS joke you heard at the gay political potluck your lover attends.

Next, remember your cultural bias and don't assume you know all about your partner's stance. Without subjecting him to bright lights and thumb screws, ask him why he feels the way he does. Don't talk him out of his position. Simply listen. Even if your disagreement continues, you will have a better understanding of your differences.

Also, remember that you can't force your lover to come out; he alone must decide to do it. Think about how unwilling you were to be pushed when you were at a similar place, and be more patient. Avoid setting up dramatic choices to test his love: "If you really love me, you'll go to the gay block party with me." Although such dialogue makes good reading in romance novels, it can ruin a relationship. Your lover needs to feel that he is coming out for himself, not because you are pressuring him emotionally.

Although we counsel against demands or coercion, we encourage you to ask for what you need and want from your partner in small, specific ways. If you find yourself fantasizing daily about your lover meeting your parents, ask him to do so. But remember the difference between a request and an ultimatum.

Just as you must not make excessive demands, so you should not give in to outrageous requests from your partner and use the side entrance because he fears the neighbors will suspect something. You must maintain your integrity and protect your own identity. If you give up your values, in the end you will resent your lover. Decide what things about yourself and your life are priorities, and where you might be flexible. If being a contact person for the gay runners' group is important to you, be one. Stand up for yourself when the alternative is to be angry and depressed.

Sometimes conflicts can be resolved by remembering that you are individuals as well as a couple. For example, if your lover does not wish to go to the gay film festival for fear of being seen there, don't make a fuss. Find some other friends or go by yourself. Don't do this to punish your lover. Such differences can actually benefit your intimacy.

Above all, look for places and occasions outside of your home where both you and your lover can be comfortable. Part of your task as a couple is to jointly construct a new culture, which you both can enjoy. This often involves finding a third choice, which respects both views, and which neither of you initially thought of. The more the two of you succeed in building a new life together, the stronger your relationship will be.

If you and your partner are at different levels of coming out, you can still have a healthy and vibrant relationship. Such disparities are opportunities for you both to grow in compassion and tolerance. They also provide excellent training in intimacy in that you are challenged to accept differences in each other—"Can I see that we have differences and still be supportive of you?" When you can answer yes to this question, you have given each other a valuable affirmation: "You do not have to be just like me in order for me to love you."

"GUESS WHO'S COMING TO DINNER"

RANDALL: "Why didn't you help me out when your mother snapped at me like that? What was wrong with her? I've never done anything to hurt her."

JAY: *"What could I do? It wouldn've looked funny if I'd jumped in. Besides, I figured you could take care of yourself. I know she's been peevish. But don't take it to heart. I think she just doesn't trust you. After all, you did take her baby boy away from her."*

RANDALL: *"She doesn't trust me? After all, you and I have only been together three years. You know, if she weren't your mother, I would've given her a taste of her own medicine. The only reason I didn't was because I didn't want you to get mad at me."*

JAY: *"Look, I'm not asking you to grovel for my benefit. But give her some time, will you? You know, this type of thing is all pretty new to her."*

In-laws are difficult to deal with for any couple but especially for a gay male couple. Some of the most challenging situations occur when your family meets your lover, without knowing that you're gay, or that you two are involved in a couple relationship. This situation can result in a comedy of errors that is not really funny and may breed serious conflict between the two of you.

A milder tension can occur when both extended families know the nature of a gay couple's relationship and on the surface seem to accept it. Nevertheless, when presented in person with the lover they have been hearing about, family members may become uneasy, confused, angry, sad, pensive, or anxious. What are the reasons for these reactions?

In Chapter 3 we discussed the grief that your family may feel when you come out. When you become involved in an intimate couple relationship, your family may relive this grief and experience it more deeply. Several factors encourage this kind of emotional reaction. Family members may have partially accepted your gayness while maintaining some denial. Perhaps they thought, "He'll snap out of it someday," "It's just a phase," or "He might still meet the right woman and change his mind." When presented with the living proof of your gayness—a lover—parents and siblings are forced to give up hope and can no longer deny their loss.

Second, the presence of a lover rocks the boat. This happens when any outside person—straight or gay—enters a family system; things are never quite the same. This imbalance is exaggerated when a gay relationship is involved, because a family is presented with decisions they never had to face before: "Should we put them in the same or separate beds?" "How will we introduce him to Grandma?" "What should we do if they kiss in front of us?" and "Are we supposed to buy him a Christmas present?" These can be anxiety-provoking questions for family members.

Trust may build more slowly between your lover and your family than it might with the same family and a hetero-sexual partner. Both sides may play a role in this distrust. Many families hold stereotypes about the short-lived nature of gay male relationships, and sometimes these ideas are strengthened by a son's or brother's string of past relationships. Such beliefs can interfere with trust building. As a mother of a gay man told one of us, "I don't want to get attached to one of my son's lovers until I'm sure that he will be around for a while. It's exhausting to get to know one and like him, only to find out a year later that you'll never see him again because the relationship is over." Your family may even go one step further in their skepticism and offend your lover as a way of testing your relationship—"Are the two of you strong enough to stand up to us?" If the two of you break up, the family may feel their worst fears were confirmed.

Many gay men also fear that their relationships will not last. This makes it hard to attach yourself to a lover's family or to introduce a lover to your family. Also, if a gay man or his lover have internalized shame, they may interpret any coolness from their families as a rejection. Recall Randall's reaction to Jay's mother, for example. Her irritability may have had nothing to do with Randall personally. He immediately felt guilty, however, and wondered what he had done wrong. Many gay men have severe difficulties with their own families because they are gay. Understandably, they are wary of having contact with another family or of introducing another gay man into their own family.

You and your lover need to understand that your relationship may intensify your families' grief about your being gay. Such awareness can keep you from taking family reactions personally, and minimize conflict between the two of you. Here are a few other suggestions for dealing with your families:

1. Don't let yourself be mistreated by your lover's family out of fear of offending him. Insist upon receiving the same courtesy that you expect from everyone else. Disrespectful behavior often stems from unresolved grief about your lover's being gay. Thus, you are doing his entire family a service by refusing to let them blame you; this forces them to confront their grief directly. In other words, you did not make your lover gay, nor did you make him leave his family. The family members need to resolve their feelings themselves. You do not have to take the blame.

2. Although you can expect support from your lover, you must be the one to stand up for yourself. He cannot do it for you. The major support you need from him is an understanding that you will not walk on eggshells with his family. If your lover doesn't agree to this, it may be better for you not to have contact with his family.

3. Your lover may also have unresolved feelings about his family, and you should not let yourself be used to express them. If you feel that you are present primarily to bait or antagonize his family, confront him with this feeling. No family will be able to accept you as long as you represent a test that they are bound to fail. Such a situation is disrespectful to you, because it involves using you to hurt others.

4. Just as you ask for respect from your lover and his family, so must you respect their ties to each other. Family loyalties are forged over many years. Recognize such loyalties and challenge them only when necessary: when they interfere with your happiness or your relationship with your lover. Don't simply test your power to see if your lover cares for you more than for his family. For example, you may be tempted to complain, "If you leave me to go to your parents' fiftieth wedding anniversary party, you love them more than me." This type of manipulation almost always backfires.

5. Remember that intimacy and trust take time. Don't rush things with a lover's family and insist that they accept you from day one. When they see that you are not a passing fancy and have your lover's best interests in mind, many families will open their hearts to you. After all, you all share a feeling of love for your partner. If both sides focus on this love, all else will follow. Learn to appreciate small changes in a family's reactions to you. This will help you wait for them to accept you.

In summary, gay male partners face a special challenge with each other's families. A gay relationship often opens unhealed wounds in a family's grief. When this happens, gay men can feel like they are at fault. With patience and wisdom, gay couples can avoid conflicts due to their families. A gay relationship can be part of a family's healing.

"ANYTHING YOU CAN DO, I CAN DO BETTER"

HOWARD: *"Did you see that man cruising me at the bar? Boy, he sure wanted to get me into bed. I bet if I had said the word, he would have taken both of us home."*

TRAVIS: *"What is that supposed to mean? That I couldn't get a trick by myself? You know there were quite a few men there tonight making eyes at me too."*

HOWARD: *"Especially that blonde near the door. I was ready to sock you, the way you were leading him on.*

TRAVIS: *"Don't get so excited. You're just jealous because the good ones always go for me."*

HOWARD: *"Yeah? Well, if it's a beauty contest you want, just wait until we go to the beach, I'll show you."*

Feelings of competition can occur in any couple. Two partners may compare sexual attractiveness, salaries, education, number of friends, physical strength, or numerous other attributes as a way of balancing power and status between them. Although such rivalries can occur in any relationship, they are more common in gay male couples. Why?

Men are socialized to be competitive and to see winning as essential to their maleness and self-worth. Some gay men overcome this training, but others find it more compelling because they doubt their masculinity and lovability. When insecure men are involved in close gay relationships, they are obsessed with beating out their partners to maintain their self-esteem. If they are not clearly more successful, desirable, or skilled than their lovers, they feel insecure and anxious. Also, it is natural to compare yourself to your lover, for he is a man you are close to and probably respect. In contrast, in traditional heterosexual relationships, partners may feel that making comparisons between them is irrelevant. Traditionally a woman is not expected to earn as much money, or to be as educated or as physically skilled as her male partner.

In *American Couples*, Blumstein and Schwarz concluded that competition in gay male couples occurred in three major arenas. First, many gay men were acutely aware of how much money they earned relative to their partner's earnings. Unlike heterosexual women, gay men were insecure and tense when their partners earned more than they did. They felt spurred on to increase their own earning potential, so they would be equal to their partners. As Blumstein and Schwarz concluded, "Because earning power is a central part of a man's identity, having more money gives a man symbolic—and therefore real—advantages over his partner . . . gay men are usually uncomfortable when being the provider or being provided for. Each man thinks he should be able to pull his own weight, but if one greatly surpasses the other, he may feel entitled to be dominant, leaving the other feeling inadequate" (p. 110).

Second, gay male couples were also more likely than other types of couples to make occupational comparisons between partners. Blumstein and Schwarz found that gay men felt most successful in their own work when their lovers were in an occupation of lesser status. Obviously, this makes it difficult for some gay men to fully support their partners' careers. As their partners become more successful, they feel less adequate.

In the third arena of competition (as shown in the conversation between Howard and Travis), gay men may compete in the area of sexual attractiveness. In part, this occurs because two lovers may be rivals for the same admirers. Blumstein and Schwarz found that gay men doubt their own handsomeness when their partners are the object of flirtations by others. Such insecurity is especially likely if the partner who feels left out has feelings of body shame. Also, according to Blumstein and Schwarz, when you think your partner is more attractive than you, you have more conflicts in a sexual relationship with him. Some men use outside sex as a way of showing their partner that they are desirable. Such contests can accelerate in a spiral of tit-for-tat affairs, which may eventually end a relationship.

Although feelings of competition with your lover are quite natural, you can keep these feelings from damaging your relationship. Learn to evaluate yourself by your own ideas of what you want rather than by your partner's accomplishments. Competition is most likely when you are insecure and need an outside standard to tell you that you are worthy. If you have clear internal standards, and can affirm yourself, there will be less need for external comparisons. You will be the judge of yourself.

Learn to enjoy receiving from your lover and depending on him. Once you know how, it can be fun not having to be the best at everything. To get some practice, choose a subject or an activity that your lover is clearly superior at, such as tennis, cooking, Spanish, or computer programming. Ask him to teach you something about it. Appreciate his expertise, as well as your first steps at learning something new. You may get upset when you are not as skilled as he is. If this happens, remember that he learns other things from you.

Keep competition in perspective by focusing on personal values, seeing your partner's successes as independent of your own, and rejoicing whenever bounty enters your relationship, be it through you or your lover.

Whenever you feel competitive, ask yourself, "Is there enough love, respect, and admiration to go around?" We believe that none of these good feelings is limited in the world; your lover's share does not decrease your own and you can rejoice in his good fortune without betraying yourself. But we recognize that this may sound too good to be true, especially if all your experience contradicts it. You must decide, is love a pie with only so many slices, or is it a river that can never be emptied?

"IT'S MY TURN TO BE ON TOP"

SIMON: *"How about if I'm on top this time? You've been on top the last three times."*

VICTOR: *"I didn't know you were counting."*

SIMON: *"Well, I like to switch around sometimes. Come on, it's only fair."*

VICTOR: *"But I don't like to get screwed. It makes me feel weird. Let's just forget it altogether."*

Tension may arise between you and your partner regarding anal sex, over who will be the active and the passive partner. This conflict often emerges early in a relationship, when a couple is working out issues of relative power and dominance. It may also arise at other times, however, and can be a signal of deeper conflicts. Sometimes similar tension arises regarding oral sex, or over who initiates sexual activity in the relationship, but this is less common.

Why is it that anal intercourse stirs up issues of dominance and reciprocity, whereas other forms of sexual activity are less likely to do so? One possibility is that the physical act of anal sex brings up these issues. You and your lover may feel more vulnerable when being penetrated anally than you do during any other sex act. Similarly, men commonly report that when they are on top, they feel active, forceful, and aggressive. Also, for many men anal sex has connotations of masculinity-femininity or dominance and submission. This can make for delicate negotiations over who will give and receive penetration. If one of you feels insecure about your masculinity, you may find being penetrated anally to be very threatening.

Conflict over anal sex in gay male couples can be related to the broader issue of competition just discussed. When Simon says, "Let's switch. It's only fair," he is really saying, "I want to be equal to you." Victor's feeling "weird" when he is penetrated may be a sign that he needs to feel more powerful than his partner. Blumstein and Schwarz found that anal sex was sometimes used to balance other perceived inequalities in gay male relationships. In some couples, the partner who earned less money and had less power in decision making would exclusively play the role of penetrator, presumably to enhance his esteem and restore equilibrium.

If Simon and Victor were to seek help with their sexual negotiations, we would suggest that they throw out their sexual score card and focus on their feelings. It is irrelevant who has done what how many times to whom. What counts is that each man feels safe in and satisfied by their sexual relationship. We would ask them to explore feelings of anger or of being treated disrespectfully by each other. Such emotions are best discussed directly, rather than being acted out in the bedroom.

We would encourage the two men to give up societal stereotypes regarding anal intercourse and other forms of sex. It is no more manly to penetrate than to be penetrated. And both of these can be pleasurable experiences. Everyone has his own sexual likes and dislikes, and it's possible that Victor may never enjoy being penetrated anally. But our hope would be that this would be due to Victor's personal preferences, not because others had told him that it was not manly to express his love for his partner in certain ways.

Victor and Simon should also explore power issues in their relationship. Victor's desire always to be on top sexually may be a sign that he is feeling powerless in other areas of the relationship. He may be helped by identifying instances when he feels out of control and discussing these with his partner.

"YOU DON'T BRING ME FLOWERS ANYMORE"

SAM: *"Did you notice my haircut?"*

JIM: *"Oh, yeah. It's real nice. He did a good job this time."*

SAM: *"I swear, sometimes I think you don't even look at me anymore."*

JIM: *"Hey, what's your problem? I'm just tired from work, that's all."*

SAM: *"You're always tired. We haven't even made love for two days. This relationship is going down the tubes fast."*

After a passionate, sometimes stormy beginning, most couples eventually go through a cooling-off phase. If you experience such a lull, you may suddenly understand such expressions as, "the honeymoon is over," "the fizz has fizzled," or "the magic is gone." Although romantic love wanes in all types of couples, many gay men feel threatened when it happens to them.

McWhirter and Mattison present an excellent description of the decline of romantic love. They connect it with the transition from stage one (blending) to stage two (nesting), and find that, in gay male couples, romantic love typically dwindles after about a year. As romantic love wanes during nesting, sexual activity decreases and partners become ambivalent as they recognize shortcomings they previously overlooked. They may feel taken for granted or want more appreciation from each other, hence the refrain of the song, "You don't bring me flowers anymore."

What causes romantic love to ebb in relationships? Most likely, you cannot have close day-to-day contact with a partner and idealize him for long. As McWhirter and Mattison explain, "Prince Charming, the object of our every desire, ends up leaving the dishes in the sink, his dirty socks on the bathroom floor, and hair in the shower drain" (p. 54). Under such circumstances, romantic illusions are dashed, and we face the task of living with a real person, warts and all. For these reasons, we see the decline of romantic love as a healthy sign in many gay male couples. Either two partners learn that they do not want to be together, or they begin the task of transforming pseudo-intimacy to intimacy. Having been romantic, they now begin to love.

If the lessening of romance is a normal and even healthy stage that occurs in many relationships, why is it so frightening to gay male couples? It bears repeating that many gay men have little confidence that they can maintain relationships. Some of this insecurity is based on past experiences with family or former lovers. Some of it may derive from believing that *all* gay male relationships are doomed. For many men the insecurity escalates to panic or serious depression. Some couples end a relationship because each man is determined not to be the one who gets left.

When a couple is concerned that their honeymoon is over, we usually congratulate them. After all, the couple is no longer relying on glitter to maintain their relationship. Each partner has made a riskier investment in a more lasting love. This can give rise to a new kind of excitement, from deeper sharing and personal growth. Such excitement may never end.

If you and your partner imagine that you are the only ones to experience the end of romantic love, you may be reassured by talking to other gay male couples. The fact is, many gay male couples stay together through the decline of romantic love, and all successful long-term relationships go through this stage. If you reach out, you may get helpful pointers from other couples. Also, by overcoming panic, you can better see the good things in their relationship.

When we work with couples who are in this stage, we encourage them to ask for and offer appreciation to each other. All of us have a tendency to take good things for granted after a while, including a wonderful lover. This can be overcome by training yourself to focus on the things you appreciate. A special thank-you when your lover does the laundry or a back rub when he is tired can make a world of difference in your relationship. Also, it is important to know when you are feeling unappreciated and to let your partner know about this. The best way is to talk about your own feelings ("I'm feeling angry and unappreciated lately"), not to accuse ("You don't love me anymore!"). We suspect Sam would have more success with Jim if he used this approach.

Also, the end of idealization does not mean that you must abandon romance completely and never again feel in love with each other. Many successful couples learn to balance trust and security with novelty and romance. As one feels safer in a relationship, there is a tendency to also be bored. Similarly, romance and novelty may be exciting and challenging, but they also make it difficult to relax and be trusting. These different qualities are difficult to blend in intimate relationships and doing so requires skill and sensitivity.

Of course, second honeymoons require time and energy. If you are feeling too tired to express appreciation to your lover or to rekindle romance, perhaps you are neglecting to care for yourself. It's hard to give what you don't have. If you wish to maintain the dew on the rose, it may be necessary to reassess life's priorities.

"YOU CAN SCREW AROUND, AS LONG AS I NEVER FIND OUT"

DAVID: *"You were awful late from work today. Bad traffic?"*
TOM: *"Do you really want to know?"*
DAVID: *"Oh, I see. No, I guess not."*
TOM: *"Why do you look so upset? I thought we had an agreement."*
DAVID: *"We do. I just don't like to be reminded. I wish you'd wait until I go out of town to trick. That's what I do."*
TOM: *"Okay, if that's what you want. I thought you just didn't want to know the details."*

Monogamy, means restricting your sexual activity to one partner in one relationship. At least prior to AIDS, gay male couples generally adopted a different stance from heterosexual society about monogamy in primary romantic relationships. Blumstein and Schwarz found that 82 percent of the gay men in their study were not monogamous and that the longer two men were a couple, the less likely they were to be monogamous. McWhirter and Mattison found even more striking results. Ninety-five percent of the gay male couples in their study permitted sex outside their relationships. Among couples who had been together five years or longer, *all* had developed some arrangement allowing for outside sexual activity. These figures were collected before the AIDS epidemic had much effect on the sexual behavior of gay men. Comparable figures today might be quite different.

We are not surprised that so few gay male couples are monogamous, for men easily separate sex from intimacy. Thus, in male couples, outside sex is more likely to be accepted and allowed. Also, although many gay men are raised to believe that sexual exclusivity is a matter of morality, they come to regard this as a matter of traditional heterosexual values. This stance makes it easier to explore nontraditional arrangements in their relationships. Finally, there is support in the gay male community for outside sex, so much so that some gay male couples complain it is difficult to maintain monogamy. For example, a client recently protested, "No one will believe that I'm monogamous!"

For some gay men, sex outside their primary relationship may serve the positive function of allowing them to explore their sexuality, overcome body shame, gain confidence in their own desirability, and become integrated in the gay male community. As mentioned in Chapter 4, these tasks belong to the period of adolescent sexual exploration, which many gay men postpone until young or middle adulthood. Some men go into a stable relationship soon after coming out. For them, nonmonogamy is a way of continuing exploration without giving up a primary relationship. The primary relationship often serves as a buffer and a home base for the stormy events of this period.

Interestingly, the frequency of outside sex does not mean that gay men never struggle with feelings of jealousy or possessiveness. McWhirter and Mattison found that 85 percent of gay male couples had their greatest conflicts over outside relationships. Also, most couples who had successfully adapted to outside sex had developed guidelines to lessen jealousy. Examples were to restrict outside sex to anonymous encounters or to "threesomes" involving one's partner. Alternatively, the members of a couple might agree not to discuss their sexual contacts with each other, on the principle that "what we don't know won't hurt us."

Obviously then, you and your partner do not need to be monogamous to maintain your relationship, although special arrangements may be necessary to deal with possessiveness. The question we would like to pose is: What effect will nonmonogamy have on the quality of intimacy in your relationship? There is no research investigating this topic, and some gay male couples have told us that outside sex has aided their relationship, whereas others feel that it has hurt them. However, there are several issues you should consider before deciding against monogamy.

There is the issue of time and energy. Intimacy is so challenging, especially in sexual relationships, that no one can simultaneously do justice to two intimate sexual relationships. One or both relationships must suffer. This is especially true in the early stages of couple relationships, when a couple is still getting to know each other. Blumstein and Schwarz found that gay male couples who were monogamous in their first two years together were more likely to stay together than couples who were not monogamous. After the first two years, monogamy was unrelated to the persistence of a relationship.

"But," you may say, "I'm not trying to have more than one intimate relationship. All of my outside sexual encounters are strictly anonymous." This gives us pause for a different reason. Recall our analogy that sexuality and intimacy are like two rivers. The longer you allow them to run in separate beds, the harder it is to unite them when you wish. Being in an intimate couple relationship, while also having anonymous sexual encounters, is like asking two rivers to run separately and together at the same time. In other words, you can't have your cake and eat it too.

Outside sex may keep you and your partner from dealing with important issues. Fears or resentments you feel but don't deal with can diminish sexual feelings for your partner. If you simply have sex with another person, instead of talking about such issues with your partner, intimacy suffers. Of course, unthinking compliance with monogamy can also stifle your feelings and your sense of individuality. Nevertheless, sexual exclusivity sometimes provides a motivation to face difficult issues in a relationship. This will aid your growth and that of your partner.

Also, consider AIDS. You and your partner may put tremendous effort into building a healthy and close relationship, but if one of you develops AIDS, the time you have to enjoy each other will probably be lessened. Monogamy is insurance on the investment you have made in your relationship.

Ultimately, you and your partner must ask yourself, "Would having sex outside our relationship bring new love into it?" If the answer is yes, as it is for some couples, you may freely choose to be monogamous or nonmonogamous. If the answer is no, you must weigh the costs of outside sex to your relationship with the benefits to yourself. Gay male couples generally determine to explore this issue on their own and not be restricted by heterosexual models.

Although one may debate the effects of nonmomogamy on relationships, sexual dishonesty is definitely detrimental to intimacy.

Sexual dishonesty consists of lies or omissions about sexual behavior that affects a relationship. A crucial distinction here is between matters that affect a relationship and those that do not. An example is whether you masturbate when apart from your lover. Assuming that your masturbation is not a compulsive habit or otherwise destructive, it is not your lover's business whether you masturbate. You may decide to tell your partner about your masturbation practices as a way of letting him know you better, but you are not obligated to, and it will not affect your intimacy if you do not.

In contrast, matters that have the potential to have an impact on your lover or your couple relationship are not your private business. An example is having sex with people other than your lover. Every time you have sex outside your relationship, you can influence your intimacy with your partner. Nowadays, this is even clearer because of AIDS. Even if you restrict your outside sexual activities to "safer" sex practices, there are health risks for you and your partner. You have the right to decide about your own risk, but not to decide for your lover. Gay men who engage in secret sex outside a primary relationship play Russian roulette with their partner's life.

Sexual dishonesty threatens intimacy because it is inherently disrespectful to your partner. In most cases, such behavior is an attempt to control a partner by not giving him all the facts. You may fear that if your lover knows you go to the baths, he will leave you. Or if your lover finds out that you do not use condoms with your tricks, he will refuse to do certain things in bed. Some gay men claim that they are actually protecting their lover's interests: "If he knew, he'd only get himself all worked up for nothing, so I won't tell him. It's for his own good." Such thinking is dishonest to others and dishonest to yourself. It also shows a mistaken conception of intimacy.

"But," you may say, "my partner has told me that he doesn't want to know about my sexual activities outside the relationship." To us, this underlines the fact that integrity is essentially a private matter that depends little on what others think. Your partner may be comfortable being lied to. You may even succeed in hiding your affairs from him. But you cannot hide them from yourself, and your falsehoods will affect the way you feel about yourself. In the end, you must decide whether your self-esteem is worth the excitement of a secret sexual encounter.

You and your partner can choose from many different arrangements about monogamy. The important thing is to be explicit and honest with each other. Sexual dishonesty may seem to be a way of maintaining intimacy while having the thrill of outside sexual encounters. But in the end, dishonesty interferes with intimacy in both current and future relationships.

"WE NEVER HAVE SEX TOGETHER ANYMORE"

Don and I stopped having sex together seven years ago. It was a gradual thing. First, he didn't want to do certain things in bed. Then he totally refused whenever I suggested making love. Finally, I stopped bringing it up altogether and we moved into separate bedrooms. Now, we don't really even hug or touch at all, but I don't mind. I always have a boyfriend on the side, although they're getting difficult to find, the older I get. I used to have fantasies of starting over, but Don and I have been together for thirty years. We have so much history behind us and our lives are so intertwined, it would be really hard to split up. It's easier to leave things as they are.

Many gay male couples continue to have passionate sexual relationships well into late adulthood, after many years of being together. However, some gay male couples show a gradual decline in their sexual activity together and eventually become nonsexual companions. Although the frequency of sex decreases in all types of couples the longer they are together, this trend is particularly pronounced in gay male couples. Blumstein and Schwarz found that after ten years together, 33 percent of gay male couples had sex together less than once a month, compared to 15 percent of heterosexual married couples. This is especially surprising because gay couples have a great deal of sex together in the early years of their relationships. And this decrease in sexual activity is cause for concern. Blumstein and Schwarz found that the more frequently a gay male couple had sex together, the happier they were with each other.

Why do so many gay male relationships become asexual with time? One possibility is that sex outside the relationship replaces or interferes with sex between partners. Once again, it is helpful to think of sexuality and intimacy as two rivers. If the two of you in a couple frequently have experiences where sexuality and intimacy are kept apart, the separate "riverbeds" will be dug more deeply. This should make it more difficult for you both to merge these processes in your relationship. If this reasoning is correct, such rules as, "You can have outside sex, but only if it's anonymous" may eventually haunt you by encouraging you to split sexuality and closeness in your relationship. Don's partner sees his outside sexual contacts as an unfortunate necessity caused by Don's refusing sex. It is likely, however, that such affairs maintain the asexual nature of their relationship.

Yet another possibility is that outside sex discourages gay couples from confronting deeper issues of anger, distrust, or jealousy that might otherwise arise. In our contacts with Don and his partner, we noticed that the two men let out a lot of anger through subtle sniping. If they were still sleeping with each other, would this continue? Or did they stop having sex together because of hidden resentments? It is impossible to tell which came first, but a couple's sex life often tells how they are dealing with deeper issues.

There is a close tie between a couple's ability to confront anger and the degree of passion in their sex lives. If you and your partner cannot be angry spontaneously, you are likely to have uninspired, boring sex. Many gay men can't imagine that anger can be constructive. This is especially true of gay men with shame about their sexuality, for shame is a potent block to anger. Men who are ashamed are excessively polite in primary relationships: "By walking on eggshells, I won't provoke his anger." Such carefulness is incompatible with passion. Remember, honesty can be an aphrodisiac.

It may also be that same-sex relationships are particularly prone to sexual boredom. Intragender empathy allows gay men to understand each other better and to know how to physically pleasure each other. However, a familiar partner of your own sex may begin to feel predictable after years of sex. Heterosexual couples may maintain more sexual excitement because the differences between men and women are mysterious and challenging.

Couples like Don and his partner have a tendency to stick with the no-sex status quo of their relationships rather than risk change; it is easier to have sex outside the relationship. Asexual couples have a host of reasons why they no longer have sex together: they are too busy with work and social activities, have different sleep schedules, or have health problems that restrict sex. Although there is usually some truth to these reasons, they often indicate a fear of looking deeper and a hopelessness that relationships can never change for the better.

Our hunch is that partners in most gay couples actually want to have sex with each other. But after long years of sexual inactivity together, it is natural for two men to feel helpless and hopeless about changing. A comfortable excuse is that sex is really not that important. But if you can admit that you are bothered by the lack of sex in your relationship and dare to expect more, the possibilities for sexual happiness are brighter.

So let's say you and your partner want to revitalize a cooling sex life together. How should you begin? If you haven't already, we suggest you first suspend outside sexual activity, at least for the time being. Do this as an experiment; see how it affects your relationship. Are you aware of feelings toward each other that you overlooked? Do you feel resentful, afraid, dependent, or sexual? These emotions may be signals of unresolved issues. Spend some time talking them through.

Even if no new feelings come up, try focusing on the nonsexual aspects of your relationship. If there are unsatisfying or worrisome areas, address these first, by yourselves or with the help of a couples therapist. One couple we knew found their sex life improved after they discussed one partner's positive HIV status. Both men had many strong feelings about this; however, they had never examined them together.

Even after you have taken care of old business, you may feel sexually awkward, uncomfortable, or turned off. Such feelings are especially likely if you have not had sex together for a long time. Don't despair. You may simply be out of practice in relating to each other sexually. Go slowly, and begin with some low-key, sensual activities. Take a bath together, or give each other a massage. Don't worry for now about orgasms, just enjoy each other's body and affection.

Finally, if all of these steps do not work, consult an experienced sex therapist. Inquire carefully before you begin, because many counselors have no experience in sex therapy. If necessary ask for a referral from AASECT (The American Association of Sex Educators, Counselors, and Therapists) 11 Dupont Circle N.W., Suite 220, Washington, DC 20036; phone: (202) 462-1171. Your persistence is admirable and is likely to be rewarded by tangible results.

CLOSING THOUGHTS

You may have gotten the idea that being in a couple is a lot of work. It is. Shouldn't it be? To be a couple, two men must acknowledge and accept the different intimacy styles and aptitudes that each learned from his family and life experiences. One partner may prefer to be alone when upset. Another to be with other people. One may be older, more closeted, or more educated. The other may be better at talking about feelings. All these differences must be blended and integrated for a couple to live together in a healthy relationship.

There are many pitfalls to this process, as you can appreciate if you've ever sung harmony with another person. First, when you are not in tune together, it is easy to feel that *you* are off key, but this is not necessarily so. Harmony is a question of balancing. Neither partner need be completely off key for a problem to arise, and getting back in tune usually requires careful listening to both parts and mutual accommodation. Second, successful harmonizing requires that you know your own part well, so that you don't get thrown off by a stronger partner. When the two of us sing harmony together, we find that each of us must occasionally plug his ears and listen to his own voice. You may find this equally true in your relationships. Sometimes singers are not properly applauded, but if they support each other they can still feel good about their duets. And when two voices blend together, the beauty can be astounding.

So you don't always do it perfectly? No one does. Each of us has had our ups and downs in couple relationships, and we continue to do so. The important things for us seem to be patience and determination. When we have dared to hope for the most in our relationships and to consistently ask for this from our partners, we have found our wildest dreams usually come true. But then again, sometimes they do not.

It has been said that marriage is not humanly possible. Well, the same may be true for gay male couple relationships. But this does not mean you should throw in the towel. Rather, recognize that there is a source of power within you and your partner and around both of you. This source can sustain you in your struggles as you learn to love one another.

And why go to all this trouble? quite simply, because it is your calling. As Thomas Merton said:

> Love is our true destiny. We do not find the meaning of life by ourselves alone—we find it with another. We do not discover the secret of our lives merely by study and calculation in our own isolated meditations. The meaning of our life is a secret that has to be revealed to us in love, *by the one we love.* And if this love is unreal, the secret will not be found, the meaning will never reveal itself, the message will never be decoded. At best, we will receive a scrambled and partial message, one that will deceive and confuse us. We will never be fully

real until we let ourselves fall in love—either with another human person or with God."[7]

NOTES TO CHAPTER 5

[1]Although the following two studies form the basis for many of the comments in this chapter, we have also made use of other studies. These will be referred to as needed and are listed in the Bibliography.

[2]M. Cardell, S. Finn, and J. Marecek. "Sex-role identity, sex-role behavior, and satisfaction in heterosexual, lesbian, and gay male couples." *Psychology of Women Quarterly*, Vol 5, (1981), pp 488–494.

[3]W. H. Masters and V. E. Johnson. *Homosexuality in Perspective* (Boston: Little, Brown, 1979), p. 213.

[4]McWhirter and Mattison, *The Male Couple*, p. 149.

[5]J. Harry and R. Lovely. "Gay marriages and communities of sexual orientation." *Alternative Lifestyles*, Vol. 2, (1979), pp. 177–200.

[6]M. S. Peck. *The Road Less Traveled*. New York: Simon & Schuster, 1978, p. 167.

[7]T. Merton. *Love and Living* (New York: Harcourt Brace Jovanovich, 1979), p. 27.

PART THREE

■

DEEPENING INTIMACY IN YOUR RELATIONSHIPS

■   ■

BUILDING INTIMACY: WHAT YOU CAN DO AS AN INDIVIDUAL

■

Once, one of us attended a ballroom dance class with much trepidation. Wondering "Who will I dance with?" only made the tension worse. Above the entrance to the class, a sign read: "Partners not required." Oh, what relief that sign brought! After all, how often can people without partners participate as equals with people in primary relationships? In this dance class, individuals learned ballroom dancing by practicing with classmates. Everyone was on an equal footing; everyone was able to learn.

Of course, not everyone who came to the class was single. But even people with partners needed to work on their individual styles. They were asked to exchange partners and dance with someone unfamiliar. They learned new steps and appreciated their partners more fully.

But it took a lot of practice.

Developing intimacy is much like learning to dance: you need somebody to dance with, but partners are not required. You may step on a lot of toes, think you have two left feet, or believe that you'll never get the rhythm. Such is life. Then, after several lessons, suddenly you can tango, waltz, cha-cha, and even make it look easy. It's really up to you to learn intimacy. You can always find somebody to practice with.

How to start? Well, suppose you were learning to dance. First, you need to practice the basic footwork without a partner: shadow dancing. This involves focusing on your own movements, mechanically learning new steps, and developing confidence in yourself without a partner. This experience may feel odd. But it is necessary, and remember, almost everyone who dances with his shadow feels self-conscious. Next, as you develop confidence in your steps, prepare to waltz and tango with other men. When you choose partners, select men who have a lot to offer and have had a few more lessons than you. You will be challenged that way. After a lot of practice, you'll say, "I can dance."

As you read this chapter and practice intimacy skills, we hope you will proudly say, "I can be intimate."

Are you ready to boogie? Time's a wastin'!

STEPS TOWARD INTIMACY

Like most of us, you may be skeptical that projects will bring you closer to others: "Mickey Mouse exercises will never help me be intimate." We are often most cynical when we are afraid of making mistakes. If this is true for you, don't worry about failing when you carry out these projects. Even screwing things up can make you laugh and bring new learning. Some of the most intimate moments occur when people make mistakes. If you want to improve your intimacy, you must not only read about the projects but actually do them. They *can* change your life.

We start with a number of projects, each of which will help you overcome a roadblock mentioned in Chapter 2. Begin by identifying your particular roadblocks, then find the corresponding projects in this chapter.

KNOWING YOURSELF ("TELL ME WHO YOU WANT ME TO BE.")

Instead of asking, "Who do *you* want me to be?" ask yourself, "Who do *I* want me to be?" For years you may have worried about what other people think of you. That's got to stop. The most important question you can ask yourself is: "Who am I?" An accurate and nonjudgmental answer to this question is the basis of self-awareness.

What is keeping you from being more self-aware? Old patterns sometimes impeded gay men from knowing themselves. If you have been terrified of the disapproval of others, you may know what others expect of you but not what you want. Or because of shame about your sexuality, you may feel there is little in you that is worthy of being explored. Clearly these patterns need to be altered. Start by telling yourself, "I am the best judge of myself," and "I am a complex person and I deserve to know myself."

Having accepted this responsibility, you may ask, "How do I become more self-aware?" We recommend two projects.

Project #1: Discovering Your Inner Self Like all of us, you put on an appearance based on how you want to be seen by yourself and others. This appearance is sometimes necessary. This outer image is only part of you, however. Beneath, there is another vital part of your identity: your inner self. This aspect consists of your feelings, thoughts, beliefs, expectations, and intuition and significantly influences important decision, such as selecting a career, deciding where to live, and choosing a lover. To be fully aware, you need to discover your inner self.

Uncovering your inner self is like solving a mystery. You need to look for clues and not get distracted, to formulate hunches, and make logical deductions. And you will need persistence and courage. Like any good detective, you can't get discouraged when the going gets rough. No matter how difficult the circumstances, solving a mystery leads to peace of mind.

Where do you look for clues? You look to yourself. Every second of your life you react to others in observable ways: your physical appearance, tone of voice, body posture, eye contact, facial expressions, and behavior patterns. All of these details say something about your inner self. Actually, without thinking about it, most of us look for these clues in other people's behavior, especially when cruising. Gay men are expert detectives!

To start this project, attend some social gathering. After a while, observe for at least fifteen minutes how you relate to others. Ask yourself: "What do I see happening in the room?" "How am I interacting with others?" and "How are other people behaving toward me?" Look for specific details. These observations are your clues. Next, ask yourself, "What do these clues tell me about my feelings, my thoughts, and my beliefs about myself?" Your hunches will lead to a discovery about yourself. After you make your discovery, tell yourself, "Congratulations, you have just solved a mystery!"

Some words of caution: you may notice that your self-scrutiny impedes spontaneity and connection with others. Sherlock Holmes had some limitations in this regard too. Such reactions mean that you are working on self-awareness. If you're disturbed by feeling disconnected from others, stop your detective work after fifteen minutes and return to the party. Also, resist all temptations to figure out other people. You are the mystery, not other people. You'll probably need to remind yourself of this again and again. Good detectives don't get distracted.

After your social outing, reflect again on what you observed and record your reactions. Sometimes it is easier to figure things out with hindsight. If you are really daring, you may ask someone else to help you figure out your reactions. Again *focus only on yourself!*

As an example, Sam went to a dance to discover his inner self. Typically, at a dance, he worried whether other men would approach him. This night was different. Instead of scrutinizing other men's behavior, he focused on his own reactions. Initially, he couldn't identify any of his reactions or feelings. Eventually he picked up some clues. He saw that he exclusively sought out attractive men, and that around them his voice faltered, he downplayed his career, and he always waited for them to make the first move. If an attractive man asked him to dance, he would imitate the movements of his partner like a puppet. After the dance he felt irritated with himself, thought of himself as spineless, and realized why other men lost respect for him. Such awareness did not leave him in a comfortable place, but he saw that his flexibility had serious drawbacks. His inner self had emerged.

Project #2: Keeping a Journal Writing a journal involves recording your journey through life. Writing what you know of your life experiences will help you recognize things about yourself that might escape you otherwise. For example, in writing this book, whenever we felt stumped, our writer's block taught us something about ourselves. It showed us that old emotional wounds were still painful, that we were having difficulties with intimacy in our current relationships, that we were overworked, or that we were mad at each other. There was joy and healing in all of these discoveries. Imagine, when you keep a journal, how much more you can discover about yourself.

Keeping a journal over a period of time also enables you to look back to identify patterns and monitor your own growth. By rereading previous entries, you may discover cycles in your life and see yourself in a different perspective. Finally, through a journal you can grieve over losses and renew your zest for living. If you find yourself missing an old lover, for example, you can go back and read about him. That will undoubtedly inspire you to put some new men in your life!

To begin this project, purchase a notebook that is large enough for you to write in. Record your feelings and perceptions when you feel inspired to do so, perhaps for fifteen minutes at the end of the day. Let your inner voice tell you when to write, and skip days when you don't feel like writing. Remember, you have no deadlines to meet, you don't have to worry about grammar, and no one will grade your work. In choosing what to write, consider three questions:

What's the most important event that happened to me today?

What am I feeling as I record my entry?

What does this event teach me about myself?

You can include all kinds of things in your journal: a poem you wrote, a news clipping, theater tickets, a recipe, dreams, erotic fantasies, some drawings, or an old sock. Anything goes! There is no right or wrong way to keep a journal. You can learn as you go along. The only rule is "listen to yourself."

You may ask, "Would it help to share my journal with someone I care about?" Clearly you have the right to keep your writing private if you choose. There may be good reasons for doing so. If you anticipate showing your writing to someone else, it may inhibit your spontaneity and interfere with self-awareness. If you want feedback from others, however, you may decide to share your journal with trusted confidants. Be sure of your purpose in revealing parts of your journal. Don't do it to impress others, hurt them, or embarrass them. Also, be careful when showing your journal to others. Remember, you are revealing your inner self.

A client of one of us once remarked, "My journal is the only place that I can truly be myself." To know ourselves, we all need such refuge.

ACCEPTING YOURSELF ("IF YOU REALLY KNEW ME, YOU'D GO AWAY.")

The roadblock of shame can be overcome by cultivating confidence in your worthiness. Friends may reassure you and compliment you, but until you can believe them, their statements will roll off of you like raindrops from an umbrella.

If you are like most gay men, you may need to accept your sexuality more fully, affirm the image you have of your body, be confident of your basic goodness, and generally, accept all aspects of your identity.

Project #1: Affirmations. Affirmations can change the way you view yourself. How you think about yourself greatly affects the core beliefs you have about yourself. Thus, if you dwell on your positive qualities, these will be more evident to yourself and others. You will tend to perceive yourself as a person of worth. At first, this may seem like circular mumbo jumbo. But we urge you to give affirmations a try. Don't take our word for it; find out for yourself.

The first step is to list affirmations that pertain to you. Here are a few examples of affirmations that have been useful to our gay male clients:

"My sexuality is a beautiful and natural part of me."

"I am a child of God. My body is perfect in God's eyes."

"I have endless beauty inside of me."

"My way of being a man is a challenge to others."

"My loving a man is an opportunity for others to understand love."

These are examples of general affirmations; they could be used for anyone. Actually, the most effective affirmations are those that are very specific to you. Thus, saying, "I am a wonderful person" may seem inappropriate. Telling yourself, "I am very sensitive to other's feelings" or "I am good at standing up for my rights" will often be more convincing, particularly if you can recall specific events that support these claims. Also, affirmations should be accurate and insightful. Don't tell yourself, "I am a responsible person" if you are twenty minutes late for almost every appointment. When you are affirming yourself, don't settle for crumbs. If you have saved someone's life, say so—"My friendship has convinced someone that life is worth living," rather than, "I am a good friend." Give yourself all the credit you deserve.

Another way to develop personal affirmations is to derive antidotes for the negative things you tell yourself. For example, instead of, "If you really knew me, you'd go away," you might substitute, "I have survived mistakes and am worth knowing." Or if you find yourself thinking, "I'm such a clumsy dancer!" instead, tell yourself, "It takes guts to do this." Again, use the results of your self-awareness projects to identify negative thoughts to change. Find the silver lining in every cloud.

Once you have made a list of affirmations, we suggest you write several on an index card each morning and carry them with you throughout the day. Choose that day's affirmations depending on your emotional state, your schedule that day, or your experiences the day before. Whenever you have a spare moment—while waiting for the bus or at the doctor's office—pull out your index card and read over your affirmations. Put them next to your bed at night and say them after rising in the morning and before going to sleep. The key to success is repetition. Say them over and over again. In this case, *saying* is believing.

Project #2: Developing Competence. Throughout our lifetimes we all must develop fundamental skills to maintain full confidence in ourselves. We need to learn numerous skills, including physical agility, personal grooming, cooking, symbolic thinking, self-assertion, and balancing a checkbook. There is no way to avoid learning these skills. If we acquire them, we gain self-acceptance; if we don't, we lack confidence. For some parts of our development, actions do speak louder than words.

Mario, a client, illustrates this point. As an adolescent, he had been sexually assaulted by a man in a park. Although he was sure that he was gay, he now had anxiety attacks whenever he had sex with men. One day, after a year of therapy, he rushed into his session and announced:

"You'll never guess what I did this week. You know how stuck I get with my panic attacks. Well, I hired a karate instructor and have taken some private lessons. I need to practice what I'm learning in therapy. I told him I'll probably panic during his instruction but that he's got to stop when I ask him to stop. I'm only a white belt and I interrupt the lessons a lot, but I am beginning to believe that I can control my fear." Mario didn't just talk about his body image—he did something about it. We all need to develop competence as part of our overall emotional development. That may have been one of the lessons you missed in high school gym class. Now's the time to learn it.

Identify one skill you have always wanted to develop: bodybuilding, wilderness camping, mountain climbing, tennis, assertiveness, or photographing wildflowers. Choose something that you are likely to follow through with. Then, find a structured way to develop your interest. Ask a buddy to join you if you can't do it alone. Then, go out and do it. Put aside all notions that you can't do it or you can't find the time. Simply enjoy your quest.

Let's say you decide to photograph wildflowers. You will need to learn a lot about F-stops and exposure timing as well as the difference between a mariposa lily and a shooting star. What's more, you'll need to be disciplined, spend time alone, and develop a sense of aesthetics. Whether you are taking a class in color photography or going on a field trip, you will make strides at developing competence in an area that's important to you personally. When you doubt your ability to face any life crisis, pull out one of your best photographs and admire it. Keep a mental picture of it wherever you go. This picture reflects your beauty within, and your ability to overcome your fear or hesitation to learn something new.

Project #3: Practicing Imperfection. Another way that shame develops is through constantly making unrealistic demands on yourself, such as "Nothing less than the best will do." None of us functions at his best all the time, so expecting it of yourself results in considerable disillusionment. It is possible to have humility and achieve greatness at the same time. Let's illustrate what we mean.

Working together for months, a group of Amish women sewed an exquisite patchwork quilt. The finished product reflected the mature needlework skills of the women and their shared love for each other. After the quilt was finished, one of the women took some brightly colored thread and made a careless stitch right in the middle of the quilt. When asked what she was doing, she answered, "That's to remind us that only God is perfect."

The Amish women knew that they had done their best and that there were imperfections in the quilt already. The bold stitch simply exaggerated these imperfections and reminded them that they didn't have to pretend to be perfect to be worthy. All of us need such acceptance.

Self-acceptance is a real bind for gay men because they are often put in a no-win situation by family and society: "I will like you if you change." Whether you change or not, you still feel unacceptable. Some gay men fantasize being perfect as the best way out of this bind. Unfortunately, believing, "I always have to be the best" carries over into personal relationships, so that at every turn you must be at peak form. Failure is inevitable. Even if you succeed, you lose. Who can stand to be around a perfect person?

If you want to accept yourself more, learn a new skill: imperfection.

Practicing imperfection, like making the bold stitch, entails deliberately doing less than what you expect of yourself. It is something you do for yourself, that does not hurt anyone, and is not manipulative. Actually, none of us needs to practice imperfection. Imperfection is all around us. In trying to be perfect, however, we become blind to our flaws. We pretend to be perfect because we fear that others will reject us and that we will not be able to cope with their reaction. Why go around being afraid? Test it out! Be imperfect!

A single friend of ours, Lloyd, had a reputation for hosting exquisite sit-down dinners with English bone china, Belgian linen, Waterford crystal, and engraved invitations. Get the idea? Several days after one of his famous dinner parties, he approached a friend and asked, "Why am I never invited to other people's houses?" His friend replied, "How can anyone compete with you?" Lloyd was irritated and visibly shaken by his friend's insight. He had often felt excluded and rather lonely. Upon further reflection, he decided to change things just a bit. With a little push from his friend, he hosted an entirely different dinner party the following month. He rounded up his guests the day before the dinner, he served soup and salad, used paper napkins and paper plates, and he didn't even have everything ready when the

guests arrived. Imagine how surprised his guests were! They
thought that Lloyd had flipped out. Some of his friends
immediately helped him out in the kitchen, some kidded him
about whether he needed his temperature taken, some specu-
lated that he had found a handsome lover, and others simply
sat in polite shock. Lloyd acted as if nothing was out of the
ordinary. He coyly asked, "Is something wrong?" During
dinner there was more chatter and laughter than ever before.
People had a ball. In fact, Lloyd couldn't get his guests to
leave until the wee hours of the morning. A week later, Lloyd
phoned his friend and blurted out that he had been asked by
an attractive man to a Texas barbecue. He hasn't been the
same person since!

There is a Lloyd in each of us. Dare to do less to be
more.

DEVELOPING SOCIAL SKILLS ("I DON'T KNOW HOW.")

Intimacy requires social skills. Expressing your own views
and feelings, listening to and empathizing with others, negotiating and valuing differences, observing rituals of respect,
and finding commonalities with others are all ways that you
acknowledge your worth and your caring for others. Such
abilities create an atmosphere of trust and safety in developing
intimacy.

Since boys are not encouraged to learn these skills, you
may have great difficulty with social know-how. Also, after
years of withholding your true feelings, you may lack confidence in emotionally relating to peers. To gain more depth in
your friendships, practice social skills with other gay men.

**Project #1: Joining and Creating Gay Men's Support
Groups.** Consider joining a gay men's support group—soon.
Oh, you'll probably be nervous if you imagine being in a
roomful of gay men. Generally the jitters subside after the
first few meetings, as honesty and closeness come more naturally. After a while, you may even feel quite comfortable!

"What can I get from gay men?" you may ask. You will
learn to feel less lonely, that you are like other people, that
there are many ways of being gay, that you are both imperfect
and worthwhile at the same time, that even big problems
have solutions, that others are attracted to you and vice versa,

and that is is possible for you to let your hair down and be yourself. Sound interesting? Such payoffs are possible in groups but may take time.

If possible, we recommend that you get involved in a group led by trained professionals. Experienced group therapists attend to the overall health of the group in a number of ways. They interview prospective group members, structure group meetings, and teach members how to communicate with each other. Typically, group facilitators don't participate in the group like other group members. As overseers, they monitor the overall group functioning and make strategic comments to keep the group focused and effective. There are many benefits to this arrangement. Group members spend less time with organizational dilemmas and have more energy for deeper sharing with one another. When a group gets bogged down in some misunderstanding, group facilitators can help get it back on track. Also, effective group leaders can help create a secure atmosphere for deeper group sharing, enabling members to face more significant personal issues. Group facilitators alone cannot make the group a success, but they can bring out the best in everyone.

When a group of gay men expresses feelings honestly, a whole new way of relating occurs. Same-sex feelings are not a secret! When sincerity is the norm, everyone seems to open up. You may be surprised at how uninhibited you are. In a support group, one person takes time to talk about himself and gets feedback from others. Several members may ask for the group's help in a given meeting. The feedback may be reassuring, instructive, puzzling, challenging, inspiring, or aggravating, all of which are valuable. Being in a group is the experience of intimacy building in its most elemental form. You don't simply make friends, you learn how to make friends.

A leaderless group also has advantages but generally demands that group members take greater responsibility for what happens in the group. It often helps to have some members with more experience, who can serve as "elders" for the group.

If there are no gay groups where you live, consider creating your own. It doesn't have to be a therapy group, but can focus on a common interest, such as, great literature, brunch, or gay history. As long as your group emphasizes friendship among members, it will improve your social skills. Through word-of-mouth and careful advertising you can find practical ways of connecting with others. Generally there is considerable untapped enthusiasm for such groups, more than you might imagine!

Let's say a word about sexuality and gay men's support groups. Unlike social groups, support groups serve many purposes. You may go to a support group to meet men, to work out emotional issues you cannot discuss elsewhere, or you may vacillate between these motives as you get to know other group members. Both motives are acceptable, but they may work against one another. For instance, you may have difficulty discussing your emotional pain if you are worrying about sexual involvements with other group members. Conversely, if you're sexually attracted to another group member, you may hesitate in approaching him because of how you will be regarded by other group members. Although sexual feelings in a support group are natural and inevitable, they can cause tension in the group. When sexual feelings are disrupting the functioning of the group, discuss them openly and move on. Such talk may seem presumptuous, but it isn't. Openly acknowledging sexual feelings often leads to less group tension.

In contrast to sexual feelings, sexual affairs have a large emotional impact on the group: jealousy, anger, distrust, or anxiety. Warranted or not, these tensions make it difficult for you to be vulnerable. For these reasons, it may be desirable to limit sexual behavior in your group. In our groups, at the first meeting, we ask members to state their expectations of the group and to set their own norms about sexual relationships between group members. Consistently, our support groups have decided that sexual relationships between group members will not be allowed during the course of the group *and* that honest expressions of sexual feelings by group members will be respected. This arrangement creates a supportive and safe atmosphere for group sharing.

If sexual expectations are not discussed openly in your group and you feel uneasy about sexual feelings or anticipated sexual demands on you, remember, support groups are not bar scenes; you can always say no. If you have tried to no avail to have your discomfort addressed by the group, it may be best to try a safer group.

LIMIT SETTING ("I CAN'T SAY NO . . . I CAN NEVER SAY YES.")

When you acknowledge your identity and needs as separate from those of another, you are setting limits. Such a boundary is not a rejection or punishment of others. Admitting to differences with other people affirms your identity and provides emotional safety. Examples of limit setting are putting a lock on your door, turning down a dinner invitation to spend time alone, or leaving a love relationship after having made many attempts to work things out. The challenge in setting limits is to protect your needs while respecting the rights of others. Thus, both flexibility and firmness are required to set healthy limits.

Some gay men have difficulty setting limits because they have always yearned to fit in with peers and fear that firm limits may lead to loneliness. Also, gay men who were hurt badly in the past may set limits that are too rigid. In any case, setting flexible limits in a relationship is crucial for intimacy. Successful limit setting requires openness with others and strength in your own convictions. Here are ways to begin developing such limits.

Project #1: Self-assertion Class. Self-assertion means standing up for your rights without violating the rights of others. The cornerstone of self-assertion is being aware of your own rights. Yes, you have rights! You might decide that:

1. *I have the right to express my attraction for other men.*

2. *I have the right to expect other people to educate themselves about same-sex feelings if they want to be close to me.*

3. *I have the right to express myself without fearing physical violence.*

When you affirm your rights, others may not agree with you, and no matter what rights you affirm, someone will be unhappy about them. A statement of personal rights is not a democratic process. You decide on your own rights, have the responsibility for defending them, and experience the consequences of asserting them. Such a stance is a normal part of being an adult.

Trusting your own judgment will enable you to maintain

your rights. If you distrust your instincts, you may need help from others in taking a firm but realistic position on your rights. If you are confused about your rights, discuss your ambivalence with a good friend. Take a stance now, even if you change your mind later. Self-examination, feedback from others, and taking a stance are critical for defining your personal rights.

In this project, list twenty-five personal rights, including some you are less sure of. Try to resolve any confusion by consulting with a friend and reading Appendices A and B of *Your Perfect Right* (by Alberti and Emmons.) Your list is the basis for setting limits.

Next, take an assertiveness training class where you will identify your personal rights, communicate your feelings and needs, and receive feedback from others. Most local mental health centers and gay rights organizations have information on self-assertion classes. If assertiveness classes are not available, consider starting your own self-help class. You can advertise in a local paper, use word of mouth, or notify a local mental health organization of your self-help group. Simply organizing such a group is itself an exercise in assertiveness.

Before you begin the class we recommend that you do some reading on self-assertion: *Your Perfect Right, Assert Yourself, When I Say No I Feel Guilty, Straight Talk.* You may fear, "They're trying to turn me into a pushy gay militant!" No, we just want to help you be more confident, so that closeness with other gay men is easier.

Project #2: Self-defense Class. Take a self-defense class. You may certainly resist this exercise: "I thought I was learning to make love, not war." Fear not. The purpose of learning to defend yourself is to build character, not to imitate Chuck Norris. Recall from Chapters 3 and 4 that many gay men distrust their bodies because they were shamed and ridiculed. A self-defense class can begin to change that view. Self-defense will help you be physically close to others, reinforce your sense of manliness, and show you that your body is reliable.

Completing Projects 1 and 2 will enable you, with the conviction of your heart and body, to say *no* and *yes.*

Project #3: Learning to Say Yes Again. Perhaps you have been burned in past relationships and feel the only way to cope is to erect psychological walls to keep everyone out. You may even be a notorious cynic. Perhaps you tell yourself, "I don't need a relationship," hoping that by not loving, you will avoid being hurt. Have we got you pegged? Well, are you in for a surprise!

Complete this exercise and you may be astonished to learn something exciting about yourself. First, list twenty-five aspects of gay life you feel most cynical about. That should be easy. For instance, you might mention:

Cynical List
1. *Gay men have only one thing on their minds: sex.*
2. *No one appreciates my interests.*
3. *Beautiful, thin, and young—that's all gay men want.*

Next, we want you to use an "I" statement so that each cynical item reflects some insight about you. *The insight must only be about you.* Finding the insight may require considerable time and self-reflection.

"I" Statements
1. *I don't trust gay men.*
2. *I worry that I'll never find a man who appreciates me.*
3. *I can't live up to gay standards.*

Finally, after more reflection, examine your "I" statements and write a phrase that honestly expresses a personal hope for each of the twenty-five items in your list of "I" statements.

Hope Statements
1. *If I'm around more gay men and keep my eyes open, maybe I can trust somebody.*
2. *Perhaps my loneliness is good; relationships are important to me.*
3. *I could worry less about what others think and have more faith in what I think.*

Compare your cynical list with your hope list. Have you discovered anything? Yes, beneath your hardened cynical mask lies an innocent young man who yearns to be loved. What is he like and what are his dreams?

Perhaps when you find your innocent gay man you may protest: "You tricked me into hoping. It's artificial anyway." Anything you put your heart to is not artificial. Still, you may object: "So I found my innocent gay man. What do I do now?" Our reply is simple: listen to him each day. For now, be thankful for finding him!

STAYING IN TOUCH WITH REALITY ("RELATIONSHIPS ARE MADE IN HEAVEN.")

Having romantic fantasies about prospective men in your life and idealizing a lover are natural parts of moving toward intimate attachments. However, when fantasizing ignores serious problems in relating to others or interferes with your individual growth, you need to take a hard look at things as they really are.

As mentioned in Chapter 3, gay men may be prone to romantic fantasies because real opportunities for relationships have often been denied them. Generally, you can be more realistic by exploring your notions of love, seeking honest feedback from others, and recalling painful choices from past relationships. Most of us need to rely on friends to separate fantasy from reality.

Project #1: Comparing Notes About Love. First, answer these questions true or false:

1. The essence of love is self-denial.
2. A boy has the same capacity to express love as an adult man.
3. When you love someone for a long time, you know exactly what is on his mind.
4. Loving your partner means that you are concerned about his growth.
5. To be in love, you must feel some zing in the relationship.
6. Feelings of excitement and jealousy are signals of true love.
7. To be loved, you must be needed.
8. When you love someone, you sometimes go through periods where you feel unavailable to your partner.
9. The person you love is the most important person in your life.
10. A commitment to love means that you are responsible for your partner's happiness.

11. True love means that you and your lover can be apart for years and still feel the same regard for each other.
12. Being firm and withholding can be a sign of deep love.
13. Fantasizing about others during sex means that your love for your partner is dying.
14. Outright rage can occur in the best relationships.
15. If your partner forgets your anniversary, he loves you less than he once did.
16. Loyalty to a lover is more important than loyalty to one's family.
17. Physical attraction is necessary for love.
18. If you really love your partner and are going out for the evening without him, you must tell him when you will be home.
19. If you can't talk to your lover about certain topics, then something is wrong.
20. The end results of years of togetherness are companionship and familiarity.

Did you puzzle over some items or get angry at the subjectiveness of the statements? Most of us want life to be black and white. It isn't. There are no right or wrong answers to this survey, but you can learn a lot from your reactions. The statements that bothered you may remind you of unresolved questions in your love life. Rekindling old pain and recognizing your confusion will prepare you to stay in touch with reality. Rather than immediately settling this confusion, be aware that in some areas of life you are still learning and need to be cautious.

Perhaps you intellectualized some answers or answered some questions "correctly" even though your behavior indicates otherwise. Those questions also warrant attention. Have a reliable friend take this inventory and compare notes. When you contrast your answers with his, listen closely to his responses, but don't argue. Ask questions when you don't understand. Find out how his understanding of love is different than yours and reflect on your discoveries. Be patient if you're confused. When you are ready to understand, you will understand.

Finally, do some basic reading on love. We recommend

The Road Less Traveled and *How to Break Your Addiction to
a Person.* By comparing notes on what you expect from
relationships with what reliable resources say about relationships, you can make more realistic decisions about loving
someone.

Project #2: Saying Good-bye to Prince Charming. Sometimes the biggest block to close relationships is your search for
the perfect lover, the mythical Prince Charming. If you hold
out for him, you will pass up many realistic relationships with
available men. Letting go of your prince is crucial for intimate sharing. For this project, you will need a large drawing
pad, some crayons, and a friend to listen to you. If this
project is too embarrassing to do with a friend, do it alone.
Close your eyes and fantasize the man of your dreams. Stay
with your image until you can visualize every detail of what
he looks like, how he acts, and what it feels to be with him.
Then, draw a portrait of your Prince Charming. Without
worrying about artistic talent, try to capture him in all of his
perfection. Is he tall or short, thin or muscular, blond or
dark? Write a list of his personal qualities on the drawing
sheet, especially qualities you have not drawn. You may
imagine him as strong, warm, tender, intelligent, and well-
hung. When you are done, show your picture to your friend.
Then, face Prince Charming for the final time and slowly
tear his image into small pieces. At any point you may stop to
examine your feelings and share them with your friend.
Gather the pieces into a pile and place them in a small grave.
Before covering the pieces, tell Prince Charming what it has
meant for you to "live" with him and what it will be like to
live without him. Then bury him. You may need to revisit
his grave from time to time to remember what his death has
meant to you.

FREEING YOURSELF FROM THE PAST ("I WON'T MAKE THAT MISTAKE AGAIN.")

Freeing yourself from the past means healing hurts from
past relationships. True healing occurs through psychologically cutting open, bleeding, and suturing old wounds. This
healing process entails grieving. You may feel shock, anger,
helplessness, depression, and serenity as you grieve. Given a

choice, most of us would avoid grief. Not allowing yourself to grieve, however, is like denying the need for lifesaving surgery; just putting it out of your mind doesn't make a tumor go away.

Gay men experience many losses throughout their lives: the loss of support from family and society in coming out, the loss of freedom to experience sexuality during teenage years, and the loss of loved ones due to AIDS. Each loss presents an opportunity for personal growth.

Project #1: Saying Good-bye to Family. Saying good-bye to family is a necessary and normal step to adulthood. This good-bye amounts to accepting your family for who they are and letting go of the family you always wanted to have. Like everyone else, gay men need to emancipate themselves from their families. Typically, this happens when gay men give up family approval of their same-sex feelings and make decisions based on their own values. In "leaving the nest," gay men often experience panic, indignation, and guilt. Nevertheless, when a gay man graduates into adulthood, it benefits him and his family.

Giving up family approval is no easy matter. This project will assist your efforts.

First, list questions you have about your upbringing, even if answers are not easily found. You might ask:

1. How did my father treat me as compared to my brothers?
2. Why didn't my mother protect me when I told her that kids picked on me at school?
3. Was there anybody with whom I could truly be myself?
4. Before I was born, what expectations did my parents have of me?
5. Who was I named after?

Second, find ways of answering your questions. Actively explore your family, as if you are a historian. You may do this in any number of ways: visit your family and have discussions you always longed for, talk to people who knew your family, return to your old school building, look through old photo albums or view home movies, reread old letters or seek out family artifacts in the attic, or write a sibling. Obviously, the closer you get to the past, the more accurate your discoveries will be.

Clearly, you will need to use discretion and keep your expectations to a minimum. Your job is simply to gather information, not make everybody feel better. Also, maintain a healthy skepticism, but don't pass judgment on what you are hearing. Simply listen. When others ask why you are raising such questions, be honest and tell them that you want more information about your childhood and you won't use this information against them. You may feel tempted to use your new insights to manipulate or injure others, but don't, because you will lose their cooperation and ultimately defeat your purpose. Be persistent; realize that others may not be ready to disclose what they know. If you feel anguish over what you learn, you have begun to grieve. Explore slowly and thoroughly for best results. Remember, your perceptions and feelings about your exploration are just as important as the new facts you discover. Your emotional reactions offer crucial evidence about your past, whether or not others cooperate with you. As all good historians know, the residues of the past are alive within us today. You simply have to open your eyes and heart.

You may still wonder how just seeing the past for what it is helps you say good-bye to your family. Actually, seeing is only a beginning, but an important one. Many of us hold on to childhood illusions about the way things were in our family. We believe we came from a perfect family that would always protect us. Or, angrily, we claim that our family gave us nothing. Neither view is true. Such illusions impede maturity and, in the long run, make life unsafe. When you see your family realistically, the stark realities of growing up prick the bubble of your illusions. This can leave you sad and distressed. Your bubble cannot be re-created. Grief ensues. But, when you give up the fantasy of an ideal or totally worthless family, you are ready to take care of yourself. Doing so heralds your adulthood. Although your family is still a part of your life, your view of them and need for them has changed. While the promise of easy living is gone, the rewards of adult living have begun.

Project #2: Saying Good-bye to Past Lovers. Nothing undermines the enthusiasm for a new relationship faster than unresolved feelings for a past lover. Hanging on to past lovers can occur in subtle ways. For example, if you tell yourself, "I won't make that mistake again," you may unknowingly expect current lovers to be flawless so they don't hurt you as a past lover did. How could anyone live up to such expectations? Is it even fair to expect this? Forgiveness and healing can free you to love again.

For this exercise, write a personal letter to the one past lover you can't let go of. It's better not to send it, because grieving is a private matter. Your letter may include what you miss most and least about him, or anything that affirms the depth of your pain. Keep in mind the letter is for your own healing. Blaming or tearing down your old lover is a put-down of your tastes. We suggest you say, "I hate your unfaithfulness" rather than "You're a sick fag." Feel your grief and rage.

Maybe what's holding you back now is guilt about the way you treated a past lover. You felt you had to get out of the relationship, but you couldn't face him then. Write him a letter now to forgive yourself.

After writing the letter, go to a high place, tear it into little pieces, and let the wind carry it away. Feel the relief and peacefulness.

Warren, a 40-year-old client, wrote a letter to Randy, his first lover. Randy and Warren met twenty years ago in a men's studies class. After a passionate five-year relationship, Randy dropped Warren the night they were about to move in together. He later refused to answer Warren's letters or phone calls or even say hello when they passed on the street. Warren wrote:

> *Dear Randy,*
> *I've hated and loved you every day for the past fifteen years. I want to rip your body to shreds for playing with my mind. You really didn't give a damn about me. You left me without saying a word. I blamed myself for twenty years. After all, wasn't it me who was fucked up? The reason you didn't want to move into that house wasn't me. You screwed the landlord and didn't have the balls to tell me. You wanted to be a saint instead. You're really a whore. I'm sure you fucked at least half the town. You disgust me.*

I've cried myself to sleep thinking about your good looks. I haven't been able to replace you. Your hair, eyes, and smile are burnt into my mind. I remember the night you first touched me and said it was O.K. I didn't know what the hell I was doing. You were tender. How could you be so loving and callous at the same time?

Well, this is it. This is where we part ways. You take your sickness with you. When I feel sad about losing you, I will cry. When I get scared of getting fucked over again, I'll remember that it wasn't my fault for being innocent. I don't need to replace you. I don't need to prove I'm worthy of a good-looking man. I don't need to prove nothing.

Warren

DEVELOPING YOUR SPIRITUALITY ("ALL THAT GLITTERS IS GOLD")

You possess an inner spirit that is sacred, powerful, and deeply lovable. It unites you with each person. You may ignore it, scorn it, or damage it. But it is still within you, waiting to be rediscovered and cherished.

You may find it hard to accept your spirituality. If you feel betrayed by organized religion or bitter about the shallowness of gay relationships, if your life is a rat race, or, if you believe all that glitters is gold, then your inner spirit may be severely depleted. You may feel completely empty inside.

All is not lost. You are not empty. Your spiritual garden may be devastated, but the roots are still there. Prove this to yourself with the following projects.

Project #1: Rediscovering Your Inner Spirit. To start, set aside some quiet time for reflection. Take the phone off the hook and eliminate any other noise in the room. Sit in a comfortable position. First, close your eyes and consider some marvels of life: the sight of a rainbow in a waterfall, the roar of the ocean in a conch shell, the smell of a sprig of lilac, the taste of homemade ice cream, and the touch of velvet. Do you recall times in your life when these experiences astonished you and inspired awe? Remember when the beauty and mystery of life seemed inexhaustable? Remember when the days were too short to discover all of the miracles of life?

Next, recall your experiences of spirituality as a child. Perhaps you were an altar boy and made a special promise to God. Maybe you buried a pet and prayed over his grave. Or watched a calf being born. Did you bow your head in prayer at a dinner table? Perhaps you asked yourself on a spring morning, "Who made all this?" Do you remember?

Now recall experiences of spirituality as an adult. Perhaps you wept before a work of art. Have you marveled at a field of summer wildflowers? Or delighted in baking bread? Perhaps you finally mastered a Beethoven piano sonata or discovered a tiny creature in the woods. Maybe you attended a candlelight vigil for persons with AIDS or learned to love one aspect of someone you hate. Do you remember?

Hold these moments in your mind for at least fifteen minutes, remembering as many of the details as you can.

Recite to yourself, "I have nurtured my spirit throughout my lifetime. I can continue to do so."

To complete this project, select an activity that renews your inner spirit. Choose one of the experiences that touched you spiritually before or any project that promotes your spirit. Work at this project for eight weeks, each session lasting at least an hour. Search for miracles in what you're doing: attending to detail, opening your heart to surprises, and surrendering yourself to the unknown. After completing your activity, ask yourself, "What have I learned about my inner spirit?" Keep a log of your answers and consider sharing your discoveries with a friend.

Let's say you decided to take up classical guitar again. First, you will need to find your instrument, dust it off, and tune it up. Notice how finely it is made, how magically the strings vibrate, what incredible sounds it produces, and how your fingers span the strings. No matter how clumsy, your fingers move across the strings as no machine can. Who created the beauty of the sounds and the beauty of your fingers? Then choose music that fits your mood, keeping your practice simple. Listen to the music. Imagine! You are experiencing the soul of Bach, Sor, or Villa-Lobos. What are these composers telling you about life? What melodies resonate within you? How does your heart beat? Improvise or practice, letting your whole body be the instrument of your expression. Listen to it. What is your spirit telling you? Then, when you are finished, put the instrument back into its velvet-lined case. After some reflection, you may record something like this in your journal:

> *Today I learned what I once knew but have long since forgotten: I have music in my soul! It's like an old friend, so neglected, yet so forgiving. My whole body shivered when I played the Bach partita. What a miracle! Through the vibratos, I felt I was hearing the heartbeat of every musician in history, the heartbeat of every person who ever lived, including my own. I was connected to everyone. For a moment, I felt God within me.*

Project #2: Service Project. Volunteering time in service to others is a way to rediscover and believe in your inner spirit. At one time or another, most of us have complained, "I feel so empty inside" or "Life has little meaning." We hunger for spiritual nourishment. Yet we make excuses: "I've always intended to do volunteer work" or "I don't have the time." Well, now's your chance. You can make time. To more fully develop your spirituality, act now.

To choose where to volunteer your time, first ask yourself, "What do I have to offer others?" "Which type of volunteer work turns me on the most?" and "How often and how long can I volunteer?" Having answered these questions, search for possible projects. You can consult with local volunteer agencies or simply contact organizations that need volunteers. Generally, it is easier to work in a structured organization that will train and supervise you. Interview prospective organizations before deciding where to invest yourself. Striking out on your own volunteer project may provide you with greater flexibility and satisfaction. It's really up to you. Don't be surprised if you have to expend both time and thought to learn which is the right project for you.

When you are involved with your service project, you may occasionally doubt your strengths or worry about being overwhelmed by the needs of others. Getting over each hump of anxiety is essential to sustaining volunteer work. First, realize that performance anxieties are normal and that you will discover your strengths as you go along. Since you are not getting a paycheck,. you may have difficulty believing that you have something valuable to give others; you are continuously challenged to answer the question: "What do I have to offer?" You will be able to answer this question, and it gets easier to do as you go along. Second, recognize your limitations in volunteering your time. It's better to commit fewer hours than to feel resentful for promising too many. If your volunteer work is fun, you will have more impact on others. When the fun stops, it is probably best to cut back. Third, read *How Can I Help?* by Ram Dass and Paul Gorman, and reflect on what it means to serve others. You will benefit from periodically reevaluating your reasons for doing so.

Serving others, while taking time for reflection, can also teach you things about yourself. For example, suppose you volunteer at a shelter for homeless people. Imagine that you are repelled by the physical appearance of one of the male residents. You secretly tell yourself that there is no possible way to connect with him because of his looks. If you allow yourself to work with him, however, you may discover that he has a dry wit, speaks French, and, like you, survived his father's cancer. How amazing to feel close to somebody who originally turned you off! After some thought, you may realize that you are as hard on yourself as you are on him. It may also dawn on you that you can see the beauty beneath appearances.

After a while, you will have completed your service project. Share your feelings about leaving with other volunteers. Although you leave a precious experience behind you, the spiritual growth resulting from your efforts will always be with you.

Our message is simple: render service to others, do it for yourself, and be prepared for miracles.

Project #3: Daily Meditation. Daily meditation is a way to discover and nurture the divine in yourself. You may experience it as a form of prayer or communication with an inner spirit, or simply as a time to be alone and enjoy silence. Trying to explain how meditation works is like describing the beauty of the Grand Canyon in words. It can't be done. You have to judge for yourself.

A few guidelines will assist your daily meditation. Begin slowly. Try meditating each day for fifteen minutes. Choose a regular time in a comfortable place where you will not be interrupted. Mornings are often best. Set a kitchen timer under a pillow so that you will not have to keep track of time. As you develop skill in meditating, increase your time to thirty minutes or longer.

How do you get ready for meditation? Preparation involves your thoughts, feelings, and body. It's best to clear your mind of thoughts from the day ahead of you and the day you've left behind. Meditation is rarely helpful when you are preoccupied with planning the future or regretting the past. Take some deep breaths and concentrate on the present moment, perhaps listening to your heartbeat, your breathing, or the silence in the room. Accept your feelings without analyzing them. Visualize that you are emptying yourself out.

What happens in meditation? The possibilities are endless. You might:

- Sit peacefully and value the silence.
- Quietly express your gratitude for the miracles in your life.
- Review the past day to discover a strength you possess.
- Read a passage from devotional literature and apply it to yourself.
- Feel the intensity of your inner pain and remind yourself of your capabilities.
- Plan to take a personal risk or make amends during the day.
- Bow your head in prayer.
- Place a special object in front of you and cherish its significance.
- Remind yourself of a time you felt especially close to God.
- Struggle to love some aspect of someone you hate.
- Experience whatever thoughts and feelings arise spontaneously.

However you decide to commune with your inner spirit is the wisest choice.

Will meditation change your life? It may. Generally, daily meditation enables you to feel more confident in your ability to cope with stress, gives you a clearer grasp of your needs and feelings, and helps you believe in the sacredness of life. These changes in you may go unnoticed, but they are very real. You don't have to convince anybody of them: your spiritual presence speaks for itself. You will also notice that meditation is not a cure-all. You will still feel stressed by work pressures, you may continue to lose your temper, and you'll probably maintain bad habits. Deeper faith in your inner spirit will improve your chances for change but not guarantee them. The true result of spiritual practice is joyful acceptance of yourself and others.

AVOIDING AND WELCOMING PERSONAL GROWTH

Everyone has some excuses for avoiding growth; they highlight the fundamental fears we all have of changing and growing. Why is it important to acknowledge your excuses? First, talking about them makes you see they are normal. After all, you can't be changing all the time. Once in a while, you need to retreat from the stresses of living without taking yourself too seriously. Having alibis is a great way to do this. Also, exploring excuses allows you to feel brotherhood with others. Your excuses are an admission that you are not perfect and are a member of the human race. Such a realization will inspire courage in facing the difficult stresses of adult living.

"IF I CHANGE, I'LL LOSE MY FRIENDS." (FEAR OF ABANDONMENT)

Being committed to your own growth can strain cherished friendships. As you develop new ideas about yourself, different ways of behaving, and more mature expectations of relationships, spending time with some old friends may feel awkward and unsatisfying. It can seem like a comfortable old glove no longer fits. These feelings may be so upsetting that you may be tempted to abandon your own growth for the sake of your friends. We can appreciate how strong this temptation is.

You face a difficult choice: Is your personal fulfillment important enough to risk losing some friends? If you choose growth, you may indeed lose people you have known for years. That would be unfortunate. If necessary, give yourself permission to grieve over these dear friends. But some friends may rise to the occasion and support your changes or use your growth as a catalyst for their own. If so, love will have triumphed over fear. In any case, your positive changes will result in having the best friend of all—yourself—someone you can't afford to lose.

"IF I CHANGE, I WILL LOSE MY LOVER." (FEAR OF THE LOSS OF LOVE)

Possibly this is the most compelling excuse of them all. Love relationships, intensified by sexuality, often have incredible power. Your self-esteem and view of life are often shaped by the give and take of relating to a lover. Your career goals may be based on the permanence and support of your partner. Even your daily moods can depend quite heavily on the ebb and flow of a love relationship. Is it any wonder that you may want to suspend positive change to avoid conflict with a partner?

Personal change need not result in a crisis. When you choose to grow as a individual, naturally you may find more traits in your partner or in yourself that are intolerable. Your lover may have similar feelings. Personal change is natural in the lives of two people who choose to grow, and there are many ways that change can be creatively accommodated in a loving relationship. Expressing feelings openly, letting go of rigid standards, acknowledging transitions, negotiating differences, and developing a sense of humor are all ways of welcoming change in a relationship. Clearly, some of these methods may not suffice and your changes may strain the relationship. Even when this is so, all is not lost.

Actually, one of the ironies of relationships is that change and exploring differences are *necessary* to maintain excitement. For your partner to find you sexy, he may need to see you as slightly less predictable. Nothing is duller than having a partner who avoids risks.

Thus, it is wise to view personal growth as risky, natural, tantalizing, and ultimately rewarding.

"I ALREADY DWELL ON MYSELF TOO MUCH." (FEAR OF SELFISHNESS)

You may feel that you are already too preoccupied with your own concerns. Perhaps you question, "If I focus more on myself, won't that make me self-centered?" or "Won't I lose my concern for others?" Such notions may cause you to fear selfishness. Also, you might be put off by self-concern because in your eyes it epitomizes the trendiness of the "me generation" and disregard for others. Possibly you believe that denying your own needs will make you a more loving and likable person. Nothing could be further from the truth.

Responsible selfishness is a natural and necessary part of self-fulfillment and does not preclude concern for others. In fact, each of us must go through necessary periods of self-centeredness several times in our life in order to develop an identity. For example, adolescents are notorious for expecting the world to revolve around them. They may primp for hours in front of the mirror, believe they have answers for everything, and exhibit their youthfulness as God's gift to the world. Such displays are simply ways of trying out new roles and eventually result in a secure identity. Even the most flamboyant experimentation can respect the rights of others. Human development follows an important rule: the more you responsibly attend to your own needs, the more you have to offer.

Embrace your responsible selfishness, experiment with life, be responsible, and prepare yourself for greater love.

"THERE ARE SOME THINGS IN MY PAST I COULD NEVER FACE." (FEAR OF BEING OVERWHELMED)

The pain of facing past emotional traumas in your life cannot be overstated. Opening such wounds can bring about depression, panic, confused thinking, health problems, job difficulties, relationship hassles, and thoughts of suicide. "Alas," you may lament, "is the cure worse than the disease?" Whether you attempt to take small steps of change alone or bigger steps with a professional helper, you must recognize that you do have some control over the situation. You can always ask questions about what is happening to you. You can always rest and take a breather. You can always scream at the top of your lungs. You can always have a friend hold your hand. And, if you believe in prayer, you can do that too. It is possible to have control over your life and feel excruciating pain at the same time. Remember, healing has an end— mending. Not healing rarely has an end.

"IT'S JUST NOT IN ME TO HAVE A POSITIVE IDENTITY." (FEAR OF FEELING WORTHY)

Sound familiar? Unfortunately, some of us get trapped in patterns that appear to prove that we are undeserving of love. We have ways of seeing the worst in everything. Most of these patterns began in childhood and continue into adulthood. Perhaps *we* have maintained them as a way of at least having some identity: "If I can't be a winner, then I'm going to be the biggest loser." All of us know kids from high school who felt like failures but chose to misbehave as a way to get recognition. Perhaps some of those kids are us. The best way to give up unworthiness is to decide to believe that you are worthy and act as if you believe it. Take small steps and develop a skill at some aspect of living. Tell yourself, "Within me God resides, and I am worthy."

ENCOURAGING WORDS

When you are facing the fears of being intimate or are feeling overwhelmed with emotional pain, it's natural to feel boxed in. If this is how you feel, let us offer some encouragement. The following eight principles frequently help us out when we are bogged down.

"BE CRAZY." (ACCEPTANCE)

Accept your limitations and enjoy the absurdity of life. You can't make other people happy. You can't make anyone love you. And you can't stop making mistakes. Pretending to be perfect is a dead end. So go ahead. Be yourself. Let it all hang out. If you're worried about what the neighbors will think, invite them over to be weird with you. If you do change anything, be crazier. Don't just put the fork in the wrong place. Spill a glass of wine, laugh when no one else is laughing, stand the wrong way in the elevator, forget to wear socks, and make a silly face. Even if you don't change a thing, enjoy yourself just as you are. Some things in life are too important to do sanely. Who knows, maybe if you can accept your craziness, you'll be able to accept anything, even love.

"TAKE MORE CHANCES." (COURAGE)

You may think that courage means never being afraid. Not true. Courage means doing something scary that you believe is in your best interests. Don't wait for the fear to go away; it often disappears through action. Of course, this will feel risky. But taking an occasional calculated risk will make your life richer and more exciting. Leave your umbrella at home on a cloudy day. Taste the spicy dish on the menu. Say what's on your mind. Call that gorgeous man who eyed you at the last party. Don't worry for now if you get soaked, burn your tongue, offend someone, or are turned down. It'll be worth it anyway; you'll find out how brave you are.

On the other hand, imagine never taking *any* risks.

"DANCE THE NIGHT AWAY." (PLAYFULNESS)

Emma Goldman once said, "If I can't dance, I don't want any part of your revolution." To be fulfilling, personal change requires a regular dose of playfulness. Laughing at ourselves, exaggerating our inadequacies, being wistful, playing pranks, telling silly jokes, tickling, whistling, and dreaming out loud are all ways we can play. When's the last time you had a squirt gun fight? Get serious!

"YOU CAN STAND IT." (RUGGEDNESS)

If you were among the fortunate children who were told by their mothers, "Now take your cod-liver oil; it's good for you", you will certainly appreciate what we mean by, "You can stand it." Unbearable then, but amusing now. Somehow we always survive. The fact that you are feeling pain does not mean that you are a failure or that you are bad. You weren't bad as a child; you're not bad now. Realistically, pain often contains a message of truth. It is up to you to listen to it. In any case, there's always an end to pain. It too shall pass. If only all of our life pains were as bearable as cod-liver oil.

"REMEMBER YOUR DEATH." (SPIRITUALITY)

During the 1987 march on Washington, D.C., thousands of people viewed the NAMES Project Quilt, dedicated to nearly 2000 people who had died of AIDS-related illnesses. Each patch was devoted to a particular person. One patch, embroidered by the parents of a gay man, said, "We miss you. We didn't understand you. We love you. You held a mirror to everything in us that we couldn't handle." Gay men are indeed challenged and blessed in facing so many differences with others. Facing death teaches us to savor each moment of life and our ties to each other. As a result of these differences, you know this lesson in your heart of hearts. But, you are also like others in a very fundamental way: you rise in the morning and retire in the evening, facing the prospect of your final day. Prepare yourself and find greater joy.

"BE A FRIEND TO HAVE A FRIEND." (GENEROSITY)

Have you ever wondered why you don't have many friends? Perhaps you've unintentionally given others the idea that you don't need their love. The best way to open yourself to being loved is to love as many people as you can.

"GIVE YOURSELF TIME." (PATIENCE)

You may plead "How long will it take me to have a man in my life who really loves me?" Well, maybe as long as it takes a snail to inch its way up Mt. Fuji. Good things take a long time. There is just no way to rush the important things of life. We often have to make many mistakes first. So you may as well relax, realize that you are not alone, and bask in the sun. Or, you may want to crawl into your shell and rest. There's a long road ahead and it's so high to climb. Enjoy every inch.

"LIGHTEN UP." (HUMOR)

At a bar, a man asked his friend, "Say, have you read the new book on gay intimacy?"

"No, is it any good?"

"It sure is. I finished it last week and I've already got a new man."

The friend acted cool and appeared to be unconcerned about this news. But he chugged his beer, gave a lame excuse, and rushed out to get a copy of this wonderful book. All the way to the store he fantasized about Sam, a hunk at his office. "Wait till I get my hands on that book—and on Sam!"

He stayed up all night to read the book from cover to cover and came up with new schemes. He planned his approach in detail and knew exactly what to say. "Sam, I'm not like all those other men, who just want to get into your pants. I know how to be intimate and am ready for some real deep sharing." How could Sam resist? He would invite him to dinner and count on candlelight and soft music for starters. But, according to the book, the real aphrodisiac was intimacy.

He made his phone call. "Sam, this is Joe from the office. I've been getting in touch with my needs for people lately and thought I would reach out to you. Would you like to come over to my place for dinner? We could open up and explore each other's feelings."

"Thanks for the invite, Joe. But I'm working on setting my boundaries. In my family I was never given permission to have my own identity. Have you seen the new book on intimacy? Tonight I'm going to do an exercise in appreciating my own body. Do you understand how I feel?"

Joe hung up the phone and threw the book in the garbage.

Sometimes the only way to deal with all this craziness is to laugh at it and at yourself.

PSYCHOTHERAPY

Sometimes enhancing intimacy defies our best efforts. You may have tried writing in a journal, socializing with new friends, taking an aerobics class, and even reading this book. Nothing seems to work. We all know that feeling. Well, take heart. You may want to consider psychotherapy as an option for developing closeness with others. After all, when home remedies for a cold fail, it's best to consult a physician.

On the other hand, don't feel that you must have a problem to see a psychotherapist. If you want to enhance your self-esteem, speed up your growth, or simply want companionship in your process of change, that is reason enough to consult a therapist. Like music, growth can be self-taught. But having an instructor is more fun.

You may object, "What, me see a therapist?" Yes, that's what we're suggesting. "But," you may say, "I'm not crazy!" Typically, people who consult therapists are not mentally ill but are dealing with problems that affect their self-esteem. "Won't he tell me I'm sick because I'm gay?[1] You and many others may regard psychiatrists, psychologists, and psychotherapists as oppressors of gay men. Indeed, gay men have been hurt and continue to be hurt by unethical professional helpers. Don't throw the baby out with the bathwater, however. A reputable and gay-sensitive psychotherapist can help you make mature and fulfilling ties with other gay men. Go to a therapist for the same reason that others do: to grow. Psychotherapy is not as mysterious and overwhelming as you may imagine.

Psychotherapy is an intimate relationship between a client and a professional helper, which is limited by a single rule: the relationship primarily serves the client's needs and facilitates his emotional well-being and independence. This restriction places the therapist in a position of power and the client in a position of vulnerability. In this way, psychotherapy resembles a parent-child relationship and is not a relationship of equals. Both people have important responsibilities, however. It is generally the client's job to set agendas for each session, talk about his views of himself, and be honest with the therapist. The therapist supports and challenges the client to reevaluate his self-image. When problems arise in the psychotherapy relationship, each partner must help resolve them.

You may want to consult a therapist for a variety of reasons. You may feel depressed and not know why, have difficulty accepting same-sex feelings, or believe you are a disappointment to your family. Relationships with men may seem like a lost cause, your career may be in shambles, or your lover may have a serious health problem.

It's natural to think that your problems are unique and no one could ever help you with them. Typically such worries are resolved over time.

A competent psychotherapist uses his biases and emotional presence to bring out the best in a client. By being honest and having your best interests at heart, a trained helper invites *you* to be honest and have your own best interests at heart. Disclosing yourself to a trained helper allows you to know and accept yourself in a meaningful way. The feedback you get from a therapist gives you information that you may not get from friends and is freer of biases because the therapist is mainly concerned with your best interests. Also, what he shows you about yourself may have a ring of truth to it because of his training and previous experience with compelling emotional issues. A good therapist–client relationship can be the most significant connection in your lifetime.

As an added bonus, psychotherapy is a safe way to practice intimacy. Because psychotherapy affects both you and your therapist in a personal way, you can practice dealing with anger, distrust, despair, sexual attraction, and boredom. Also you can listen to how your therapist feels about you. As a client, you will not be punished or rejected for expressing negative feelings to your therapist. Having your true feelings show, however imperfectly, allows you to accept parts of yourself that have remained hidden. Thus, you become a more competent person.

There are different modes of psychotherapy: individual, couple, family, and group psychotherapy. Generally, individual psychotherapy is a good place to start and provides an intense learning experience in intimacy building. Couple's therapy is recommended when you want to resolve issues with a particular partner. Family therapy involves family members in the process of healing emotional wounds and is a valuable adjunct to individual psychotherapy. Group psychotherapy is a friendly, anxiety-producing, and dynamic way to socialize with others while working on personal issues. Group psychotherapy is like asking a bunch of your friends to help you move; you sweat, but it's a lot of fun and you never forget the experience. If you're ready to socialize with other men, group therapy is recommended.

From reading this book you already know a great deal about intimacy—what it is, how it leads to growth, when it is being undermined and when it is being enriched, and what role sexuality plays in closeness. You have the basic tools to evaluate an intimate relationship. Use them in choosing a therapist!

To start psychotherapy, call a reliable therapist for an initial appointment. If you don't know one, consult friends who have had positive experiences with a therapist or call a professional organization (American Psychological Association, Association of Marriage and Family Therapists) for referrals. Recognize that the therapist you choose will influence your entire personal identity. So, interview a prospective psychotherapist, asking such questions as these:

1. What are your views about gay identity?
2. What training and experiences have you had with helping gay men?
3. How would you respond if I talk explicitly about my sexuality?
4. If the therapy gets bogged down, how would you handle it?
5. How would you respond if I expressed negative feeling to you?
6. Will you confront me if I am avoiding an important issue?
7. What are your views on the use of medication, psychological testing, and resources outside of therapy?
8. Do you have training helping people with my particular issue?

It may feel awkward and frightening to interview a psychotherapist at an initial meeting. Our questions may seem like overkill. But, it's worth the effort to select a therapist carefully. An initial interview is no time to be thinking that relationships are made in heaven. Choosing a therapist is probably the single most important decision you make in healing.

As you can tell from these questions, whether your therapist is gay or straight, a man or a woman, is not nearly as important as whether the professional you consult has experience and training with gay-life issues and is capable of being professionally intimate. All you know about intimacy will guide you in selecting this person. When you begin psychotherapy, realize you have the right to evaluate and, if necessary, to terminate that relationship at any point. You can decide this completely on your own.

If you don't have a favorable connection with a therapist after the first three sessions *and* have discussed your feelings with this professional to no avail, it's best to move on. Trust your intuition.

Use your psychotherapy relationship for all it is worth. You are there for you. Use the whole hour to focus on yourself. You may need to show your pain, weep or scream as necessary, talk about your dreams, uncover your self-hatred, or simply chit-chat. Remember, you are paying for this time with your money and sweat. So make it count! Also, a word to the wise. Go as far as you can before each session to solve your own problems and then ask for feedback from your therapist. Don't let your therapist steal your thunder. Allow time before and after each session to be with yourself, to identify what you need to discuss and what you have learned about yourself. Finally, remember the cardinal rule of intimacy building: it's okay to express a difference of opinion. How else will your therapist learn anything?

The best laid plans of mice and men often go awry. You may reach a point in therapy where you and your therapist are not seeing eye to eye on some important issue. Even the most successful psychotherapy relationships have such trouble spots. When these crises are not resolved, the psychotherapy relationship may turn into a draining power struggle or a threatening truce. Although it may be unnerving to discuss these difficulties with your therapist, you must. Oddly enough, healing these differences can be the most significant experience in your therapy. Normal trouble spots can be springboards for personal growth.

Some crises are not normal, however. For example,

sometimes a client is sexually or emotionally exploited by his therapist. We hesitate to discuss the gory details, for fear that you'll be frightened of therapy. Such abuses are not common. But if and when it does occur, exploitation results in serious harm to clients and needs to be remedied as soon as possible. That's why we've chosen to talk about these situations. Besides, there is a lot you can do to stop and protect yourself from these traumas. Frequently these conflicts are resolved by *not* seeing your therapist and consulting with professional and legal resources outside your therapy. It is possible to heal from a damaging psychotherapy relationship. Here's how you can cope with these difficulties.

"WHOSE THERAPY IS IT ANYWAY?" (PATERNALISM)

Initially, it is natural to regard a therapist as an all-knowing authority figure. After all, he's the one who's supposed to have all the answers and you are the one with the emotional problems. Putting him on a pedestal is perfectly understandable and resembles the idealization of parent–child relationships. But, for psychotherapy to be effective this idealization must progress into honesty.

When your therapy is honest, here are some ways you might view your work:

1. I am the best judge of what's good for me. No therapist will ever know me as well as I know myself.
2. I make myself feel better. My therapist may help, but the responsibility and credit for my therapy primarily belong to me.
3. My mistakes are always more valuable than other people's approval. I am my best teacher.
4. My therapist is only human. He makes mistakes also, and I may have something to teach him.

Such beliefs enable you to be responsible for your own growth and dignity.

When these beliefs are not part of your therapy, paternalism may result. Paternalism is based on the assumption that "father knows best." Paternalistic therapists think they know what is best for you, promise they can make you feel better, and expect that you will do things their way, or else. Clients of such therapists often act helpless, think their therapists can do no wrong, and deceive themselves by believing that a strong therapist will make them strong. Actually, being patronized makes you feel insecure.

If paternalism is interfering with your therapy, discuss your feelings with your therapist. If you don't feel understood after repeated efforts, it is best to move on and start over again.

"DO I HAVE TO LET HIM TOUCH ME?" (SEXUAL EXPLOITATION)

No! You don't have to let anyone touch you or come on to you against your wishes.

If you've been touched by your therapist and have not been traumatized by the encounter, then you probably don't feel sexually exploited. Clearly, comforting and appropriate touch is a healing part of therapy.

When touch feels intrusive, out of context, secretive, obligatory, or shameful, then it is wise to ask, "Do I have to let him touch me?" Most clients cannot and do not want to be sexual with their therapist even if they are no longer seeing that therapist, no matter how long ago therapy occurred. Even if you have been hurt by your therapist, you may resist acknowledging this pain. In fact, it is quite common for clients who have been sexual with their therapists to blame themselves and feel protective of their therapist. *Such denial will not protect you.* A sexual relationship with your therapist is not healthy no matter how good it may feel. When you are both your therapist's client and his lover, both relationships suffer in the long run. As a client, you rely on your therapist to give you feedback that serves your needs and not his. A sexual relationship generally removes that guarantee, and trust is permanently breached. Also, having a loving relationship requires partners to be equals; psychotherapy is inherently an unequal relationship. Sex with a therapist is not an affair—it is exploitation.

Even if you were active in seducing your therapist, he is always and completely responsible to resist and not be sexual with you. He has all the training and power to do so. Generally, his professional organization and the state in which he practices forbids him from being sexual with clients. When a therapist defies his training, breaches the standards of his profession, and betrays your trust in him, he is acting out of his own selfish interests. Although he may appear strong and concerned about you, he isn't.

When you have been sexually exploited by a therapist, it is important to stop therapy immediately and consult with the appropriate professional organization to get professional and legal help. It is best to discuss your concerns with professionals who have worked with clients who have been sexually abused by their therapists. Your emotional life and the lives of other men depend on it.

"OH NO, I'M FALLING IN LOVE WITH MY THERAPIST!" (SEXUAL FEELINGS)

Having sexual feelings for your therapist and vice versa is completely natural. Feelings are different than actions. In fact, almost all good psychotherapy relationships include times when you fantasize about "marrying" your therapist and he feels that he wants to "marry" his client. Because sexual feelings occur in a nonsexual relationship, most of us are embarrassed by such feelings and prefer to keep them secret. Sometimes the secret keeping makes the feelings even more embarrassing (and titillating!).

When you think about it, why shouldn't two people have sexual feelings for each other when they have shared intense personal moments together? Such feelings never have to be acted out and they often go away naturally.

Sometimes these feelings may persist or interfere in the therapy relationship. Perhaps you resisted talking about a new lover because you were afraid of making your therapist jealous. Perhaps you missed some appointments because your therapist ignored your new Yves St. Laurent shirt. Perhaps the crush on your therapist has become more important than your personal growth. When these signals last longer than a month, it is best to discuss your sexual feelings with your therapist. Such openness is not a come-on but a part of the honest sharing of an intimate relationship. You will feel a lot better after you have opened up. Just remember, sexual feelings for your therapist are not based on a thorough knowledge of who he is. Besides, being sexual with available men is a lot more fun!

"HOW COULD I EVER TALK TO MY THERAPIST ABOUT THAT!" (SHAME)

There may be parts of yourself that you suspect are best kept under wraps. To some extent, this feeling is normal in therapy, especially if your psychotherapy relationship is rather new. All of us need time to fully reveal ourselves. However, if there is some aspect of your personal life about which you need help and you are purposely holding back that information from your therapist, you owe it to yourself to talk about it. The fear that you will offend, disappoint, or shock your therapist is probably unrealistic. It's most likely that your therapist will respond calmly and with reassurance. Perhaps you are more critical than your therapist is. In any case, we encourage you to share yourself fully when you are ready to do so. The integrity of your therapy depends on it.

Conversely, if your therapist is disapproving or judgmental of your disclosure, then it is best to find a therapist who can accept you. After all, why have a therapist who can't be around you at your worst?

"DOES IT MATTER IF MY THERAPIST USED TO DATE MY PARTNER?" (CONFLICT OF INTEREST)

If you are asking this question, a conflict of interest probably exists. Ignoring this concern may keep you from fully trusting your therapist, even though he may be completely trustworthy. You may fruitlessly worry that feedback from your therapist is tainted by feelings he has for your partner. How can you ever know for sure what to believe? There are other reasons to be concerned about a conflict of interest. Suppose you wanted to bring your partner into a session. Could you trust your therapist to be fair? Suppose your partner wants to take your therapist out for lunch? By now, you may be telling yourself, "This is a fine mess I've gotten myself into."

Many types of conflicts of interest may arise in therapy. Your therapist may go to the same aerobics class you go to. He may attend the same church you do. Through the grapevine, you may have heard that his former lover was an alcoholic. There may be rumblings in the community about his sexual escapades. Being gay can sometimes feel like a small-town experience—everybody is related to somebody else.

Don't despair. There are ways to handle such situations.

First, recognize that any uneasy feelings you have about a conflict of interest are warranted and not anybody's fault. Such dilemmas are common in therapy, especially if your therapist is gay. Therapists are trained to recognize and deal with them openly and honestly. Remember, your therapist has a part in this mix-up and is responsible for helping you unravel it.

Second, describe the conflict of interest to your therapist and discuss your mixed feelings about seeing him. After exploring these feelings, you may decide to continue with your present helper. There is no right or wrong way to decide. If you continue to distrust your therapy, it is probably best to move on.

When possible, allow yourself to see a therapist who has no outside connection to you. In that way, hidden agendas in your psychotherapy relationship are minimized. As with any intimate relationship, safety and integrity are at least as crucial as endearment to a therapist.

Treat your growth like a precious child! Share it with others. Widen its horizons. Laugh and cry with its antics. But remember that you are ultimately responsible for it and should take most of the credit for it.

NOTE TO CHAPTER 6

[1]In order to simplify the text in this section, we use masculine pronouns when referring to psychotherapists. We believe gay men can be helped by psychotherapists of either gender.

BUILDING INTIMACY: WHAT YOU CAN DO AS A COUPLE

INTIMACY EXERCISES FOR COUPLES

The following exercises are included so you and your partner can have fun playing together, learn more about each other, and deepen your intimacy. They are an enjoyable way to improve your relationship. Don't worry if you encounter difficulties when doing the exercises; even if you botch them up, you'll feel closer to each other.

MAKING LOVE (SEX AND AFFECTION)

Even Ginger Rogers and Fred Astaire could learn new steps, and any couple can benefit from jointly examining their love life. The two of you may find these projects especially useful if your sex life is waning. New couples will also enjoy these exercises.

Project #1: Sensuality Exercise. Want to expand your sexual responsiveness and overcome sexual rigidity? Want to decrease any shame you have about your body? If so, this is the exercise for you. Sensuality is crucial to any healthy sexual relationship, so learn to enjoy each other's bodies in a way that is affectionate and sensual but does not involve genital sex.

Choose a time when you will not be disturbed. Unplug your phone, turn off the TV, and create a relaxed atmosphere by dimming lights, lighting a fire in the fireplace, or doing whatever makes you comfortable. Take off your clothes and decide which of you will be the giver and which the receiver. The giver should begin by caressing, massaging, or fondling the receiver, while not touching the genital area. If you are the giver, don't worry for now about how well you are doing. Simply enjoy touching your partner. The receiver's role is to enjoy being touched. His sole responsibility is to tell his partner if any touch is uncomfortable, irritating, or distracting. Otherwise, the receiver is not required to say anything, even to comment on what feels good, although spontaneous "oohs" and "mmmm's" are permitted. If the receiver wants to be touched in a certain area, he should let his partner know by asking, or by moving his hand to the desired place. When one of you is finished with your role, switch and let the receiver become the giver. Do the exercise again. The same rules apply. Just enjoy touching and being touched.

Project #2: Sexuality Communication Project. An essential part of making love is letting each other know what pleases you and what does not. Even though intragender empathy will help you make guesses about this, each of you has sexual likes and dislikes that the other may not recognize. Talking together about your sexual tastes is a way of strengthening your relationship and improving your sex life.

If you have never discussed sexual matters openly before, you may find them embarrassing. If so, it is better to communicate indirectly rather than not at all. If necessary, write notes to each other about your sexual desires. After a while, your embarrassment may diminish and you can discuss sexual matters directly.

Will you offend each other if you give honest appraisals of your sex life together? Perhaps. It can deflate your ego to find out that the hot sexual moves you are so proud of actually annoy your partner. But remember, your lover's sexual tastes are no reflection on you, and you cannot know them without his telling you. The most skilled lovers are open to feedback and direction. And speaking more frankly about sexuality, even when it is not reassuring, draws you closer to each other.

Of course, be sure that you are not using sexual honesty to hurt each other or express anger indirectly. Never give sexual appraisals of each other during a fight. Recall how you feel when you receive such feedback and always be gentle and tactful when discussing sex together. And don't gossip about your sex life with friends. This is a private area of your relationship; share it only with each other.

Will discussing your sexual tastes make lovemaking mechanical, predictable, and unspontaneous? Usually not. No matter how specific your directions are to each other, there is still room for imagination. In fact, once you know the basic outlines of each other's sexual tastes, you may find you are freer and more inventive. How else will you discover intriguing, novel possibilities if you don't discuss these things?

One last piece of advice: *don't discuss your sexual likes and dislikes during sex.* This can make you both feel self-conscious and put a damper on your lovemaking. Wait until another time, when you are feeling close and safe with each other. Then discuss your sex life frankly. Use the following questions as a guide:

The most sensitive parts of my body are . . .
The sexual act I enjoy most with you is . . .
The best sex we ever had was when . . .
When we are having sex, I don't like it when you . . .
Something I have never done with you, but fantasize about is . . .

The sensuality exercise will help you answer these questions.

Project #3: Novelty Exercise. It bears repeating that novelty is an important way to keep sexual excitement alive in a relationship. This does not mean that you must search for strange and bizarre ways to have ecstatic sex. Nor are we saying that comfortable, familiar sex with each other is bad for your relationship. Nevertheless, most couples are happier if they experiment with new ways to be sexual with each other.

Let's be specific. Sexual novelty can be found in the following ways:

1. Make love at a time of day when you normally don't. If you always have sex at night before going to sleep, make love first thing in the morning, or midafternoon.

2. Make love in a place that is different. Is your sex typically restricted to the bedroom? Make love in the living room, the kitchen, the shower, on the dining room table, or swinging from the chandelier.

3. Make love in a way that is different. Does your sex follow a predictable routine in what you do and the order in which you do it? Use the information you gained from the communication exercise and try different ways of being sexual together.

4. Use fantasy to enhance your lovemaking. Some gay men have a deep, dark secret, for which they feel tremendously guilty: occasionally, when making love with their partners, they fantasize about someone else. Well, if this is true for you, relax. Not only is this common and completely natural, it does not signal the end of your attraction for each other. Sometimes fantasizing about a hot man while you are with your partner can make sex more exciting. Such fantasizing is a way to bring new sexual energy into your relationship. It can also be a substitute for playing around. You can sleep with Robert Redford, Warren Beatty, or the man down the street without ever straying from home. And you don't even have to tell each other when or what you are fantasizing about. A warning, though: if your fantasizing doesn't feel good or you find it impossible to have sex together without fantasizing, something is wrong. Limit your fantasizing and consult a sex therapist.

When pursuing new and exciting ways of making love, remember that your sex should feel safe to both of you. Tying each other up may be a novel sexual act, but we discourage it unless you both truly desire it. Similarly, you may find it exciting to make love in public places, but that is asking for trouble. Although such behavior may enliven your sex life, it could land you in jail. Novelty in intimate relationships must always be carefully balanced with safety and good judgment.

FIGHTING FAIR (ANGER)

Like most people, you probably did not come into your current relationship being a master at expressing anger. Some gay male couples face a particular problem with anger: because they believe that gay relationships are fragile, they work hard to avoid all conflict. If this is true for the two of you, you can best help your relationship by learning how to disagree. Practice makes perfect. Also, dealing with unresolved anger can spice up your sex life.

Project #1: Setting Ground Rules for Arguments. For disagreements to be productive, you must first establish some joint guidelines about what is fair in an argument. We suggest that the two of you sit down together and explicitly discuss these rules. Some guidelines may be applicable to all your relationships. Others will be specific to your couple relationship.

Here are ten ground rules for fighting fair:

1. If you are angry at your partner, stop and see what you're angry about. If you can't identify why you are angry, tell your partner that you are upset and that you need to discuss your feelings later. Don't just hold in your anger because it's difficult to communicate.

2. When you know what is bothering you, discuss it as soon as you can do so without attacking your partner. You may wish to schedule a regular meeting where grievances can be aired before they accumulate.

3. If you feel yourself losing control (e.g., becoming physically violent or bitingly sarcastic), stop, leave the room, and spend time alone until you cool off. Similarly, if your partner loses control, insist on a "time out." The best way to avoid abuse is by not participating in abusive fighting. *Never* strike or throw things at each other.

4. Don't bring up old hurts when discussing a current issue. Stick to the matter at hand. If you wish to discuss an old grievance, do so at another time. Also, fight about a single current issue at a time. Instead of dragging out a list of complaints, say, "Let's talk about one gripe at a time. Do you want to go first?"

5. Talk about your own feelings and don't make assumptions about how your partner is feeling. "I've been feeling unappreciated lately" is more helpful than "You don't love me anymore." Be as specific as possible when making a complaint. "You never do anything around the house" is probably inaccurate. "I've been angry because I always do the laundry" is more accurate and to the point. Also, state what you want directly, don't just complain. If you are angry about the laundry, make a request: "I'd like you to do your own laundry," or "Will you do the laundry every other week?"

6. Don't mention third persons as a way of supporting your point of view. This fight is between the two of you. Instead of saying: "My friends say I deserve to be taken out once in a while," or "My old lover and I used to go out every weekend," ask: "Would you be willing to go out more often?"

7. Open your heart to your partner if you feel it is safe to do so. Perhaps you are angry because you feel hurt, betrayed, shocked, abandoned, disappointed, or distrustful. If you convey these feelings, as well as your anger, it will help your partner understand and respect your hurt feelings.

8. Don't try to talk your partner out of his feelings. Examples of this are, "You have no reason to feel like that" or "You're crazy. I never . . ." Your partner's feelings are real, even if they seem wrong to you. Your job is to try to understand his feelings and to share your own with him.

9. Don't make threats, such as "If you don't start doing more of the housework, I'm moving out." Threats drastically interfere with trust in a relationship and make it difficult to resolve conflicts. Of course it is your right to make ultimatums, but don't make them until you have decided to go though with them.

10. If one of you repeatedly deviates from a mutually accepted guideline for arguing, stop, point that out, and start over. But don't use this tactic as a way to score points. Remember, both of you are learning how to express anger, and you are bound to make mistakes. If you want to improve communication, be generous in your appraisals of each other.

Apart from these general guidelines, we encourage you to set personal guidelines for arguments. For example, you may get upset when your partner raises his voice. This may remind you of an abusive parent, or it may simply frighten you. It may be appropriate to ask your partner to keep his voice down when arguing; continuous loud shouting is not necessary for the honest expression of anger. Similarly, a man we know resented being greeted after work by his lover's long list of complaints. He was tired and preoccupied and needed time to recuperate from his job. He asked his lover to bring up grievances at another time, unless a matter was urgent. In drawing up such personal guidelines, each of you must first decide separately what you require to feel safe when fighting. Then, discuss these needs with each other and try to agree on joint guidelines.

Your guidelines may seem like a lot to remember, especially when you are feeling hot under the collar, but you don't have to do each one perfectly. In our culture, most people have difficulty expressing anger, and you are bound to make mistakes at first. These errors are not disasters, just a way you learn and help each other grow. With the exception of physical or emotional violence, any mistake you make expressing anger is better than holding it inside. And dealing with anger over molehills will get you in practice for the mountains.

Project #2: Anger Communication Project. Now that you have set some guidelines, you are ready to express some anger with each other. Perhaps the best way is to wait for an opportunity when some conflict arises between you. If you are harboring old hurts or facing an issue that has already come up, however, simply schedule a time to do this exercise. You will need a quiet place to talk, where you can sit facing each other, and a kitchen timer. Remember to follow the guidelines you established in the previous exercise.

One of the hardest things to do when arguing or expressing anger is to listen carefully to what the other person says. This exercise is designed to help the two of you do this. Decide who will begin talking and set the kitchen timer for five minutes. During this time, one person will express his feelings, using the guidelines that you agreed upon together in the preceding section. *Without interrupting*, the other partner is to listen to his lover's point of view. There will be a strong temptation to jump in and make a comment, but it's essential not to do this. After five minutes, reset the timer, and let the other person have his turn, again without being interrupted. Continue switching back and forth, in listening and talking modes, until you have made some progress together.

Using the timer may feel artificial and limiting at first, but it is useful if you are afraid of anger and unsure of where it will lead. After several sessions using the timer, try resolving differences without it. If either of you feels he has a problem listening or being listened to, you can always go back to using the timer.

PLAY

Play is the creative use of fantasy, spontaneity, and humor to interact with another person. It is one of the best ways to strengthen your relationship. Play increases trust, renews energy, and teaches you a great deal about each other. Some gay male couples find it difficult to play together. Perhaps one or both men had negative experiences with play in childhood. Or sometimes body shame gets in the way. In any case, the following projects should prove fun and exciting.

Project #1: Pillow Fight. For gay men, one of the most healing kinds of play is rough-and-tumble activity. Football, wrestling, and snowball fights are all recommended, but may be too threatening if you are beginners at physical play. Therefore, we suggest the two of you stage a pillow fight.

As with the anger exercise, a few guidelines will help. Agree that either of you can stop the play at any time if you feel scared, tired, or overwhelmed. No explanations are required. You may restrict the location of your game, so as not to smash the expensive crystal in the living room. And set limits on where to hit each other, for example, only below the shoulders, only below the belt, anywhere but the genital area.

We do not recommend this exercise if you have a history of physical violence in relationships or one of you has a physical disability that can result in injury. Stop the exercise if either of you is hurt.

As you fight, remember that good play depends on spontaneity, creativity, fairness, and humor. Find ways of surprising each other, within the guidelines the two of you set. Let your imaginations run wild.

Afterward, stop and notice how you are feeling. Are you angry? Sometimes play uncovers resentments. Sexual? It can be a powerful stimulant. Learn from your reactions and perhaps discuss them together.

If you want some inspiration for future pillow fights, we recommend the film, *My Brilliant Career.* It contains a world-class pillow fight between two lovers. You can find it on videotape at many stores.

Project #2: Travel Adventure. One of the most useful things you can do for your relationship is to vacation periodically together. Such holidays are opportunities to relax, talk, and play with each other. They also can be shared adventures, and we recommend them as a way of getting to know each other better. A successful vacation does not require a week at a luxury resort in Mexico. If you can afford this, fine. But some of the best vacations take place in a friend's cabin in the woods, the campground of a state park, or in an inexpensive motel. The important ingredients are a break in your usual routine and time (at least two days) to focus on each other.

A second consideration is how planned your adventure should be. If you are inexperienced travelers or visiting New Orleans at Mardi Gras, you may wish to at least reserve your overnight accommodations in advance. As you get more practice, it is fun to just go wherever your hearts lead you. Again, adventure must be balanced with good judgment.

There is an old saying, "The best test of a relationship is to travel together." You may find that parts of your vacation are stressful. You will get practice at negotiation ("Where will we eat?" "Where will we stay?" "What do we want to do with our time?"). You will find the limit of your own and your partner's patience ("You have to go to the bathroom again!"). And you may discover which of you is better at reading a map. Remember, both of you are out of your ordinary surroundings. This is part of what is so revealing and so difficult about travel.

Above all, keep a sense of humor when things do not go as expected. This is all part of the adventure. That rainy bike ride will provide amusing stories for years to come, and even a lumpy bed or a wrong turn in the bush can be romantic. This is your chance to demonstrate your resourcefulness and mutual support.

COMMITMENT AND RITUAL

Commitment is an alarming word for some gay men. It conjures up visions of boredom, dying relationships, and loss of freedom. But there are positive signs of commitment: appreciating your history together and marking important transitions in your life as a couple. Both of these tasks are neglected by gay male couples, in part because gay relationships are regarded as illegitmate by our society. Also many gay men do not recognize the importance of celebrating their partnerships. The exercises in this section will add security and strength to your relationship.

Project #1: Creating Couple Traditions. We mentioned in Chapter 5 that being a couple involves creating a new culture together. Couple traditions are essential to this undertaking and form a supporting structure for relationships. What are couple traditions? They are special routines that celebrate your relationship and show your love for each other. Typically, they are performed at special times and have personal meaning. Here are some examples to get you started:

- You and your partner spend each Friday night at home together, reading, talking, and catching up from a busy week.
- Every year at Christmas you prepare a meal together with holiday foods that were special in each of your families.
- On Saturday afternoons, you always go for a long walk together.
- At Thanksgiving, you eat dinner with your lover's family. On Passover, you visit your family.
- You host a costume party together each Halloween and invite your friends.
- Every year, you exchange gifts on the anniversary of your first date.
- You go to a certain resort for a week's vacation each summer.

Notice that traditions are not necessarily handed down from generation to generation. Sometimes, like special holiday foods, they are. But other traditions will be novel and highly specific to your relationship. They will primarily have meaning for the two of you.

Couple traditions are like other aspects of relationships: you can open your heart to them, but you cannot make them happen. The best traditions arise spontaneously and sometimes mysteriously from your life together. Although we cannot give you a recipe, we can describe some of the ingredients of a good tradition:

1. A good couple tradition is enjoyable to both partners.

You may look forward to bowling on Wednesday nights. But if your lover dislikes all sports, bowling is a poor candidate for a tradition.

2. Traditions often blend the individual personalities of the two partners. In one couple we know, one partner was raised Catholic and the other Jewish. They have both a Menorah and a Christmas tree in their home and exchange gifts on both Hannukah and Christmas.

3. Successful traditions are repeated consistently, with each partner taking the initiative to participate. If the two of you reserve a certain night to be at home with each other, but often cancel or reschedule your plans, the arrangement will not grow into a firm tradition. This will also be true if one of you must remind the other of your agreement.

4. Although consistency is important, healthy traditions are flexible, so they can be changed or discontinued if necessary. If your lover becomes a vegetarian, drop the usual French meat pie from the Christmas menu and substitute another dish that you both enjoy. Similarly, if the two of you recently moved from Vermont to Texas, considering changing the annual ski trip to a week at the beach. Traditions that are inflexible often grow meaningless and empty with time. Each time you prepare for a tradition, reflect on whether it is still meaningful or can be improved.

In their study of gay male couples, McWhirter and Mattison found that traditions were comforting and reassuring, especially when partners felt insecure about their relationship. As we have cautioned, however, security must be kept in perspective. It would be possible to standardize every aspect of life with your partner, including what you did every night of the week and what you ate for dinner, but such traditions would be oppressive and boring. Similarly, you can make sexual negotiations safer by agreeing to make love only on Tuesdays and Thursdays, but then you will lack practice in asking, offering, and saying no. Couple traditions embody your commitment to each other, but they are not replacements for the real thing. When traditions express your joy in being together and do not cover up other issues, they benefit your relationship.

Project #2: Couple Rituals. A ritual is different from a tradition in that it is often done only once. Rituals derive their meaning from ceremony and symbolic action rather than from repetition and consistency. Rituals are useful in relationships as a way of labeling the bonds between two partners and deepening their attachment. We encourage you to jointly create rituals to mark major events in your relationship like the following:

- After signing the papers for their new house, Tim and Bob drink a bottle of champagne in front of the fireplace. They talk about their hopes for the new home and their fears about this new commitment.
- John and Tom celebrate their fifth anniversary with a dinner for all their friends. After dessert, each guest presents the couple with a gift representing a hope for John and Tom's relationship. After all the gifts have been explained, everyone joins hands and sings a song.
- Bart and Jerry announce their commitment to each other at a special party attended by family and friends. In the middle of the party, the men gather their guests around them and read poems they have written to each other. They exchange rings and flowers and kiss as their friends cheer.

You may think, "Now they are telling us that we should get married!" This is not what we are saying. One ritual you might consider is a ceremony celebrating your commitment to each other. But the important thing is that any ritual you create be an honest expression of your relationship. Don't write vows professing undying love and read them in the presence of your friends if you've only known each other for two months. Instead, think of a ritual that will realistically express the hopes and fears of your young relationship. A good ritual takes stock of where you are now and commemorates that place.

You may notice from the examples that rituals often, but not necessarily, involve other people. Including close friends and family in a ritual can make the experience more moving and powerful. But some rituals are best kept between the two of you. If you stop to think carefully, you can decide if you want to include others.

Also, let your joint creativity express itself in composing a ritual. Music, dance, art, and food are often useful in such ceremonies. Choose elements that are meaningful to you and that feel just right. Although you should both agree on the major parts of the ritual, there may be parts that represent your individuality as well as your relationship. Plan beforehand, but leave room for last-minute inspiration.

A final caution is, have fun but don't take rituals lightly. A friend who is an expert on ritual once said, "Participate in a ritual only if you are willing to be changed by it." By naming the status of your relationship and enacting and symbolizing that relationship in a ritual, you open yourselves to growth, change, and new insights. Is this what you want? Ritual is a powerful tool that can teach you much about being together.

SPIRITUALITY

Relationships based on a shared spiritual understanding possess a distinctive depth and solidity. Gay male couples often find it difficult to develop a common spirituality because one or both partners has been hurt by traditional religion. Also, your spiritual beliefs are an intensely private part of your life, and it can feel embarrassing to discuss them with a lover or partner. The exercises in this section will help you to share your spiritual journeys with each other.

Project #1: Exploring Spiritual Communities. There are three goals to this project: to help the two of you understand each other's spiritual experiences while growing up, to stimulate discussions of spiritual matters together, and to aid you in your search for a spiritual support group.

Begin by sharing with your partner a significant aspect of your spiritual or religious history. Don't simply talk about some experience; do something active together. If you were raised in a particular church, visit a church of that denomination. If you and your partner were raised in the same religious tradition, visit these congregations. If you did not attend church while growing up, or find the thought of going to church distasteful, think of some other experience that was spiritual for you and share that with your partner. For example, take a walk in the woods, listen to Beethoven's Ninth Symphony, or read a favorite book together. When you make your religious experiences concrete to each other, it is easier to appreciate your present view of spirituality.

After your joint outing, use it as an opportunity to understand each other better. Discuss your responses to the experience and see if you can appreciate each other's reactions. If you are the visiting partner, keep your comments nonjudgmental and try to find things you both like and dislike about the experience. If you are the host for this experience, listen to your partner's impressions without getting defensive. His reactions are not a reflection on you. Most important, don't use these outings to try to convert each other to your own points of view. Use them to learn about each other's spiritual life.

Now that you have shared a part of your personal spiritual histories together, we encourage you to embark on additional spiritual outings together. Begin by making a list of spiritual experiences you each wish to explore. Your list may include traditional churches, gay religious groups, spiritual advisers, lecturers, meditation groups, or books that you are anxious to read. Set aside time once or twice a month as a couple to pursue these activities. Again, after each experience, take time to fully discuss your reactions and to learn more about each other. Listen for commonalities in your perspectives and respect differences of opinion. Remember, spirituality is a multifaceted jewel. If you find an experience that feels special to you both, repeat it. Such situations can be strong spiritual supports for your relationship.

Project #2: Meditating Together. In Chapter 6, we presented some guidelines for meditating on your own. You may now wish to try meditating with each other. Meditating with another person is a powerful way to develop a shared spirituality. It is especially useful when you are from different religious backgrounds or hold different spiritual beliefs, because meditation transcends words and is found in many religious traditions. If you and your partner meditate regularly together, it will increase your intimacy.

As with meditating alone, find a time and place when the two of you will not be disturbed. Initially you may try fifteen minutes of meditation, but ten or twenty minutes will do as well. Sit in a place where you can be physically close, either next to or across from each other. Some couples enjoy holding hands as they meditate, whereas others find this distracting.

To be successful with this exercise, you must first realize how joint meditation differs from meditating alone. Physical proximity alone will not produce a sense of spiritual union. Rather, you must cultivate an openness to each other while you meditate, while remaining focused within yourselves. This shared spiritual awareness is what makes meditating together special. Here are some techniques that may be useful in developing this spiritual accessibility:

- While you meditate, picture yourself and your partner holding hands, laughing, or playing together. What scene do you see?
- Imagine a golden thread joining you and your partner. Where are you connected and what does the thread look like?
- Before you meditate, choose a question together that touches upon your relationship. Contemplate this question in your meditation. What answer(s) do you receive? This technique is especially useful when the two of you face a major decision together.

After the agreed time has elapsed, end the meditation with a hug or some other touch. Sit quietly for a moment and bask in the peaceful feeling. If you wish, spend a few minutes talking about your individual experiences during the silence. You may be amazed at how similar your thoughts or images were.

Like individual meditation, joint meditation requires consistent practice to be useful. You probably won't realize the full value of the experience the first time. You may notice, however, that meditation with your partner is quite special. The fact that you know each other well and are close to each other makes joint meditation a powerful and enriching experience. It will also benefit your relationship by providing a shared spiritual experience that is simply beyond words.

"GENERATIVITY"

You and your lover may yearn to leave a legacy of your relationship to others. This is the desire for generativity, a normal characteristic of adult relationships. In heterosexual couples, generativity is partly expressed by having children. As a gay male couple, the two of you may need other ways to make your mark on the world. The projects in this section will help you do this.

Besides being a normal part of adult life, it will benefit you and your partner to share your relationship with others. You are likely to encounter people who do not share your values and this will help you examine yourselves and your relationship. Sharing your relationship with others will prevent you from becoming isolated, which is a real danger given the attitudes of society toward same-sex couples. And as you reevaluate yourselves and the quality of your life together, unfinished parts of your identity and flaws in your relationship have another chance to mend.

Project #1: A Joint Service Project. Undertaking a joint act of charity is very different from helping as an individual. You may be supported and challenged as a couple in ways that you never were individually: you have someone to observe and give you feedback, you can share reactions with someone who knows the situation, and you can learn new ways of handling difficult tasks. Also, the presence of someone you trust makes it possible to take bigger risks; you can serve in ways that would be too unnerving to do alone. Even more important, a joint service project brings you closer together. You are likely to share intense feelings of joy and disappointment and discover previously unknown aspects of each other.

The crucial step is the first one: choosing the project you will do together. Thoughtfully consider different options. Is there a project that feels right to both of you? Ideally, it should involve a cause you both feel committed to and require no more time or money than you have to give. Consider also whether you can be open about your relationship in the setting you choose. Your task will be less rewarding if you must hide the fact that you are a couple.

Here are examples of projects that gay male couples can do together:

• Richard and Bill are buddies to a person with AIDS and his lover.

- Paul and Tom sort food one day a month for a church that gives groceries to the poor.
- Bob and John coordinate religious education classes for children in the church they attend.
- Alan and Mark are heavily involved in the sanctuary movement for Central American refugees.
- Sam and Alex run errands for an elderly woman next door. They mow her lawn in summer and shovel her walk in the winter.
- Peter and Steve are foster parents to a gay teenager.
- Jim and Jack are co-chairs of the local gay political action committee.

Don't be limited by these examples. The possibilities for service are endless. Listen to your hearts!

Once you get involved in your project, don't be surprised if the two of you sometimes feel different degrees of enthusiasm about it. There will be ups and downs for each of you. One of the benefits of working together is that you can support each other when you are discouraged. But to do so, it must be safe to admit that your commitment is wavering and your spirits are low.

While serving, you can use your couple relationship as a medium to help others. Be more than co-workers or close friends. Remember that you are lovers. For example, Richard and Bill found that their AIDS buddies appreciated hearing about some of the struggles in their own relationship. This gave the two men hope that difficulties could be worked through. Similarly, Peter and Steve know that their relationship is an important model for their foster son. The love you show between you will be seen by others and can have a healing effect on them.

Finally, easy does it. Don't get so overextended with helping people that you have no time or energy for each other. Remember, one reason you became involved in this project is to nurture your relationship. In times of sickness or stress, it is especially important to turn your attention homeward and cut back on other commitments. In the end, balancing your energies will also help your service project. There is a saying: "The love we give is the overflow of love we receive." When your primary relationship is full of caring, it's easy to care for others.

Project #2: Getting to Know Another Gay Male Couple.
You and your lover also can express the generativity of your
relationship by becoming friends with another gay male couple. There are many good reasons to form this kind of tie: it
will prevent relationship isolation, benefit the other couple,
give you a fresh look at another gay male relationship, and
teach you how much the two of you have to offer. It is often
especially rewarding when older and younger gay male couples become friends. The younger couple benefits from the
experience and solidity of the older couple, who in turn are
exposed to a vital, new relationship. Such connections foster
intimacy on both sides.

"Fine," you may say, "but where are we supposed to
find such a couple?" If you live in a major urban area, it's
easy. Even if you live in a small community, don't be discouraged. To start, simply keep your eyes open. The two men
who live down the street, belong to your church, or shop in
your grocery store may be a couple. A warm greeting and
some discreet questions will determine if your hunch is correct. If so, follow up with a dinner invitation. This is a good
way to begin a friendship.

As with making individual friends, it may take several
tries before you find people with whom you are compatible.
Don't be discouraged; keep on trying. Once you have found a
couple, make use of the connection to benefit your relationship. Have you wondered how other gay male couples handle
sex outside their relationships? Don't be shy, ask! Tell stories
about your first dates, and drag out the picture albums.
Which do you think will astonish you more: how similar the
other couple is or how different? Both the similarities and
differences provide valuable lessons.

As you get to know each other, it is possible that sexual
feelings will arise among the four of you. This is very common and natural in gay friendships, and you must decide
how to handle these feelings. It's our experience that the
friendship is most likely to succeed if members of different
couples decide not to be sexual with each other. If one or
both of you has an affair, you may be afraid to make friends
with another couple, should the opportunity arise again.

As an example of the rewards you can reap from becoming friends with another gay male couple, we share the
following letter.

Dear Tony and James,

We just wanted to write and thank you both for coming to our cabin last weekend. We both agreed that it's been years since we laughed so much. We feel younger from being around the two of you. Watching you nuzzle on the couch reminded us of our earlier days together and how good they were. Thanks for the inspiration. We were serious about lending you furniture for your new house. Call us when you're ready to have us drop some things off.

Love,
Tom and Harold

Although you may find special value in getting to know other gay male couples, many of the same benefits can be found in friendships with lesbian or heterosexual couples. So if you have trouble finding another gay male couple who's compatible, you may want to explore a friendship with a lesbian or heterosexual couple.

COUPLES THERAPY

The preceding exercises are designed to enhance the intimacy in your relationship. However, there may be times when you need professional help in relating to each other. This is common in any growing relationship, and we urge you to consider couples therapy (also called conjoint therapy) as a way of addressing problems. You may also seek the input of a professional when there are no major problems in your relationship, as a way to challenge yourselves and your ability to love.

Couples therapy can take any of several forms: couples groups, couples enrichment seminars, and joint sessions between a couple and one or two counselors. All these methods are different from individual psychotherapy in important ways.

First, the goals differ. The focus of couples therapy is your relationship. The focus of individual therapy is you as an individual. Obviously, individual problems can affect your relationship, and faulty relationship patterns may cause difficulties in other areas of your life. Thus you may be in individual and couples therapy at the same time.

The two types of therapy also differ in the relationship that forms between therapist and client or clients. In individual therapy, you and your therapist may spend a great deal of time examining the interactions between you. This is a part of intimacy and helps shed light on your intimacy patterns in other relationships. In couples therapy, the relationship between clients and therapist is often less intense. A therapist is likely to watch how you and your partner interact in sessions in order to understand your relationship. Less attention may be paid to how you interact with the therapist.

If you enter individual therapy, it is probably because you want help with a personal problem. In contrast, many couples enter conjoint therapy with each partner feeling, "I'm okay, but you're not okay." Typically, neither is totally at fault. Most of us find it hard to think in terms of relationships and mutuality, so we tend to blame ourselves or somebody else. Would it surprise you if the troubles do not stem completely from your partner's faults, or if you are not totally to blame?

The power of couples therapy comes from its focus on relationships. By subjecting yourselves to the scrutiny of an unbiased third person, you can identify strengths and weaknesses in your patterns of relating, learn what part each of you plays in creating or prolonging problems in your relationship, and find ways to keep individual problems from interfering with your life together. Couples therapy can help you both develop and maintain a passionate, spontaneous, trusting, and loving relationship. It will also challenge you as individuals. Frequently couple therapy leads you to acknowledge personal issues from childhood and scars from previous relationships. When these come to light, you may decide to discuss them in individual therapy.

Choosing a couple therapist is similar to choosing an individual therapist. Look for someone who is comfortable working with gay men and familiar with the issues faced by gay male couples. The therapist may be a gay man, but this is not necessary. Also, choose someone who has professional training and credentials. If you are unsure about the licensing of therapists in your local area, contact your state mental health association. Seek out a therapist who has experience working with couples. Ask friends for recommendations and shop around.

Both of you should feel comfortable with the couples therapist you choose, but your feelings may fluctuate during the therapy. At different times, the therapist may seem to take sides, switch sides, or be neutral. This is all part of good couples work. The best couples therapists support each of you in a balanced way and acknowledge your individuality. Each of you has a role in the difficulties in your relationship, and you will be shortchanged if only one side is discussed.

This leads to a common question: should the individual therapist of one of you see both of you for conjoint therapy? We have found problems with this arrangement. As you might imagine, the partner who has not previously seen the therapist for individual therapy often feels distrustful and left out. And even a good therapist may identify more with the individual client and take his side in an argument. Furthermore, such complications can damage the individual therapy relationship. For these reasons, it's probably wiser to seek a couples therapist who is not offering one of you individual therapy. The exception is when both of you are in individual therapy with different therapists; then conjoint sessions with both therapists may work well.

A good couples therapist helps each of you make informed decisions about your relationship but doesn't make decisions for you. Unfortunately, some therapists gauge the success of their work by whether a couple stays together. This criterion puts undo pressure on a couple to hang in there, perhaps long after they are ready to throw in the towel. Expect your therapist to bring out the very best in your relationship and to help each of you grow as individuals, with or without your relationship.

Apart from the qualities and skill of the therapist, the most important determinants of your experience will be the attitudes you bring to the therapy.

1. Be clear beforehand what each of you wants for yourself from the therapy. "I want him to be more physically affectionate with me" is a goal that involves changing your partner, not you. "I want to feel less frustrated and more secure" is a goal for yourself.

2. Expect to learn something about how you are contributing to problems and how you can change to help the relationship. It is natural for you to have a harder time seeing both sides; that is why you need an objective third party to help.

3. Practice new ways of being with each other in the therapy sessions, where you can feel safe because of the presence of the therapist. If you are afraid to fight, have your first argument there. If you want to learn a new way to communicate, try it out there. Take risks.

4. Take what you have learned in the sessions and practice when you are alone. Don't save up everything until you are in your therapist's office. Remember, the eventual goal is to communicate well on your own.

5. Record your experiences of the relationship in separate journals during the week and bring them to the couple's sessions. Use your journals to learn, not to score points against each other.

6. Don't hesitate to consult a therapist when difficulties first arise or to go back to a therapist if problems reappear. Some couples adopt a couples therapist like a family doctor and go in for periodic checkups. Your chances of success are greater if you get help as soon as you need it.

7. Address misunderstandings that arise with your couple's therapist. These are natural. Open discussion can lead to important revelations and will prepare you to deal with each other more honestly.

In summary, many successful gay male couples make use of couples therapy at some point in their relationships. As with individual or group psychotherapy, choose a therapist carefully and know what you want from the experience. If you and your partner follow these guidelines, couples therapy can be a valuable tool in resolving difficulties and furthering intimacy in your relationship.

ENDING COUPLE RELATIONSHIPS

It may seem odd to you that a book on intimacy includes a section on ending relationships. But let's face it, sometimes no matter how hard you try, a relationship simply doesn't work out. And in spite of what others say, leaving a lover is not easy. It takes the same care to end a relationship as it does to begin one or maintain it. You may prefer to simply drop off the key and skip town. If this is the best you can do, fine. But first read this section because how you end relationships has tremendous importance for your intimacy in future relationships.

Ending a relationship can be a mature act of love in itself. Love does not always mean togetherness, and togetherness does not always lead to growth. Honestly telling each other where you stand and compassionately listening to each other's feelings is loving. Staying together when you are consistently unhappy is not. Breaking up may be the most loving thing you do together.

Although we have written this section for couples, we realize that you may have to implement it on your own. Breaking up is best done together, but if your partner cannot or will not participate, you have no option but to proceed on your own. You can still do what you need to do.

A common question about ending relationships is: "How do I know if I should break up with my partner or try to stay together?" Like other questions about intimacy, answering this one requires significant personal reflection and a realistic understanding of your own feelings. It is courageous simply to ask the question. Let's share a few examples of how gay men decide to end a relationship.

- Bob is involved in an Al-Anon group and has come to realize he cannot make Mike stop drinking. Their couples therapist refuses to see them because of Mike's continued abuse of alcohol. Mike continues to make empty promises. Bob feels he must leave the relationship or die.
- Buzz and Robbie have received job offers in different cities. Although they enjoyed their time living together, neither of them is willing to give up his job for the relationship. They agree to part.
- Stan and John have been seeing a couples therapist for six months. John has begun to suspect that he never really loved Stan; he simply was afraid to be alone after he left home. With much reluctance and fear, Stan proposes a trial separation to John.

If you are struggling with the decision of ending a relationship and you still have questions after reading this far, we refer you to *How to Break Your Addiction to a Person*, and *Love and Addiction*. This section is for those who have already decided to end a relationship and wish to know how to proceed, or for those who have been informed by a lover that he is ending their relationship.

<hr>

INITIATING A BREAKUP

<hr>

Let's imagine you've been thinking for weeks or months that it's time for you and your lover to separate. Most likely this thought has come and gone, and you've tried the various ways outlined in this book to overcome the problems you see in the relationship. Maybe you've struggled on your own or have talked things over with him. You've tried the intimacy exercises, or he wants no part of them. In any case, you now are certain that you no longer wish to be in this couple relationship. How should you responsibly proceed?

First, be as clear in your own mind as you can be about your reasons for splitting. This step is difficult and may take months. But if you know now why you are ending the relationship, you will be better off.

Next, decide on a reasonable way to tell your partner. Take into account your physical safety: it is unwise to tell a physically abusive lover face-to-face that you are moving out, or where you are going. But only in such dire circumstances should you cut off contact without saying anything. Push yourself to communicate openly with your lover. If you cannot face him directly, write a letter or make a phone call. You don't have to do it perfectly, just do the best you can.

When telling your partner your decision, be prepared for shock, anger, or depression on his part. Remember, you needed time to get used to the idea of separating; so will your partner. If you are able, answer his questions, discuss your feelings, and explain why you are not willing to try other options. Once you have made yourself clear, you are under no obligation to continue to explain yourself. It is now up to your partner to accept your decision. He must seek emotional support from other sources. You cannot be responsible for consoling him or making him feel better. This will only confuse him and in the end, prolong the separation.

You may ask, "Why should I go to all this trouble? Once

I have made my decision, I simply want to get the hell out of here." We understand such feelings and that you may need to leave and then discuss your feelings with your partner. It's hard to deal with endings, especially when someone you care about is upset. But whether you do so now or later, it's worthwhile to take part in a frank discussion. Men who have a history of abruptly ending relationships often have difficulty getting close to others. Perhaps they expect someone to abandon them, or are afraid of hurting anyone else again. Or they never finish grieving over past relationships. You need to make the separation into a clear ending. And even though the relationship didn't work out, you had deep, loving feelings for your lover at one time. Take care of your emotional needs first, while trying not to get even with him. The more care you invest in separations, the better you will feel about yourself and the better your future relationships will be.

Bob, a former client, realized this during his therapy. Several years earlier, he ended a five-year relationship with Doug, an alcoholic lover, by suddenly leaving town without notice. Since that time Bob had never had an intimate love relationship. In one session he confessed:

> We've talked about me being afraid of getting hurt again, like I was with Doug. But this week I was thinking about how badly I treated him. I owed Doug more at the end than simply skipping out. He could've taken it if I'd told him I was leaving. At the time, I thought I was making it easier for him. But I just didn't want to cope with it myself. Now, I wake up in the middle of the night sometimes and start wondering where he is and how he's doing. Do you think I should try to contact him?

You can avoid Bob's sleepless nights and loneliness by dealing responsibly with your partner about your decision to break up. And if, like Bob, you find yourself worrying repeatedly over a past relationship, you need to explore your feelings about the relationship, whether or not you recontact your old lover.

IF YOUR PARTNER INITIATES A BREAKUP

You may be terribly shocked when your partner decides to end your relationship, or it may be something you expected and wanted for some time. In either case, your task is to accept, survive, and learn from your lover's decision.

It's common to feel embarrassed because you didn't make the break first. You may wonder if your partner hurts as much as you do. Rest assured, you are both feeling pain, even if appearances tell you otherwise.

If you didn't anticipate the breakup, the first step is to realize that the relationship is indeed ending. This step can be a major task in itself. You are entitled to ask for explanations and to express your feelings. Don't subject your lover to angry harangues or try to change his mind, however. Put yourself in his place. And remember, intimacy requires two willing participants. If your partner doesn't want to be close to you, you can't force intimacy. The sooner you accept his decision, the better.

Even if you desired the breakup, it is common to feel rejected and panicky when your lover announces a decision to leave the relationship. Paradoxically, the fact that he is leaving may make him seem more precious than he ever did before. You may want to plead with him to stay. When this urge comes upon you, remember that you also had many doubts about the relationship.

Whether or not you anticipated the end, you will need lots of emotional support as you go through the separation. This is especially true since you did not initiate the breakup. Now is the time to turn to friends. If you've neglected friends and other support networks during your relationship, swallow your pride and contact them anyway. They may be willing to forgive and start over. Or seek help from a psychotherapist.

SUGGESTIONS FOR BOTH OF YOU

Although you will both need to get on with living and rebuilding your lives apart, take time to grieve over your past relationship. Feelings of shock, sadness, rage, helplessness, confusion, guilt, despair, relief, and serenity are natural parts of ending a relationship. Many years ago, after a relationship ended, one of us coped by getting extremely busy with work in the following months. Not surprisingly, when an extended vacation came along seven months later, the suppressed feelings were all there waiting to be felt. You cannot run away from grief, you only put it on hold. Read *How to Survive the Loss of Love* and fully experience this time of mourning.

Another temptation is to become romantically involved soon after the separation. Typically such rebound relationships are escapes from the sadness and loneliness of a breakup. Although they sometimes succeed, such romances have a poor track record. Take time to be single again. Regroup and rethink your previous relationship.

Several months after the initial separation, try talking again with each other about your feelings and reasons for the separation. This is not a chance to get back together. Rather, you may have insights or feelings you were unable to express initially. Talking about the breakup can help you both to heal and move on with your lives.

If one or both of you is having a great deal of trouble separating, consider seeing a couples therapist together for "separation counseling." This typically involves a small number—usually two to five—joint sessions and is aimed at clearing up remaining issues and helping the two of you make a clean and healthy break. It may seem strange to invest time and money for conjoint therapy once a relationship is over. But if this is necessary for you to be at peace about a separation and to ensure your ability to become intimate in future relationships, it is worth every penny.

Can We Still Be Friends? Many couples manage to transform their attachment from a romantic relationship to a friendship, rather than ending it altogether. If you can do this, you can keep aspects of the intimacy you worked hard to establish. But this may be impossible, for several reasons. You may have little in common outside your sexual relationship. You may find it too painful to see each other. Or you may simply find it easier to make a clean break. There is no obligation to be friends with your old lover and it will not lessen the pain of your separation.

Even if both of you agree to remain friends, take time apart before attempting this. How much time away you need depends on how long you were together, how strong you felt about each other, and how difficult the breakup was. In most cases you will need several months away from each other. This interval allows emotional pain to subside and yields fresh perspective. You may continue to discuss your old relationship, just as you find new ways to be with each other.

Who Gets the Dog? Among the more painful aspects of a separation are dividing joint property, changing legal documents, and dealing with other practical matters. The longer you have been together, the more difficult these tasks are. Such practical matters are further complicated in gay male couples by the lack of legal recognition of same-sex partnerships. There are no foolproof guidelines for making practical aspects of a separation easier. However, a few principles will help you when you get stuck.

1. *The way you handle practical aspects of a separation can affect your self-esteem for years to come.* If you throw in the towel and do not ask for what you deserve, you will kick yourself long afterward. Similarly, if you take advantage of your lover, guilt feelings may haunt you long after the relationship has ended. Your self-esteem is more important than any piece of property or amount of money. It's in your own interest to be fair to yourself and your lover in these negotiations.

2. *When negotiations break down, deal with the underlying issues.* If one of you feels resentful and abused in the relationship, it will be difficult to divide up joint property. Similarly, you may encounter repeated snags in changing the title on the house you jointly own if one of you is still hoping to get back together. When you run into such problems, talk over your feelings about the separation. You don't have to clear up all remaining issues, just make enough of a dent to bypass the current log jam. You may stay stuck on practical aspects of a breakup until enough emotional healing has taken place to allow you to move on.

3. *If necessary, get help from an objective third party.* If the two of you cannot agree about practical aspects of the separation, ask one or more people to help you with your negotiations. Ideally, this mediator should be someone with whom you both feel comfortable, who is not closer to one of you than the other. A mutual friend is rarely the best choice, because he or she can feel caught in the middle. If the two of you belong to a church and are open about your relationship, you might consider asking a minister to mediate. Or seek help from a professional mediation service. Mediators are trained professionals who help people resolve disputes that might otherwise take them into court. Many metropolitan areas have low-cost mediation services. Some have experience with same-sex couples. As a last resort, consult an attorney.

When Will I Stop Hurting? Your pain over this separation may seem unbearable and without end. But by grieving over the old relationship, you are doing exactly what is necessary to get through the pain and go on with intimacy. The more intimate the relationship, the greater the pain of the breakup. So don't criticize yourself for grieving; it's a sign of your ability to love. There is no short cut through it. Sometimes it takes months or years to recover from a ruptured relationship. You can stand it. Grief is not fatal.

Having heard this, if you find your pain about a past relationship does not lessen with time and you are preoccupied with an old lover, seek professional help. Letting go of old hurts requires figuring out what went wrong and how to do better the next time. An experienced therapist can help.

A RITUAL FOR ENDING RELATIONSHIPS

Consider planning a ritual to mark the ending of your relationship. It may take months or years of healing before you can even consider such a ceremony. But ending rituals have incredible healing potential, and can help you move on from a relationship. An ending ritual is best if you yourselves decide on the structure. Thus, we will give you only general guidelines and examples of what some other couples have done. Conrad and Lance ended a stormy seven-year relationship with a great deal of bitterness on both sides. Lance felt attacked and threatened by Conrad's incessant complaints and angry outbursts. Conrad was furious at Lance's financial irresponsibility and felt shortchanged in the relationship. Three years after the separation, both men barely spoke to each other and continued to disagree about whether Lance owed Conrad money. After attempting to resolve the matter on their own, the men finally sought help from a church group they had attended together. The group appointed a committee of four people to meet with the two men. After several lengthy meetings full of anger and tears, Lance and Conrad finally reached an agreement about the money. They also better understood what had gone wrong in their relationship. Although these were great improvements, the committee members agreed that more was needed to finish the matter. One person suggested a separation ritual, and Lance and Conrad planned one with the help of the committee.

One evening, Conrad and Lance each came with their closest friends to the home of a committee member. They went into separate rooms, and their friends helped them dress and prepare for the ritual. When they were ready, the two men entered the main room and stood together with their friends in a circle around them. A friend of Lance and a friend of Conrad then took a ball of twine and wrapped it around and around the two men. When they were done, the two friends announced that this represented the links between the former couple. Then both Conrad and Lance were given scissors and, with the help of their friends, proceeded to cut themselves out of the twine. As each strand was cut, Lance or Conrad would say, "I free myself from the ties that bind us, keeping only those that will help me in my journey." When they were totally loosed, they turned and hugged and said, "I forgive you and I forgive myself." They then walked into the waiting arms of their friends, who cheered and spontaneously carried them out of the house by different doors. The two men then went to their separate houses, where they celebrated over dinner with friends.

Obviously, the ritual we described had the cooperation and participation of both former partners. Sometimes, this is not possible; one partner has died, moved away, or is simply unwilling to participate in a separation ritual. Or the hurt in the relationship may have been so great that you simply cannot bear the thought of having contact with your former lover again. If so, plan and execute a ritual of your own, without your former lover. Ask a friend to be a proxy for your ex or do the whole thing yourself. Your letting go need not depend on your former partner's willingness or ability to do the same.

And if it takes you decades to do this ritual, that's still better than not doing it at all.

LAST-MINUTE ADVICE

This chapter contains many tips for improving the intimacy in your couple relationship. We have tried to make suggestions that are straightforward and appear simple; one danger is that you may think they will also be easy. Clearly the advice we have presented would be difficult for anyone to follow. Don't worry about doing it perfectly; just do it.

As you are better able to be close to each other, have patience and appreciate small signs of progress. Fritz Perls, a famous psychotherapist, described growth as follows: "Two steps forward, one step backward." This applies to relationships as well as to individuals.

Just because this is a self-help book, don't think you have to do it all yourself. Help is all around you. Ask for it and accept it.

8

SUMMARY AND GOOD-BYE

In finishing this book, we became aware of two conflicting feelings. In each of us, a voice exclaimed, "Thank God we're done. We've had enough of each other." Another warned, "But, if we're done writing the book together, what will become of our friendship?" These feelings are the very core of what impedes intimacy: the fear of being overwhelmed and the fear of being abandoned. In closing, it's very fitting for us to reexperience these fears, yet be confident of overcoming them.

We are also led by these feelings.

Let's face the music. We are ending with you as well as ending with each other. We may meet again, but everything will be different then. Now is now. Finishing is both sad and somewhat exciting. In saying good-bye, we have decided to talk about ourselves and to recap some major ideas of the book.

John: Throughout this book I've been perplexed. One part of me would nervously ask, "As a straight man, what am I doing writing a book about gay relationships?" Another part would protest, "What difference does it make?" Clearly my inner struggle reflects essential mysteries of gay relationships: being like everybody else and being different. The ups and downs of this struggle have allowed me to enjoy my inner spirit more fully. We are all in this together. Were it not for a very dear friendship with my co-author, this book would surely have driven me over the edge. Instead, I am so proud of playing a part in teaching others how to love more deeply. I have picked up many lessons for myself along the way. I am sad to see this end.

Steve: Writing this book has stretched me in ways I never expected. Every time I thought I had reached the end of my enthusiasm, energy, and wisdom, there was more to be found. Because I learned to be open to new resources within and around me, my life is richer and more complete. This project has also changed my relationships. John and I began this book as good friends. I now feel a deep respect and love between us. My lover, Jim, has been an essential support for my work, and our love has matured from a deeper understanding of intimacy. Now every part of me is crying, "Enough! Finished! Time to let go!" But ending has its own challenge. Will this book be helpful? Will other people like it? I can only trust and hope.

WHAT IT'S ALL ABOUT

- Think of intimacy as a precious jewel. Although rare, it can be possessed, and you will treasure it for the rest of your life. Of course rare jewels are not easily acquired. The jewel of intimacy is hewn from rough stone and is cut and polished throughout your life. Releasing the gem from the stone demands the very best of you. Its glow reflects your inner beauty and enables you to feel real, worthy, and whole. And although it becomes more and more brilliant, the jewel can always benefit from further polishing. When the storms of life wash over the jewel, it endures like a diamond. It can never be lost or stolen. Its beauty will last forever.
- Discover the part of you that does not want to be intimate and embrace it. We all have a This-is-too-much-work and I-can't-stand-it part of us. As an old AA slogan goes, "I'm not okay. You're not okay. But that's okay." It is possible for us to love, to be responsible for, and to appreciate our avoidance of intimacy.
- See your striving for closeness as part of a larger picture. You were raised male and your sexual feelings

were not the norm. What does that have to do with the price of tea in China? Everything and nothing. Being male taught you to keep your distance from other men. Being gay taught you to give that idea a second thought. In any case, recognize how you have been affected by the larger picture, but go on anyway. Never let the failure of others be a reflection on you. Do your duty to yourself even when others goof off or don't like you. Blame no one. Excel.

- Celebrate the rich development of your sexuality! Sexuality occurs over your lifetime, extends to nearly every part of your day, and unites you with God. Expand the boundaries of your sexuality to include caring for the health of your body, developing your athletic capacities, offering and accepting sensuous touch, and accepting your same-sex feelings. Your body image is not skin deep. Work on your insides and the outside will be just fine. Each step of enhancing your sexuality is a coming out.

- Work toward uniting sexuality and intimacy in a single relationship. Even when opportunity knocks, you may chose to refrain from being sexual. Sex is never an emergency and it's not a crime to save yourself for a special man. Waiting will allow you to grow in other ways and prepare you for intimacy.

- Look for the best in gay relationships and you will find it. Look for the worst and you will find that too. Gay relationships teach everyone how to love more deeply and freely. What are the lessons of gay relationships? That the essence of love goes beyond our stereotypes of men and women, accepting differences and the unpredictability of life are ongoing requirements of love, and God's place in our life is essential. The possibilities for learning are infinite.

- Prepare for intimacy, as an individual, as if your life depended on it—it does. Intimacy is crucial for your life to have meaning and for you to feel good about yourself. There are specific skills and projects you can work on daily to help yourself grow. As a result of your efforts, you may feel pain and grief. You can't escape these feelings. They often precede personal growth. When you work on your offerings to others and on respecting yourself, friendship will find you.

- Seek psychotherapy when you want help with growing. An intimate professional relationship with a trained helper can enable you to grow by leaps and bounds. A caring therapeutic relationship is energizing, disarming, affirming, and joyous.
- Enrich your couple relationship daily while accepting its limitations. Breathe new life into it: expand sensuality, fight fair, explore rituals and traditions, extend yourself to others, and play a lot. Seek professional help when you are stuck or are considering a separation.
- See gay relationships as a window to God. What better way to learn that life is not within your control, that the essence of love goes beyond roles, and that differences can be a source of pleasure and fellowship! Your gay feelings taught you that you cannot love yourself by winning the approval of others. Could you have understood the mysteries of life without first accepting the mysteries within yourself?

GOOD-BYE

We have already expressed our feelings about ending. What about your feelings about finishing this book? Leave time at the end for reflection. What were your reactions? Were you jarred, disappointed, angry, inspired, or challenged? Were there parts of the text that disturbed you? Which ones? If you felt like criticizing part of the text, perhaps something important was being stirred up within you. What was it? What can you learn about yourself? You now have new ways of thinking about intimacy, sexuality, and being gay. What are these new ideas? Write them down or tell others about your discoveries. Continue your reflections. What was it like for you to learn from us? What did you like the most and the least about our writing? Is there something you need to tell us? Let us know.

Having gathered your thoughts, tell someone you trust what it was like to read this book. Ask that person for support and feedback. Whether you reacted with pain or joy, feel it for God's sake. You are alive and real. It doesn't get any better than this.

BIBLIOGRAPHY

ALBERTI, R.E., AND M.L. EMMONS. *Your Perfect Right.* San Luis Obispo, CA: Impact, 1974.

BELL, A.P., M.S., WEINBERG, AND S.K. HAMMER-SMITH. *Sexual Preference: Its Development in Men and Women.* Bloomington: Indiana University Press, 1981.

BLUMSTEIN, P., AND P. SCHWARZ. *American Couples.* New York: William Morrow, 1983.

CARDELL, M., S., FINN, AND J. MARECEK. "Sex-role identity, sex-role behavior, and satisfaction in heterosexual, lesbian, and gay male couples." *Psychology of Women Quarterly,* Vol. 5 (1981), pp. 488-494.

CHODOROW, N. *The Reproduction of Mothering: Psychoanaysis and the Sociology of Gender.* Berkeley: University of California Press, 1978.

DASS, R., AND P. GORMAN. *How Can I Help?* New York: Knopf, 1985.

COLGROVE, M., H.H., BLUMFIELD, and P. MCWILLIAMS. *How to Survive the Loss of Love.* New York: Bantam Books, 1976.

ERIKSON, E.H. *Childhood and Society.* New York: W.W. Norton, 1950.

ERIKSON, E.H. *Identity and the Life Cycle.* New York: W.W. Norton, 1980.

FINKELHOR, D. *Sexually Victimized Children.* New York: Macmillan, 1979.

FIELDS, R., R., WEYLER, AND R. INGRASCI. *Chop Wood, Carry Water.* New York: St. Martin's Press, 1984.

FRITZ, G., K. STOLL, AND N. WAGNER, "A comparison of males and females who were sexually molested as children." *Journal of Sex and Marital Therapy,* Vol. 7 (1981), pp. 54-59.

GALASSI, M.D., AND J.P. GALASSI. *Assert Yourself.* New York: Human Sciences Press, 1977.

GILLIGAN, C. *In a Different Voice.* Cambridge: Harvard University Press, 1982.

GREEN, R. *The "Sissy Boy Syndrome" and the Development of Homosexuality.* New Haven: Yale University Press, 1987.

HALPERN, H. *How to Break Your Addiction to a Person.* New York: McGraw-Hill, 1982.

HARRY, J., AND R. LOVELY. "Gay marriages and communities of sexual orientation." *Alternative Lifestyles,* Vol. 2 (1979), pp. 177-200.

KOPP, S. AND C. FLANDERS. *No Hidden Meanings.* Palo Alto, CA: Science and Behavior Books, Inc., 1975.

KOPP, S. AND C. FLANDERS. *What Took You So Long?* Palo Alto, CA: Science and Behavior Books, Inc., 1979.

LEWIS, C.S. *The Four Loves.* New York: Harcourt Brace Jovanovich, 1960.

MASTERS, W.H., AND V.E. JOHNSON. *Homosexuality in Perspective.* Boston: Little, Brown, 1979.

MCNEILL, J.J. "Homosexuality: Challenging the church to grow." *The Christian Century,* (March 11, 1987), pp. 242-246.

MCWHIRTER, D.P. AND A.M. MATTISON. *The Male Couple: How Relationships Develop.* Englewood Cliffs, NJ: Prentice-Hall, 1984.

MERTON, T. *Love and Living.* New York: Harcourt Brace Jovanovich, 1979.

MILLER, S., D. WACKMAN, AND C. SALINE. *Straight Talk.* New York: New American Library, 1982.

MONEY, J. "Sin, sickness, or status? Homosexual gender identity and psychoneuroendocrinology." *American Psychologist,* Vol. 42 (1987), pp. 384-399.

NELSON, J.E. *Embodiment: An Approach to Sexuality and Christian Theology.* Minneapolis: Augsburg Press, 1978.

PECK, M.S. *The Road Less Traveled.* New York: Simon & Schuster, 1978.

PEELE, S., AND A. BRODSKY. *Love and Addiction.* New York: New American Library, 1975.

RAMIREZ, M. "Biculturalism/multiculturalism in the Americas." In R. Diaz-Guerrero (Ed.), *Cross-cultural and National Studies in Social Psychology.* Amsterdam: North-Holland, 1985.

ROFES, E.E. (Ed.) *Gay Life: Leisure, Love, and Living for the Contemporary Gay Male.* Garden City, NY: Doubleday, 1986.

SAGHIR, M. AND E. ROBINS. *Male and Female Sexuality.* Baltimore: Williams & Wilkins, 1973.

SMEDES, L.B. *Forgive and Forget.* New York: Pocket Books, 1984.

SMITH, M.J. *When I Say No I Feel Guilty.* New York: Bantam, 1975.

THOMPSON, M. *Gay Spirit: Myth and Meaning.* New York: St. Martin's Press, 1987.

WHITAM, F. "The pre-homosexual child in three societies: The United States, Guatemala, Brazil." *Archives of Sexual Behavior,* Vol. 9, pp. 87-99.